And Where Do We Live When We Get Older?
THE FUTURE OF THE RETIREMENT HOME AND ALTERNATIVE LIVING OPTIONS

RALPH VILLMAN

AND WHERE DO WE LIVE WHEN WE GET OLDER?
The Future of the Retirement Home and Alternative Living Options

Copyright © 2016 by Ralph Villman

All rights reserved. This book or any portion thereof may not be reproduced or used in any manner whatsoever without the express written permission of the publisher except for the use of brief quotations in a book review.

DISCLAIMER
The views expressed in this book are solely those of the author and do not necessarily reflect those of the publisher and/or the reader. The reader may be advised to use his or her own discretion in the different subjects before applying any information given in this book. The author expressively disclaims any responsibility for the content. The author has the rights of this book, and any part hereof cannot be used elsewhere without the written permission of the author. Because of the dynamic of the internet, any links or websites or citations given in this book may have changed or discontinued and may no longer be valid. Further, any information given from the internet has not been verified as its accuracy, and may not been relied on by the reader.

Printed in the United States of America

ISBN 978-0-9950493-0-7

First Printing, 2016
20 19 18 17 16 / 10 9 8 7 6 5 4 3 2 1

Published by: 7114583 Canada Ltd

RalphVillman.com

Table of Contents

	Introduction	1
CHAPTER 1	**Staying at Home—The Best Alternative?**	5
	How it all began	7
	Development in the States	8
	From the fear of dying to the joy of living	9
	Development in Europe	10
	What's the difference between active adult and independent living?	11
	Quality of Living: *Advancing age in relation to various living arrangements*	12
CHAPTER 2	**The Future of Retirement Homes in a Changing Climate**	15
	So where does all this rent money go?	15
	The cost of living at home	18
	Where are seniors living?	20
	When should one consider moving?	21
	Affordability	23
	The future of rates and rents	25
	Staffing and other costs	26
	Night shift staffing	28
	Management salaries	30
	Summary of rates and rents	30
CHAPTER 3	**Running Out of Funds**	32
CHAPTER 4	**The Missing Link**	36
	The retirement residence as a 'home'?	36
	Holistic wellness	39
	Community	40
CHAPTER 5	**The Retirement Home and Growing Spiritual Awareness**	42
CHAPTER 6	**Operational Challenges**	50
	How beneficial is living in a retirement home for the elderly person?	53
	How long do people stay in retirement homes?	63
	When residents require care beyond the ability of the retirement home to provide adequately	65
	Ownership	67

CHAPTER 7	Where Does Home Care Fit In?	69
CHAPTER 8	**Looking Ahead Into the Future**	78
	To hire a live-in-caregiver	82
CHAPTER 9	**Rules, Regulations and Permits**	83
	Too many rules and regulations?	83
	Permits	90
CHAPTER 10	**Medical Emergencies and Their Cost**	93
CHAPTER 11	**Outbreaks**	103
CHAPTER 12	**Considerations for a Future-Oriented Housing Model**	105
	Attempts to look at ways to pay for care—once the senior population explodes	110
	Care giving robots	115
	Senior living options agencies	117
	Are retirement home residents free to leave the home anytime?	119
	Couples aging gracefully together	120
	A few thoughts on location of future oriented senior communities: City or Country?	122
CHAPTER 13	**Alternative Living Options**	126
	The Senior Daycare Centre	126
	Senior Shared Housing Arrangement	127
	Senior Co-Housing	128
	Senior Co-ops	136
	Abbeyfield House	137
	Senior Suite as Condo Unit?	141
	Shared Intergenerational Community Housing Model	144
	Community Living in purposefully built Multi-Unit Residences, or Intentional Senior Housing Community	150
	Community Living designed as Sacred Places	155
	Senior Community Living in Tiny Homes	157
	Building Methods	163
	Living Abroad	163
CHAPTER 14	**How the Ideas Came About in My Own Experience**	165
	Marketing	171
CHAPTER 15	**The Concept Takes Form**	173
	Ten components to make housing of seniors a desirable way to live	175
	Other considerations	206

Introduction

The retirement home industry is the only known industry which consistently offers services most of its customers do not want. Moreover, what the customers wants or even requires, is not what the industry offers, or is even able to offer.

All along, as Mom and Pop are getting older, they watch the marketing efforts by the various retirement homes, but moving in one of those is totally out of the question. They live happily at home, are independent and healthy, and do not 'need' to move into one of those places. As Pop passes on, and Mom is getting lonely, the thought of moving comes up again, but is just as quickly tossed out, after the question of affordability is looked into. Rates are unaffordable. Then, something unexpected happened to Mom, and after a longer hospital stay, the doctors advised Mom that it is impossible for her to go back home—from here on, she has to be looked after in a nursing home. Trouble is, nursing homes have long waiting periods, perhaps a year. Family is devastated. How can this happen, and so quickly and unexpected?

After all, Mom is only eighty-five?

A year might be an awful long time, if making it through the day becomes the challenge on hand. Fear sets in, that perhaps Mom does not even live long enough to see the nursing home from inside. Then again, this was never envisioned too much to begin with.

Ah, the retirement home. This will bridge the waiting time. Now, the 'need' is there, the time has come.

Little does Mom or the family understand that, while this is a typical scenario, this is not the customer, or resident, the home wants, caters to and serves to. Yet, it is common perception. Everyone believes this is what retirement homes are for. Or are they?

Perhaps an alternative living option should be looked into. But as it turns out, there are hardly any available, let alone known of. One does not even know how and where to start looking for one.

At the same time, the burden of nursing homes is constantly busting their seams, so retirement homes seem like a very good alternative, at least for the time being, until a nursing home place becomes available. Even so it has to be paid for privately. The rent money necessary just has to be scraped up somehow.

The fact that a growing, huge number of older people needing assistance let the construction of retirement homes boom; while at the same time, clouding over the disparity between services offered and services needed.

The same growing number does also cloud over the fact that most people do not want to leave home, only if they must. As retirement homes are sprouting up everywhere it seems like they are so popular. Fact is, they are not. Statistics tell us different. For the retirement home industry to sustain its very existence, something has to give. And something, actually quite a number of things, must be changed, to make them for their future customer more attractive to become an alternative living option, and not be the extended arm of a nursing home. Then again, this may be just the service retirement homes may offer in order to continue to exist.

But there are larger problems looming on the horizon, and as a society, we would do well to anticipate these problems, and perhaps give it some thought as to how to solve them, before we are overcome by them.

The very fact is that this huge number of care requiring seniors can hardly be looked after today, and provided for, today, let alone tomorrow, when the number of seniors doubles or more. Dwindling resources make a retirement home living for the majority for the older folks simply not obtainable.

The solution to all problems, it seems, came into being 25 years ago, when the first time around it was recognized that looking after older folks in nursing homes proved just too expensive—the solutions was the "invention" of the home care services.

In Europe, home care services were alive and well for at least 25 years prior to that. However, this solution, as it has matured into today, is at best a band-aid, and the entire set-up is constantly strained by funding cut-backs. At the same time, announcements of more money poured into the home care service industry are publicized.

What's not announced, is, that the number of seniors to be looked after is growing rapidly, and on a per person basis, there are cut backs despite all additional funding. Announcements of new funding lets people relax in the knowing that they will be looked after, one day, and they do not have to leave their beloved home. Trouble is, this is dangerous thinking at best. In North America we also have the added problem of the population living far more spread out than in Europe, and travel time and added expense is another issue. Especially keeping in mind that diminishing oil resources may force us all to re-think our travel habits one day, and on that day we also have to re-think the perceived need to travel for miles to old people just to help them brush their teeth.

Simply multiplying constructions of retirement homes is not the answer either, because in the future, private funds will be less and less available to pay for those services, especially if the current trend of exploding cost and rental charges continues. Even if, and especially if, the industry decides to gear up for increased care requiring residents, which means nothing more than increase staff levels, which no doubt leads again into higher rental rates. A vicious cycle.

Simply multiplying constructions of nursing homes is not the answer either, because, who should pay for those, including the growing staffing requirements? Governments are strained to pay for the existing ones. We may run out of the option of taxing the working population, to pay for all of those care requiring seniors. Because there are simply not enough pay cheques around to be taxed, in order to pay for all this. And its not just the nursing home cost. There is medical cost, which is also spiralling upwards. Cost of doctors, hospitals and associated medical therapies applied for larger population of elderlies cannot be paid for with today's ways of taxations.

Something has to give.

For these reasons, this book has been written.

And it has been written in a style which reflects the urgency of the matter. It is critical, and addresses many wrongs with present rules and regulations just to make the point. This is not written to cover up potential problems, but addresses those. It is to be regarded as a wake-up call, and the time to act is now. We simply cannot afford to bury the head in the sand and continue with business as usual. If we do not make decisions, there might be a time when decisions are being made for us, which we may not want to see. The first ripples can already be felt.

For more than two decades I am observing the retirement home industry maturing. But it matures in the wrong direction. While it was always expensive, and so only affordable for a certain number of people, the cost has mushroomed lately, and the gap widens. There is no hint of this gap getting any closer anytime soon, rather the opposite.

In an attempt to address these problems, alternative living options are introduced, at rates and prices which are much more affordable than what is being offered today in North America's retirement homes. After all, there are other options available—everywhere but here.

A solution must be found to house older people in a type living option they actually want to live in and move into, not because they must. A solution must be found to correct the built-in short comings of the typical retirement home set-up, including sky rocketing cost. A solution must be found to have those living options made affordable. A solution must be found to establish these supportive living options in a way which does not strip the elderly person of their life long savings within the last few years of their lives.

It will be pointed out that it is very well possible to overcome all these problems, but not without growing pains. A model has been developed to address most of the problems, but again, only with the underlying assumption that a number of well-established rules and regulations are dismantled.

As a society, we still have time, but we have to act now. Simply because there is work to be done beforehand. The playing field must be levelled. Numerous rules and regulations, of which we are so proud of to have established, must be reversed or simply scrapped. These are also looked into, and the effect being expected. As it is today, we are stumbling over our own feet. Any entrepreneurial spirit as to find solutions to these difficulties are nipped in the bud, because the proposed set-up turns out to be illegal in one way or another, or otherwise not doable. As soon as we believe to have found a way of solving problems, we find out and immediately it becomes apparent that this solution, too, is not according to established rules and regulations and so comes to a grinding halt. So, if we really want to tackle these problems, and actually solve them, we have to look a little deeper into what must be done, instead of trying to fix everything by throwing money at it. As money becomes scarcer, the problems really will hit home, unless we act in different ways—and most importantly, act now.

Under the assumption of dismantling some laws, a workable, attractive senior housing model is introduced very detailed—one in which you and I would love to live in. Not when the need arises, but long before that.

The urgency is in the air—we have to act now.

CHAPTER 1

Staying at Home— The Best Alternative?

"*I am not ready yet...*" might be the most often used phrase when someone is asked if they would consider a move into a senior residence. And the obvious goes without saying—staying at home is the best alternative there is, at least at first sight. After all, their house is paid for. Actually the mortgage was paid off 30 years ago, so living there does come cheap. The same cannot be said for living in a retirement home. "Besides, I'm really fit and don't need anyone to look after me. Now, when my health deteriorates, and I really can't make it on my own, I'll consider moving. But before that, ten horses couldn't drag me out of here".

This is the most common attitude. Common means more than 92% of all seniors keep living in their own home.

Curious 85 or even 90 year old folks come to us for a tour, just to see what it's like to live in a retirement home, "Just in case…".

Of course, a move is out of the question, because "they are not ready—yet".

Well, folks, if this is you, or your loved one, I invite you to ponder a few insights:

First, the family home which served well in the last 50 years, does not serve so well anymore once we get older.

Sure, the family has been raised, and everything with the house is great. Well, almost everything.

Of course, it's way too big now, especially since Dad passed away. Mom really lives in two rooms only, and recently, the stairs are not manageable anymore, so the living room is used as the bedroom. 'Sonny' and his boys came in and did the move. The entire upstairs rooms are not used anymore, neither is the basement, of course. Mom hasn't been there since Dad passed away.

Things are otherwise falling apart, too. Dad has always looked after all that, but not anymore.

"Sonny promised to fix things, but gosh, he is so busy. My other son is long retired, and he was never good with his hands, anyway. Dad always said he'd better get a contractor in if he had to put up a picture."

And so the house will need more and more repairs, which are not really looked after very well—actually, not at all. So it is with the yard, the shed and the garage, never mind the pot holes in the driveway.

"But being so alone really hurts me most—all I can do is think, think, think. The TV runs constantly, but they only have garbage on that, not something worth watching, something interesting like they used to have.

And besides, why am I still here? I should go and follow Dad, I feel so useless. I don't want to be a bother to the family. Sure, family comes in once in a while, but only for an hour or two, and then I am alone, again; gosh, they are all so busy...."

From now on, we will see a lot more problems, which Mom never mentioned. She is not telling, she just does not want to be a bother...

Her arthritis hurts so much, and she has to constantly take painkillers. But when exactly the last time was, she cannot remember, so she takes another one, just to be sure.

Really, if one would look over her shoulder, her entire medication management is nothing short of a mess. But the good thing is, there is nobody there to look over her shoulder, so everything is just fine.

The other day the wind blew a door shut, and Mom was not able to turn the knob to open it. The arthritis, you know. So effectively she locked herself in. But she managed to call the neighbors; they are really nice people, so everything is just fine.

"They come over anyways all the time, to bring the groceries. They have done that for two years now, since they told me I can't have my license renewed anymore. Silly, these people, I have been driving for 50 years without an accident. What are they thinking? I hope my neighbor doesn't move. They were over the other day, because the smoke detector went off and kept beeping. They thought I had a fire in the house. I really don't know how that happened. These things go off once in a while. They must have a mind of their own. Perhaps it had something to do with the stove. Sometimes I forget to turn it off, the arthritis, you know. Good thing the neighbor heard it, because I didn't. Sonny really never asks how I get my groceries, or how I heat up my soup, but that's ok. He doesn't need to know everything. But really, I don't struggle. It's just, things around the house are getting more difficult to handle for me. He would just worry, I don't know why. Gosh, he is so busy..."

Well, folks, I could go on and on, and we hear new variations of all this every day. The point is, Mom is not as independent as she thinks she is.

The fact is she needs half a dozen people to get through her day, but she won't admit it. Besides, she loves talking to them anyway, and they are all so nice.

When Mom finally thinks of moving into a retirement home, it is when some health issue arises, and living alone can no longer be managed.

It is then, and only then, when people knock on our doors, or the doors of other retirement homes.

Bluntly spoken, she should have come 10 years ago, when Dad passed away. This way we—and any other home—could have provided her with a wonderful last part of her life, one she would never imagined. As it is, she was just hanging in at home and waiting to follow Dad.

That old house, Mom's house, became unsuitable for her to live in, simply because the requirements of living in it have changed, and do so constantly, more and more, as time goes on. There is always something, which has worked well for so long, but all of a sudden, it does not work any longer. It has to be changed, or adjusted, or replaced or amended, with something more senior friendly. It is then when a move shall be considered, expensive as it is. But it may be remembered that Mom sits on perhaps half a million dollars' worth of property, unless, with more time passing and maintenance neglected, the house becomes a fixer upper. Repairs tend to be over valued by potential buyers in the other direction, that is, in lower prices. That could be a big loss, so living in the old house and remaining there might not be so cheap, after all. While at first sight it is cheap to live in, it is also true that it represents dead capital. If utilized, it could go a long way towards the cost of alternative living. So, retirement living never entered Mom's mind, because, that's only for old folks, not for Mom, and also because nobody has laid out to her that it might be a valuable option. This is where professional advice comes in. And the family might not be a good idea.

First off, they are likely not too familiar with today's financing tools, and also, it may not be in their interest to see Mom in an expensive retirement home. Then again, perhaps they want for Mom only the best. It really might prove to be too expensive, or the advisor or consultant can see that it is feasible and doable, but it did not appear that way at first. If that half a million dollars' worth of Moms house happen to sit in a not so hot area, perhaps in a rural area, far away from urban centres, it's value might be not half a million dollars at all. Perhaps the other end of the spectrum; $62,500.00 asking price, stretching it. And the listing may sit there till the realtor sign fades from the sun shining on it every summer!

(I know what I am talking about. At one point, I was a buyer of what's called 'stale' or 'dead-end' listings, and was on the lookout for faded out signs. At another point, I was a broker and had dead-end listings myself. This time I made sure I had the signs replaced every year!)

Still, it is certainly worth it to sit down, take stock, and see if retirement home living can be financially managed. If not, there are cheaper options, but not many.

As it is today in North America, one can only chose between one expensive retirement home or another expensive retirement home. But this will change. More on that in a later chapter.

How it all began

The retirement home industry in North America is fairly young—less than 50 years old. It came into being because of the need of family members, who in the post war industrial development found themselves getting jobs away from their home town, farther and farther away. Relocating to different cities, provinces or even to the States became the norm. Although family members had families of their own, they traditionally stayed in the same town or city where their parents lived. This was changing now. With jobs further and further away, family members would move. However, this move also meant that nobody was at home any more for Mom and Dad.

That was ok because the older couple did just fine, albeit perhaps they would have liked to be together more often. As time went on, and Dad passed away, there was no way for Mom to cope alone at home. Some sort of arrangement had to be found, and this was the birth of the retirement home.

From the very beginning, the retirement home had a bad stigma which it still has today. Viewed by many as an old folks home, the common perception was that this was not good. And sadly, this holds true for many older folks of today, who still carry this stigma with them.

From these meager beginnings, it soon had become a catch-all-institution for everyone who needed assistance to get through the day. Well distinguished from the nursing home, it still had a bad ring to it and was, and sadly enough still is, often considered a last resort, no getting out, the final place. It is seen as everything but a nice home to live in and enjoy life. Actual living conditions for its inhabitants, or residents, were described between not likeable and horrible. In short, something to be avoided at all cost.

Prices were modest, with cheap labour, since they were uneducated and abundant.

Many of those earlier circumstances have improved, to the point where the pendulum is now swinging more and more in the opposite direction. But let's slow down a bit.

This was in Canada, in the sixties and seventies.

Development in the States

In the United States, the development had a different twist, since in the States the nursing home care has to be paid for privately. This, of course, is a broad statement, because it is only partially true. Retirement homes then had the task of acting as a privately paid nursing home, too.

This has vast implications. First, the population in general expected a much higher level of care, since it was and is privately paid. Along with it came the expectation of first class accommodation, services and amenities, for the same reason. Further, because of the cost, only a certain percentage of people were able to afford such a place. However, for the ones who were able, this was indeed quite a different living option as the retirement home living in Canada. From the operator's view point, the homes have to be as large as possible, because of the high nursing home cost expected for some of the residents. In large numbers lies salvation, because of the economics of scale. In a way, this is like insurance. Everyone has to pay, and the ones who needed care later were partially paid for by the ones who did not, or passed away before they needed it. I am very familiar with the retirement home industry in North Carolina back in the eighties. The usual 'entry fee', as this cost was called, was between U$ 75,000 and U$ 300,000. With the payment of this fee, you get in the door. Then there was the monthly fee, which covered ongoing cost and services, and the range here of course was very broad. The majority of the residences charged in the range of $2,000 to $4,000/month, with some notable exceptions. I found homes even back then with monthly rental charges of $ 10,000.

While this seems staggeringly high, it might be well noted what these places offered. Many of these retirement residences can be described only as full-time resort-style living. The living options, the services provided and the amendments are endless. It became kind of an obsession of mine to tour those communities, even as I was studying 'Building Designs for Senior Living', in North Carolina a few years later.

From the fear of dying to the joy of living

It was quite an experience to tour and witness what these residences had aspired to, even their sheer size. Grounds were often several hundred acres in size. Many residences, communities, or even villages as they were called, featured many hundred residents, some with even more than a thousand senior living units. Amendments and services provided for the residents other than personal assistance and care, such as well-developed and coordinated activities were the norm. There were scheduled buses running in these park like grounds, and tons of golf carts coming and going to and fro in all directions. In larger communities one could literally pick what one desired for the day, and join that group. At lunch time, from the golf courses there might be 20 or so golf carts heading towards the dining room buildings and restaurants, and there were quite a few of them, like ducks in a row.

For other groups, it might be exercise in the gym, or a bus going to town for shopping, or another bus leaving for a walk in the park. Yet another group would be going golfing, while another goes for an outing. If the resident feels like staying at home, perhaps he or she might go to the swimming pool. There were manmade pools and ponds and bridges and walkways. Waterfalls and fountains. The possibilities were endless.

And then, of course, there were different living unit styles. Virtually every style of housing was available. A part of the grounds may be designed to house regular 1–2-bedroom semi-detached homes, with garden and landscaping all tended to by paid landscaping staff. There were link homes. Then there are apartments in larger buildings for rent, or perhaps condo units to buy. And of course, there were rooms only for those who need more care, in dedicated buildings. Here they were offered health related services provided by the residence's own care staff, nurses and even doctors.

Then there were shopping opportunities, stores, restaurants, perhaps marinas if the community was on waterfront, which was also artificially created. Independent houses had their own docks and waterways in the back, for the residents who are also boat owners. Of course, there were golf courses, tons of those, because golfing and North Carolina go well together. In short, nothing was missing. They often even had their own firefighting garage and equipment. These full size retirement communities were almost like small towns on their own, all planned and intentionally developed.

But then again, that is the States, and everything is possible. There is only one limiting factor in this wonderful world—the money. It comes as no surprise that with what these wonderful residences have to offer, affluent seniors can't wait to live in one. For this reason, there is a huge difference between the age of the senior who moves into a retirement community in the States, or into one in Canada. In fact, the difference is slightly more than twelve years. The average age for an American senior to move into a retirement home is 69, while in Canada it is 81. It may be noted here that these statistics are about 20 years old, stemming from a time when I did the research; this is just to make the point. The trend, however, is that the age at the time of admission is going upwards very similarly in both countries, but for different reasons. In Canada, it is because seniors want to stay at home longer, in fact as long as possible, and the introduction of home care services allows for that, while in the States, it is simply the lack of money, or the fear of running out of funds in years to come. After all, including the 'entry fee', if one lives 20 years in one of those residences, the price tag can easily exceed a million dollars. That's a lot to pay for the last part of one's life. From the owner or operator's point of view, multiply that million by 1000 residents and see that this is big business, indeed.

Development in Europe

By contrast, Europe experienced, and still does experience, quite a different development. There are none of these super retirement home communities as there are in the States. This is not necessary, because governments pay for nursing care. Again, this is a broad and general statement, and differs from country to country, and even within each country, to various degrees. In Germany, for instance, it's an arm of the government, an insurance company. Everyone who works and receives a pay cheque during their working years has a certain portion deducted for old age care insurance. That portion is at 21% nothing to sneeze at. Besides the taxes, monthly deductions of pay cheques are therefore huge. But then, this huge amount of money pools for old age care cost.

For demonstration purposes only, this is to show that there is not necessarily a need for this kind of resort style senior housing developments.

But there are other reasons too, why there are no such super developments. First, there is no space. There are no several hundred acres available to build such a place. If there were, it would not be feasible for such development because of the cost of land. Then, family members have traditionally not been parted to the extent this happened in North America. And distances to travel are far shorter, so even if sonny works somewhere else, it is possible to visit Mom Friday afternoon. So family members are still able to look after Mom and Dad, at least for visiting them, which reduces the loneliness aspect.

For basic assistance and care, there is and was 'home care'.

The invention of North America's "home care services" as it was touted back in the nineties is a long time practice in Europe, and not new at all. As a matter of fact, my wife was a 'travelling nurse' back in the seventies in Germany, and she is quite surprised to learn that this concept needed another 20 years to come to North America. I might mention that the term travelling nurse has a different meaning today than in the last sentence; it is used to describe nothing else but home care.

And then, there are quite a few different types of living arrangements available for older people in Europe, thus, retirement home residences are by and large not needed. Hence the entire retirement home industry, while present, plays only a small role in Europe. We look at them later.

What's the difference between active adult and independent living?

(*Source:* Aplaceformom.com/blog)

Active adult communities house seniors who need less care with daily tasks than residents requiring assisted living. This type of housing is also known as resort communities, 55 plus or adult lifestyle communities. Active adult living communities can be single-family homes, mobile or manufactured homes, cluster housing, condo style housing or special subdivisions. Occupants lease or purchase the residence and enjoy an independent lifestyle with their neighbors. These housing options have features and activities that independent seniors find fulfilling and enjoyable. From indoor swimming pools and lush golf courses to onsite shopping and transportation, active adult communities suit the needs of healthy and active seniors.

Independent living facilities, on another hand, are housing units designed specifically for seniors, often with an age limit around 65. Residents of independent living facilities care for themselves and live independently in a secure environment of their peers. These residents usually do not require assistance with day-to-day activities, but may use services of a care provider as required.

The key difference between independent living and other housing options is the degree of overall assistance in daily living activities. While seniors in independent living homes take care of the majority of their own needs, they may be offered meals, laundry services, linen delivery and planned activities. However, if one requires round-the-clock help with eating, dressing, and using the toilet, or requires regular medical assistance, other housing options such as assisted living or nursing homes may be a better option. Active adult living is limited in the type of care options available to seniors and the focus of housing is on seniors who are, as implied by the name, very active.

Independent living offers a good deal of comfort, security and safety but medical care is limited. Meals, housekeeping, transportation, and planned social activities are offered to seniors. There are many types of independent living facilities, from apartment complexes to separate houses. Continuing care retirement facilities provide independent living as well as other types of senior housing with more services at the same facility.

Here, I'd like to point out the following: Throughout this book you will find the reference to the term 'Retirement Home Industry'.

However this is somewhat an unfortunate term, albeit widely used. The definition of industry is the production of goods and services within an economy. Smoke stacks and blue collar workers come to mind. Some goods are produced, perhaps for our own use, perhaps for export. Somehow, I feel that in relation to retirement homes, this is a poor choice of words. However, I am bowing to commonly used terminology.

Ditto for the word 'community', especially as in retirement community. Again, this is a misnomer, because the very set-up of a top-down managed retirement home is everything else but a community. I will outline more details on that later.

Also, the widespread use and readily understood word 'senior' is also frequently used. Here again, I prefer a different word, for instance, elderly, or elderly person, because this contains an element of respect.

Let's look at it this way: Everyone who becomes old enough, perhaps 80 or 90 years and more, and proved to the world that he or she tackled all tasks life has presented them, is worthy to be respected.

After all, life is not easy—at least for most of us.

Quality of Living: *Advancing age in relation to various living arrangements*

This chart is for demonstration purposes only, not to show actual facts. The chart shows graphically that living at home is not the best option, although widely thought of it is.

- GREEN – high quality of living
- ORANGE – diminishing quality of living, due to failing health and assistance required
- RED – low quality of living, assistance and/or care required

a) Living at Home

b) Living at Home with Home Care Services

c) Moving into an assisted living retirement home

d) Moving into an assisted living community style living arrangement (*not retirement home*)

Living at Home
The above graph shows drastically that living at home, albeit widely thought of, is not the best option at a time in life where increasing assistance is required.

Since most people at this stage denying this fact and view themselves as independent, the thought of moving does not even enter their mind—a sadly misunderstood common belief.

In addition, options are not many.

Living at Home with Home Care Services
The same common belief holds that no matter what, if I happen to need care and can't live totally independent any longer, there is home care—they will look after me. This way I can stay home, and avoid going into one of these dreaded old folks homes.

Unfortunately, this is also is sadly misunderstood. While it is true to some extent, experience shows that home care, at least the part paid by the Government, is absolutely minimum with tendency to further cut backs. This is what it is. Quality of living is no doubt increased as opposed to coping at home with no services, however, it is not the best option, and only to be regarded as a band aid. To stay at home is the most widely viewed ultimate goal, however, familiarity with the known is not the same with high quality of living the last part of life.

Retirement Home Living

While this type living can be attractive, there are inherent short falls with this kind of living arrangement, as well. First, there is cost. By definition, only a part of society is able to afford it.

As a society, we have to ask if this set-up is sustainable. In addition, with runaway costs, the writing is on the wall. In the future, there will be less older folks who are able to afford retirement home living. But because baby boomers are on their way and the numbers of potential residents will increase dramatically, this will obscure that fact. But there is more. The approach of "fee for service" should be questioned. If this fee becomes out of proportion with services provided, and the general view of "let's milk them while we can" is becoming obvious, then we have to question ourselves if the entire concept of having older folks pay younger folks to have to look after them is a sustainable concept, indeed.

Community Style Living Arrangements with assistance provided by Live-in Care Givers

This will no doubt be the most desired living arrangement of the future. Trouble is, these are presently not around. At least not in this part of the world. That is because the very set-up would infringe on too many rules and regulations, and so cannot come to fruition. In this set-up, while some staff is paid, many or even most are not. Here are living 50-70 year olds who are able, willing and even eager to help others, perhaps in their eighties and nineties, who need some kind of assistance. However, with the present thinking and mindset this cannot happen. As we will see further on in chapter 15, there are certainly more advantages to this kind of living than any other form practiced today. If we were to allow this kind of arrangement to happen, a lot of our so called advances of society have to be dismantled.

Perhaps because of the many advantages, including the highest quality of living for an older person, we as a society or country may have sooner or later to discover that this dismantling is necessary to assist the bulging part of our elder population in a sustainable way, and in an affordable way.

CHAPTER 2

The Future of Retirement Homes in a Changing Climate

Everyone is saying that the retirement home industry is the future. Everyone is saying that it is a good business to be in, because lots of money can be made. Everyone is saying that it holds very good career opportunities for decades to come. Well, folks, if you are among those 'everyone's', let me tell you that you are all wrong.

Today in North America, we experience the beginning of the baby boomers generation seeking accommodations in retirement communities.

Compound that with the fact that people are living longer, and there is a perfect recipe for growth.

That fact alone sparked for retirement homes popping out of the ground wherever you go. A glut of these residences have been built and continue to be built. That's great, looking from that angle.

But I invite you to check the vacancy rates even today. In larger cities like Toronto, Montreal or Ottawa to name a few hot spots, these cities are showing residence's vacancy rates of around 18–20% with increasing trend. Compare that with apartment home vacancy rates, which are only a few percent, if that, despite all new home construction. That should raise a red flag, and it is hard to understand why developers in charge keep building these residences, despite these warning signs. The body in charge of statistics in Canada is the CHMC, Canadian Housing and Mortgage Corporation, which keeps excellent studies and trends on their site, for public use.

Larger residences are increasingly owned by chains and corresponding large corporations. One thing is for sure. If smaller homes would show a vacancy rate of 18–20%, they could not survive. There are tons of retirement homes closing down, especially the smaller ones. They can't keep up. They go the way of small scale shops or milk stores or the like of the past, if you are old enough to remember those.

So where does all this rent money go?

At first sight, it is indeed the large amount of rent which makes an outsider wonder how much profit is in this kind of business. And it certainly looks that way. But if one crunches a few numbers, the world looks not all that rosy, after all.

The majority of the rent cheque goes into the payroll. This is not hard to do. Although people may think that there are tons of care hours being paid for per person, it might come as a surprise to learn that the retirement industry builds its budget on *one hour per day per resident*. Even LTCs' (Long Term Care homes, formerly known as nursing homes) care loads provided are not much higher than this. These numbers, by the way, are no secret and are disclosed on appropriate web pages from the government. Very few people, though, know this. They think that nurses and care staff are buzzing around their loved ones all day. The part which is true is that they are indeed buzzing around, just not for one resident only. At only one hour/day at let's say $20/hr including employers cost, this hour alone costs $600/mth. That's the productive work. But training is another matter, so is the cost of the nurse. Once seen as an added benefit, the nurse is now the key person of the entire staff. And because she belongs to the category of high income earners, in our case the above figure increases to about $800.00 of care staffing cost per resident per month.

Meal preparation is another big item, and runs (in our home) to the tune of 35 minutes of staff time per day per resident. Then there are a number of services required which are less time consuming, like cleaning, laundry, running errands, maintenance related work in the home as well as snow removal and lawn care. Finally, administration, once with 4% of the payroll and hardly on the books, nowadays, because of consistently increasing red tape, is a noticeable item of the payroll. All told, we try to run the home with a little less than a total of 2.9 paid staff hours per day, per resident. And we are lucky enough to be not unionized, because if we were, our cost of the payroll would actually exceed our revenue figure. As it is, we have, at about $16/hr for care staff cost including employers contributions, a staff cost of $1,400.00 in wages per resident per month. But wages are not everything. The mortgage on the home is another big ticket item. Unfortunately, we are classified as commercial and as such, do not have the luxury of paying 3% or so interest for the mortgage, as is common these days for residential mortgages.

Commercial mortgages are more like 7–8% or more in interest. Each bedroom is around $70,000 so the mortgage payment alone is more than $400/door/month. Electricity cost is astonishingly high at around $160/door/month on average, despite numerous measures to save electricity. Heating, taxes, insurance, upkeep and food cost for the resident runs about the same as the mortgage payment. These all totalled up is close to $1,000.00 per resident/month. Add to that the staffing cost as calculated above with $1,400 and we are in the range of 2,400/month in expenses alone.

Our rent structure starts at $1,700 per month, with the majority of the rooms between $2,300 and $2,500/mth. You do the math. If you are looking for a retirement home which costs less than that per month, you can see easily that this is only possible if some of the above described services provided are simply not provided. Period.

It is then no wonder that smaller homes have to use a sharp pencil indeed, if they want to stay afloat. Actually, many don't. For these reasons the homes are getting larger and larger, but as you can see from above, some of the cost is the same proportional no matter how large a home is. Newly built residences have the added difficulty that they cannot build for less than $100 k/door, and sometimes considerably more, but their salvation lies in access to cheaper mortgage money than smaller homes have.

So much for this being a good business to be in.

The larger ones do survive, at this point, even thrive, and some of them are incredibly profitable. However, just in case you wanted to buy one, or build one, these residences are outside of reasonable price ranges. As mentioned above, especially in larger cities we see building prices of $120,000 and more per door. Multiply that by a 100 resident bed retirement home, and you have a price tag of $12 million. But it's the size that matters. Salvation is in economics of scale. In Ontario for instance, the average home size is approaching 90 rooms per home. Just to clear up one question we are asked frequently, no, there are no shared rooms. All rooms are private. This is common practise, as opposed to LTCs, where semi rooms and perhaps even wards with 4 residents/room are common.

Incidentally, nobody is asking how the residents feel living in such large complexes. The 'homey' atmosphere is not existent any more. It cannot be. To reach the dining room, one has to tackle that dreaded long walk in the never ending long hall way. Walking is not what it used to be, which was fun. Now it's pain. But that's only one of many minor inconveniences. Insecurity with the sheer size, intimidated by staff members running back and forth, a call bell ringing here and there, and you have all the ingredients for why the resident never wanted to live here to begin with. Staff turnover is another. Again, the sheer size of the operation calls for constant replacing and revolving of staff members. From the residents view point, no sooner that they get used to a certain care giver, she is gone and there is another one on her way. There is an unwanted but unavoidable fast turnover in staff, at least in the age bracket of the 20–30 year olds.

Once the caregiver is older, apparently care giving is considered more permanent employment, and her calling is found. Changing of jobs is not so much an issue, anymore. Just another reason personally I prefer having more mature staff employed.

The service of providing meals is also changing rapidly. We as a smaller home proudly provide home cooked meals, most of the time prepared from scratch. This is the niche we are promoting, and as expected, is well received. This is one area where we can be ahead of the competition, that is, larger homes. Still, many of the residents have special dietary needs and requirements such as prescribed diets, or are diabetics or have other preferences which have to be met. In smaller homes, we can deal with this, but for how long? Look out! There are dark clouds on the horizon. Larger homes tend to rationalize dietary staff cost and efforts, and as a result prefer more and more the use of precooked and prepackaged meals-large quantities produced by large commercial kitchens, hospital style.

Another advantage is that it is relatively easy, as opposed to home cooked meals, to provide alternatives. No doubt there are advantages from the provider's view, especially keeping in mind that it is not quite cheap to create meals for 100–200 persons from scratch in a regular commercial kitchen on a regular basis. That almost guarantees to have production cost like restaurants, and they are known to have small, if any, profit margins. But if we are talking for each resident 90 meals a month, plus snacks in between, and calculate $12/ meal, that results in more than $1,000/month, surely totally out of reality. Even at $9/meal we have $810/month, way too much to feed a person, so something has to give. Somewhere money has to be saved, and a lot. But how, and keeping a high standard in food quality and quantity?

Official rates are different. The allowance for meals in LTC's (nursing homes) per person is $8 per *day*, or $2.66 per meal. This number compared to retirement home budgets speak volumes. That includes snacks in between the meals. So it is no surprise that smaller homes have to give their best, and more, to survive the increasing pressure of larger homes which can do better and more cheaply. Of course, they do not care too much about the quality served, and do not have to, because they serve what's produced by someone else. But then again, the large scale commercial providers are doing *their* best to create tasty meals. After all, *they* have competitors, as well.

But the real danger comes in the form of government regulations, which do not like the idea of home cooked meals. In contrast, they do like the idea of precooked meals. The rationale here is that with home cooked meals there is the risk of possible food borne illnesses and cross contamination which may pose a real risk to the residents in the smaller scale operations. So far, no regulations to that effect are in place, but are talked about. How long will it take?

Once in effect, smaller scale operations get another knife in the back.

So much for a good business to be in.

The cost of living at home

In an effort to convince folks that living at home is not at all that cheap, with the premise that living in a retirement home is not so expensive after all, I am always amused how marketers of retirement homes do their calculations.

Yes, one can rattle off all kinds of expenses retirement homes have and assumingly they could be construed in a way that suggests private home owners have these costs as well.

Trouble is, nobody believes it.

For instance, the cost of security. Well, I have not seen a home owner yet who has to pay for his own security guard. But some retirement homes have to pay for security, and so, safety of the residents is being provided, and therefore must be paid for. In a retirement home, yes, perhaps, but this expense is not something a private home owner would have.

Food is of course, another good example. It is true that this is one reason folks like retirement homes, and this is an excellent drawing card. Meals provided are assumingly well done, balanced, and nutritious and feature a low rate of rotation. The same can certainly not be said for the lonely senior at home. In fact, the opposite is true. Folks at home get by with minimum cost, simply because their quality of their diet went down in the drain, with increasing age and immobility. Cooking for one person is not easy to begin with, but add to that not feeling well enough to cook and, not having a variety of food items on hand because shopping is at best a chore, then the diet seniors provide for themselves needs a lot of improvement, to say it in a nice way.

The longer coping at home is practised, the worse it gets. And that is only the tip of the iceberg. If you want to know more details, I am not going there. I fear that the dear reader might get the wrong impression about what is really going on, if seniors, mostly older seniors that is, or perhaps seniors with beginning dementia, are in charge of their own diet. That's not to say that every senior has diets like this. But there are surely plenty of sad stories out there to tell.

Given these parameters, the cost of food for the one who stays at home is very small indeed.

The housing cost, also very low, since the mortgage on the old home was paid for long ago, is just taxes and insurance. Of course, nobody is asking what the house would yield if it were to be sold, and therefore, the senior lives on non-utilized capital. But selling was always out of the question, because sonny and his sister are already waiting in the wings for their inheritance.

What follows is that living at home is very cheap, indeed. Or so it seems.

Here comes along all the marketers of retirement homes with their calculations on how expensive it is to live at home. Surely, it can be calculated that way. But if true or not, if reasonable or not, one has to do his own math, and this will reveal, indeed, that living at home is not really all that cheap, after all.

What I observe, however, is quite different from what these cost calculations show, which may include costs of 'security guards'. Truth is there are many expenses included which will continue to be. For instance, taxes for the house still have to be paid for if the house is kept. So does basic cost for electricity and insurance. Car expenses will continue, if car driving is not given up, yet. Moving into a retirement residence does not mean that automatically all other expenses are not existent anymore. One has to do one's own calculations.

In my opinion, the loss of income by sitting on the house is a big income loss, indeed. And the other big expense item is the cost of repair and maintenance, which in my observation is in many cases grossly neglected, and this will bite back sooner or later. Probably later, when the 'kids' divide up the proceeds of the sale of the house, and discover that the house, because of its obsolete functionality, has not yielded what they thought it would.

Where are seniors living?

The vast majority of seniors—despite all attempts from the retirement home industry—are still living at home.

Currently there are about 50 million seniors over the age of 65 living in North America, with about 45 million of those in the US.

Statistics from Canada show that of the about 5 million seniors over 65 years, an astonishing 92, 8% are living at home. That leaves only 7. 2% of all seniors living in other accommodations, presumably the majority of those in retirement homes, since there are hardly any alternatives—a subject which will be visited further below.

This is a surprising number, but this of course changes once we look at seniors in their 90's, with fewer living now at home. But this number is even more astonishing. A full 56% of those old folks in their 90's are still living at home, half of those, 28% by themselves—and alone. While many do fine at home, surprisingly many do not.

I have been at numerous private homes, usually to pick up potential residents for a tour through our residence, and so I have witnessed many a condition these folks live in. And many are so horrible I could not describe them. But I also tell you the truth, which is not so nice, if you want to know it or not. I have visited private homes where folks literally eat out of cans, for simplicity reasons. Perhaps they didn't feel like making that peanut butter sandwich. Same can tomorrow, too, since it was too much to eat today. But it gets worse. Are you ready? If they run out of cans, they eat the cat food. You might think this is exaggerated. I can assure you it's not. You might think this is an isolated case, one in thousands. I can assure you it's not. Perhaps only dement people would do that? Yes, in some cases for sure, but not all, by far not.

Suffice to say that this is a testimony of a society which still has a lot of work ahead. How can we look at that, and believe everything is ok? Or worse, look the other way? How can we have 28% of people over 90 years of age living alone? If you ask them they would not want it any other way. But unless they are reasonably able to do so, we can call that 'coping at home' because there cannot be any quality left in living like this anymore.

We are all looking in a different direction, and think this is all ok.

I believe this needs some serious revamping.

But there is some good news. Important to remember is the difference in perspective.

One is that horrible as these places or circumstances may be, it is all relative, because many a folk living there are actually quite happy. And not even ten horses could drag Mom out, and for her to move. This is just the way the home is, and the way the living circumstances have been created, and so Mom got used to them. And so Mom is indeed quite happy there.

Another aspect of good news is that many of those older folks are actually looked after, even if no statistic shows that. Sort of.

Not even if you ask them, because they all tell you proudly they live 'independently'. However, it does not take much to see that the so-called independence really means that these old folks need half a dozen friends and neighbours to give them assistance for whatever, just to get them through their day!

In the States, it's not much better, but the numbers indicate that retirement home living is much more attractive, because in the above age bracket, 'only' 41% live at home (statistics here shows 85+ years, so it's a bit lower than the statistic I found for Canada, so a bit harder to compare). The rest are living in alternative living options; again probably mostly in retirement homes.

When should one consider moving?

Quick answer: When the thought occurs the first time…

Sometimes it is refreshing to have folks perhaps in their seventies coming through our door, who tell us they are concerned about the future. They are concerned what will happen in their later years, and evaluate their options once they are getting older, and perhaps in need of assistance.

They would say—quite correctly—if they would move in a residence today, they basically buy the security needed in case some day assistance is needed. But if they would wait another 10 years before such a decision is made, they most likely can't afford it anymore. Chances are these folks are living alone, and perhaps feel lonely, too. This is a prudent view, and should be adapted by many.

It is this view which gives rise to the implementation of the concept of what I call 'the independent living option'. With this option, care is not charged at a time when not needed. But it is the availability, the entire infrastructure, which is available at any time. Once required, the regular rent, including assistance, is charged. Kind of a user fee. Hence, with this model it is quite possible to shift the largest burden of the monthly rent cheque—the cost of the care staff—ahead into the future once or even if ever needed.

This philosophy is not unknown of, but by and large not practiced today. You move in—you pay. For all services which are offered. If you need any particular service or not. Within the framework of retirement homes, there could be a model established which allows for this. In a way, but not quite, this is practiced today with the application of all add-on charges. The big difference is that the resident usually does not know or understand, so these extra charges come as a surprise.

From the view as the operator, as a pleasant side effect, the retirement home would by applying of this principle finally attract the type of people they really like to have. Younger and able people, who enjoy what's being offered.

RETIREMENT HOME LIVING ?
"I AM NOT READY, YET"

Your house has served you so well over the years—so why are things different now?

> *"When I really need help, I might consider moving into a retirement residence ... but for now, I am not ready, yet."*

This is the standard reply, but please consider this:

Moving into a retirement residence is a *life style choice* you may make—once you think you need help, or even care, most likely this is the moment where help or care you need is only available in an institutional setting—which is NOT what retirement residences provide.

Unfortunately, most people are waiting too long—and mostly the reason is that a move simply seems overwhelming, if not scary and "expensive"

Sometimes, there is also the comment "I can't afford it".

If you think this is you, please talk to us—we might be able to accommodate you after all, and show you it's not as "expensive" as you think it is.

Also, often we hear the comment "I wish I would have discovered living at Golden Pond much earlier", indeed we do everything we can to provide you with a unique lifestyle in wonderful surroundings.

Care Staff are dedicated to provide you with all your needs.

Meals are mostly home made, the way you come to know it over the years.

We are a small home, and as such, provide individual 'specials' other residences cannot do—they are too large. Here, we are one big family.

Here is a little self-test, designed for prospective residents, which is commonly used for independent people to evaluate themselves in regards to moving into a retirement home:

YES NO	ARE YOU BORED AND/OR LONELY AT TIMES?
YES NO	DOES YOUR SOCIAL LIFE REVOLVE AROUND THE TV?
YES NO	IS YOUR CIRCLE OF FRIENDS SHRINKING?
YES NO	DID SOCIAL CONTACTS CHANGE ONCE YOU COULDN'T DRIVE CAR ANYMORE?
YES NO	COULD YOU USE MORE EXERCISE?
YES NO	IS HOME MAINTENANCE A BURDEN AND EXPENSE YOU ARE TIRED OF?
YES NO	ARE HOUSEKEEPING CHORES NOT AS EASY AS THEY USED TO BE?
YES NO	HAVE YOU LATELY FORGOTTEN TO SWITCH OFF THE STOVE?

YES	NO	ARE YOU CARING FOR A SPOUSE WHICH WEARS YOU OUT? (The caring not the spouse.)
YES	NO	ARE YOU EATING POORLY? HAVE YOUR EATING HABITS CHANGED?
YES	NO	ARE YOU EATING ALONE? DO YOU STILL COOK FOR YOURSELF?
YES	NO	DO YOU WORRY ABOUT NEEDING HELP AND NOT GETTING ASSISTANCE?
YES	NO	DO YOU WANT TO ENJOY BETTER HEALTH?
YES	NO	WOULD YOU BE MORE COMFORTABLE IF YOU HAD HEALTH SERVICES?
YES	NO	HAVE YOU LATELY FORGOTTEN TO TAKE SOME OF YOUR MEDS?
YES	NO	ARE YOU RELYING ON FRIENDS, NEIGHBORS AND FAMILY TO GET THINGS DONE FOR YOU?
YES	NO	IS THIS REPEATING ITSELF AND BECOMES A BURDEN TO THEM?

If any of these questions have been answered with "yes", think about moving into a retirement residence.

Affordability

So, then, we really have a two tier society. There are the ones who rely for their old age expenses solely on government assistance, like government Old Age pensions and a host of different subsidies, just the same. By definition, this part of the population is simply not able to afford retirement home living. Period.

Is there any way that this segment of the population is able to enjoy retirement home living?

This is the key question I ask myself since I am involved in (alternative) senior living arrangements.

The answer is yes, but these concepts are still quite a few years away. Part of the reason is that society has to change some of its fundamental views and that is not likely to happen soon. However, I am convinced that it will happen. In the section on alternative options we will touch on those elements a bit more. It should be noted here loud and clear that the retirement home industry is not interested in the answer to this question. Simply, because, at least at current times, there is enough money out there so this is not relevant. They are interested in recruiting the market of folks with money. However, this available pool of money will shrink, and perhaps one day to the point where the retirement home industry is indeed forced to look at potential residents with less income—much less.

But we are not there, yet.

The other segments are the ones who have additional income in any form. We find because many investment vehicles do not pay substantial amounts any more, that most of our residents pay their way by means of additional company retirement contributions earned in their earlier, active years. While this is ok today, it may not be tomorrow, given today's trend of companies to cut back on benefits, including pension payments.

Company pensions or contributions simply may not be around in the future, for sure not to the extent they are today. This may be just enough to not being able to afford retirement home living tomorrow.

And then there is one more source of additional income to pay for those additional services:

Real estate appreciation. Consider a farm, being bought by a working couple in the mid of the century. This farm has long been paid off. Now, either the next generation is willing to operate it—or not. If not, it might be put up for sale. By now, money is flowing. Even a small farm is worth a lot, measured in millions of dollars. This is the money pool expensive retirement homes are after. Even the value of a regular single family home has appreciated to the extent that retirement home living can easily be paid for. There is one caveat however. Real estate today will most likely not appreciate tomorrow the same way as it did in the past. That means less in the kitty for the new generations to tap from.

There is one more source for Mom to be able to move into a retirement home. You may not want to hear this, so I left it for last:

Family chips in.

Again, we see this more and more, and I believe this will happen even more in the future, if the trend of rapidly increasing retirement home rates is not slowed or even reversed.

In the States things have cooled down a bit. In Canada, we are still trying to catch up with these kinds of developments, but it looks we will not have a chance to catch up. There are dark clouds on the horizon.

Research shows that money will be getting scarcer in just one or two generations.

The reasons shall not be investigated here any further. Suffice to say that investment income has even at the present time dwindled down to negligible returns. Company induced retirement plans are also sharply reduced, if not cut out, leaving the population more or less to their own devices to look after their families, when assistance is needed or required. Compound with that the fact that our population will continue to get older, with increased life expectancy. Today they talk about the bulging baby boomers generation. They call it the 'silver tsunami'. Care insurances are a fairly unknown vehicle to pay for care cost, but you practically have to sign up, and pay as a young adult, in order to receive payments when you need it, perhaps 50 years later. I cannot imagine that this set-up will attract many young people. For this reason, it is and will remain only a small portion of payments to come in later years. Other ways will have to be found to make younger people pay into such insurances. Again, I point to Europeans, who have had this arrangement for decades, and it works. The simple answer is, that contributions into such insurances are *compulsive and the law*. This way, like it or not, every younger adult have to pay contributions for old age care cost.

What about family members chip in to help their parents pay for their stay in retirement homes?

This is a really interesting question. In my experience, this is something family members seem never to have thought about. This is something which apparently is to be avoided as the plague. Perhaps it's only in my experience, and I have no data from Canada as to back this up.

It's different in the States. A full 42% of Americans worry about not being able to afford retirement home living for their parents. And with good reason. Of all residents living in retirement homes, 36% of all Americans do already provide financial support to house their parents. That is, more than one third. That's today. What will it look like tomorrow? And how come we in Canada seem to have never had that idea?

The future of rates and rents

Rates of retirement homes keep spiraling upwards into unknown realms.

Reasons are many. Cost of construction has risen dramatically, compounded by two important factors. One is, that new residences are getting fancier, larger by number and larger by individual size unit all the time. They also tend to become more and more elaborate. All this must be paid for. And second, the increased requirements in observing and obeying rules and regulations. They are coming out of nowhere like mushrooms, and growing in the same way. And it seems, there are here to stay. All of them costing money on an ongoing basis and these expenses have to be absorbed. New retirement home regulations in Ontario, for instance, are prohibitively expensive to meet, at least for the smaller operators who have to comply just the same. There will be more on that later under 'Rules and Regulations'. Add to this the increased cost of staffing and staffing educational and training requirements, and here is the recipe for rates going up drastically. The question then becomes, where is all this money going to come from?

If you are on the lookout of comparing retirement home rates, a word of caution. There is a new twist out there and here it is.

The rates quoted are not all inclusive, as it was in the past, but tiered according to services required. While at first this makes a lot of sense, and is especially well suited to the one who says "I don't need care anyways, and when I do, I pay", so this set-up is well received.

Trouble is, reality looks different. The initial low ball rate of $1,600/month proves that there is really only the *availability of care staff* included. As soon as actual care is required, the clock starts ticking.

No doubt this idea came up with how home care services are constructed today. Every move they make is being billed. In real time. This is why home care staff starts entering in their smart phone: Mrs. Smith 'combing' $2.35, 'brushing hair' $1.75, 'assistance with dressing' etc. Since this works so well, retirement homes are just copying invoicing practises by home care companies, which, of course, invoices the Ministry and not the resident. But it's a nice way to have low rental rates shown upfront.

By the time the invoice is printed out, the resident gets a 5 page invoice. I just hope this practise will falter before it develops any further.

For the majority of all residents, even if they feel differently, it is safe to say that they require 'care' rather sooner than later.

And one more point to clarify. In general text, including this book, we read about *care* providing by retirement homes. It should be made clear that the mandate of retirement home is *not* to provide care, but rather *assistance for the activities of daily living*. These are well defined as feeding-grooming-hygiene-dressing-toileting and some others. Then there are 'instrumental ADL's' which fall outside the scope provided.

So retirement homes are in the end very reluctant to provide *care*, although widely advertised.

The main difference is the amount of time required to provide assistance versus to provide care. Also, the frequency plays a role in this definition.

Staffing and other costs

In the old days we would hire care staff who by age, experience and compassion were very good at giving care for elderly residents. Plus, they were in an age group which was not the target age group for other industries. So they practically had no choice of finding a job somewhere else. For us as well as the older staff, it was a win-win situation. All that has changed. Care staff is now required to have credentials, something an older job holder may not be able or willing to obtain. Younger job seekers do. Now, the market is flooded with so-called Personal Support Workers. They are being churned out like they are coming out of a puppy mill. Trouble is, they are being told by the teaching colleges that this is the most sought after and well paid career path of the future. Truth is, while there certainly is increased need for in the future, it's hardly a well-paid career. Taking care of our elderly population should not be reduced to or regarded as being a well-paid career. The money is not raised in any meaningful way, like in the production industry, but paid for out of savings of their own grandparents. But indeed, these young girls do earn more than older, more experienced workers. And that increases the payroll cost of the home.

All residences are now required to employ *qualified* staff not only in the care sector, but also in dietary.

Gone are the times when you had a house mum, advanced in age, cooking for the residence-one who knew how to, and cooked very well, at that. Today, only qualified dietary staff will do. And in larger homes, meals are purchased precooked, hospital style, anyways.

When we have a job opening seeking a PSW, we usually have 20, sometimes 30 or more applicants within a few days.

However, we are very reluctant to hire a younger person, for a number of reasons. Unlike larger homes which want personal care workers in that function only, in our small home this job also includes dietary jobs, meaning cooking, as well as housekeeping, meaning cleaning and doing laundry. Girls coming from school or college are surprised to learn that. "What, I have to clean, too? Cooking? Never done that! Baking? At home, my Mom always does that!"

You would be surprised when I tell you how many young ladies in their twenties have no idea about cooking a meal. No doubt fueled by the fast food movement, apparently cooking is not 'in' anymore. We have a fair share of applicants who told us in no uncertain terms that they never cooked or baked in their lives. This is astonishing. I thought they taught that in schools! Also, it might appear easy for someone to be able to swing a mop or broom, but once you watch some of those newly hired girls do that job, you wonder how or if they ever cleaned their own place.

But, as the law goes, we have to have PSW's, which, by the way, is today not even a recognized or regulated occupation.

We are also looking for a quality in a job seeker called *compassion*. But it is difficult to check with a job application or within an interview. For personal reasons and because of the privacy act it is not even allowed to look into this, much less to talk about it.

So, this 'Quality' remains unspoken, but is yet an important segment of our hiring policy. Society just does not speak about those things. Again, younger job seekers, by definition not by judgment, are less able to fill this niche, with some notable exceptions. So much for endless job opportunities for PSW's. This might only materialize if the current trend of living in retirement homes grows, as it will for a while. After the pinnacle is reached, and baby boomers are on their way out, it is then when this industry will shrink, simply because available income is not available any more, and to pay for this fairly expensive option of living.

Larger homes, actually even our size homes, face additional pressure by labour unions aggressively recruiting staff of retirement homes as new targets. This fact alone puts tremendous pressure on the financial ability of the homes, which now must pay wages similar to hospitals-that's the wage level the unions are striving for, which by definition is impossible to reach. After all, hospital wages (in Canada) are in the final analysis paid for by the tax payer, not privately. Seen any hospital making profit lately? And it will be harder and harder to keep up with higher and higher wages, and so this expense is in the end paid for by the senior resident in the form of rent.

Just one quick number. The average cost in a retirement residence, for assisted living and not including any further nursing care, has risen in the last 10 years in Ontario from 1,640 per month to $2,380 per month in 2010. The figure only one year later rose to $2,540/month. In 2012 we are having $2,840. The last figure published by CHMC for 2013 shows the threshold of $3,000/month has surpassed. The average rent payment sits at $3,204/month, and that's the average cost of a retirement home place in Ontario. Compare that to the rise in cost caused by inflation, which is next to nil. Compare that with the official rate of cost increase, the index, which is 0.8%/year +/– for the last few years.

There are now more and more homes whose rates are exceeding $5,000/mth, and I have seen places which charge $10,000 per month. Where does it end?

It is easy to see that the gap between available income and cost of living in retirement homes is getting wider and wider, by a large margin, and surprisingly fast, too.

Night shift staffing

Do retirement homes need night shift staffing? There is no clear cut answer, but the following elements should help clear that question;

- *Size*: A 100 bed retirement home is much more likely, actually ten times as much likely, to have night shift staff than a 10 bed retirement home
- *Care requirements of residents*: the more care is to be provided, then the need of night time attention increases. Chances are there is night shift staff necessary.
- In smaller homes, sometimes owners live onsite and can be called in a case of emergency. This is much more common today than it used to be.

Interesting to note, that in general there is a much wider acceptance of the concept of night time staffing.

The explanation for this is that on one hand, full service is simply expected from the consumer's viewpoint, especially keeping in mind the price tag of rents charged. But also, because retirement homes have now much more care cases requiring attention during the night time than they used to. This kind of assistance was at one point considered care and the provision of which was left up to nursing homes. Still there are many smaller homes out there which have night staff available only on call, perhaps even the owner.

This is not without reason-cost.

After all, this is not a hospital, or even nursing home, where night calls are expected in the routine of the business. Retirement homes are a bit different. In theory, we should not get any calls at all, except in case of emergency. This is what the 'call bell' system is all about.

Reality looks different. Some retirement homes are actually charging for each call. This is done in an attempt to curb nuisance calls and have only real emergency calls coming in. That's one way, the cost of which you may find only in small print. In one larger residence in our vicinity, the charge is $38 for each call made. It may succeed at that. But then, it makes also residents hesitant to call when there is an actual emergency, or even in instances where a call is appropriate.

User type charges, with a basic rent payment which looks attractive, but all assistance services like personal care etc. are on top—in this case, even the use of the call bell. This new practise is borrowed from the home care industry, which has adapted a similar model, as mentioned above.

I believe this is not very 'user-friendly' at all, if you allow me to use that term in this context.

While it is true that the majorities of residents don't use the call bells excessively for assistance, there are always a few who do; they think it's for room service. They need the attention, and ring half a dozen times a night. Their definition of emergency is quite different from the rest of us. They call if they can't find their glasses, or they need a drink of water. Or their cat needs to be petted, while it's laying on their lap in bed. In such 'emergencies', they may lean on that button until someone shows up. And because it worked so flawlessly the last time, they try that again and again. By the end of the night, they are really proud of themselves in having the night staff trained so well-she appears within minutes every time she calls!

And that's the problem. Night shift has to be onsite, awake and at the resident's room within minutes. In case of a real emergency. But then again, in a small home this probability is not very high, in fact so small that the question comes up, if the cost justifies the expense. This cost, however wasn't always so high. What happened?

I remember being in real estate back in the eighties, and had many listings as I was in the specialized niche of small businesses, suitable for immigrants to purchase and with this financial commitment to be able to immigrate into Canada.

As a result, I had many smaller mom and pop businesses listed, including retirement homes, and had insight of their financials. I remember a good many small operations had paid a back then common wage of $25 for the night shift—round and accepted number. This was at a time when people earned $6 or 7/hour, so this wage meant about half of the night time paid, the rest of the night was unpaid. From the viewpoint of the operator, it was because no work was performed.

That view, of course, is not in line with today's view. If an employee spends her time at the facility and is on standby for any emergency, this is regarded as working time and as such, has to be paid. The Employments Standard Act says that this time would be considered on-call time, and that shall be reimbursed with the commonly paid wage-the entire time, not just the time when actual work was performed.

With this development, other means have to be found to occupy the otherwise idle night shift with productive work. One thought is to employ them in other sectors, but this only works marginally. Cleaning for instance is one way to have night shift workers occupy their unused time, but it stops dead at for instance vacuuming. Baking pies and such is an option, but it turns out to be the most expensive pies in town.

Thus smaller operations have a hard time justifying this expense from a viewpoint of value for money. Hence it is mostly smaller homes which have to scramble for cheaper solutions, knowing that even standby time must be paid for. To demonstrate the impact of paid night shift staff: In our home the monthly rent payment for the residents could be reduced by $200 per month, if we had no night shift. That's the impact.

In my proposed future oriented senior housing model, searching for ways to offer more inexpensive senior living, I propose workable solutions to this problem, actually with the payroll cost of all employed staff.

Management salaries

Just for information purposes, here are some numbers in case you ever wondered how much the managers of all these fancy places make:

The generally accepted figure for management salaries is 4% of the revenue.

While this number is quite substantial in larger homes, and reaches into the low six figures, it might be remembered that the workload in larger homes quickly increases to the point where this figure may be split among 2 or even more managers—called job splitting.

Come to think of it, even in our home we have this kind of set-up between my wife and me. And in our case, the number is $22,000/year, which we share 50/50.

Summary of rents and rates

To summarize, the rents in retirement homes are going up over and above the average of other industries, because of numerous specific reasons:
- The homes are now becoming larger per unit, and more residences are getting fancier and fancier. Read: more expensive for the tenant
- Increased rules and regulations take a bigger bite out of the profitability, and these costs must be passed on. Read: more expensive for the tenant.
- The hype of job seekers that this industry is the career path of the future, which relates to higher education jobs and thus, salaries. In addition, higher qualified staff such as nurses to look after the increased load on medical care provided must be employed, which was not on so much the case in the past. As a result, staffing cost and wages are on the increase. Read: more expensive for the tenant.
- Increased safety features of the home must be met. Commercial elevators instead of stair lifts, add-on sprinkler systems, increased safety equipment

such as a beefed up fire alarm system, additional fire doors, wander guard systems, emergency generators and many more safety measures have to be installed, to name but a few. It all has to be installed and maintained—all at an additional cost. Read: more expensive for the tenant.

- Safety is becoming a more and more pressing issue. Staff training in safety measures including evacuation of the home is increasingly checked up upon from official agencies. Example: Once upon a time, annual fire drills were common. Now it's once a month, for each staff member to participate. So is tested and witnessed evacuation procedures. This means they have to be called in just for the training purposes. That results in additional cost. Read: more expensive for the tenant.
- Unions are aggressively targeting retirement homes, and, once successfully established, the entire cost of payroll increases dramatically. Read: more expensive for the tenant. This, actually, is a very big one.
- Losing ground in its ability to attract sufficient tenant occupancies results in more advertising, more aggressive marketing to bid for fewer tenant prospects, which increases cost. In addition, services offered must do so increasingly competitively. The thought that once a tenant is attracted and moves in, the tenants stay till the end of their lives, is wrong thinking. Despite the difficulties and logistics involved, unhappy tenants do move out and to other residences. As a result, operators have to be alert and must give their very best—which of course, is what competitive business is all about.
- The residences are more and more being taking over by American companies, presumably not for interests of providing welfare—good profit margins are expected, as the American business world is well known to do—along with big salaries and management cost which must be paid. Read: more expensive for the tenant.

CHAPTER 3

Running Out of Funds

In Europe, at least in most western countries, the monthly contributions from each employee's paycheque to pay for old age care and medical cost is much higher than in North America. While these funds are on political level arguably also mismanaged, a similar problem like this here exists—namely, never enough funds available. It should be noted that it only makes sense to pay for one's old age cost by monthly 'savings' in their productive years, a concept younger people have no idea of. Vehicles to do that are abound, albeit not well known and not sufficient. But studies show that saving is not 'in' anymore. Probably because it is difficult enough to make ends meet as it is. Even savings for a rainy day, like a car repair etc. is hardly practised. The reality is that available income hardly pays the bills, let alone save! Quite often, earners are only one paycheque away from catastrophic events. This was not always so. I grew up with the concept of having 6 months' worth of living expenses in the bank account, for a 'rainy day'. Wow! Tell anyone that today and see what happens. Although my Dad practised this, me, I was guilty all my earning years when I was only able to have 1 month of living expenses in the account—when I was lucky.

When good old German chancellor Otto von Bismarck introduced the "old age pension" system in 1880, there were only 3% of all the population which reached the age of 65 and were able to collect actual pension cheques. And these 3% did so not for long. That of course, is different today, very different. It is no problem to withdraw from government coffers an amount of pension which way exceeds what ever has been paid in in 40 or even 50 years of productive earnings and contributions. It does not take a scientist to figure out that this fact is totally out of focus and unsustainable. Some folks actually take out several times the amount which has ever been paid in. And then the seniors are still complaining that their cheque is not enough to cover their present day living expenses. No wonder that something is about to give, if not crash.

While it is true that old folks pension may not enough to live on, but who says it must? It must be remembered that perhaps it is questionable that in years to come, governments may not even pay out what they pay out today. Much less. The writing, of course, is on the wall. Younger people are well advised to consider looking after they own old age pension. This is a tall order, in particular if living expenses cannot be met today, let alone "save" a dollar for every dollar spent for old age support. There are ways of doing just that, and the younger a person is, the easier it is. But who looks into these possibilities, and who actually is disciplined enough and adheres to these self-appointed promises of making monthly contributions for a time frame of perhaps 40 years of earnings?

The answer is, of course, not many. Hence I believe this entire set-up needs to be revamped. If governments tell us how tight the pension fund is, and even more so in the future, then it must give the earning population vehicles to earn their own way for their retirement years. It might be argued that these vehicles are in place, but while this is true, they are a far cry away of what I am talking here. Just not taxing a part of the income, as in RRSP plans, are just not attractive enough, and certainly cannot pay for 30 years of retirement.

Again, the notion must be considered that in years to come, everyone is on their own. Everyone has to look after their own finances in their later, not earnable years. That's with today's long life expectancy quite an amount, if you do the math. No government pension funds in the kitty any more.

And while for instance in Germany the common way of funding old age pensions is by a sort of government backed insurance, this is in some ways of benefit; as opposed to direct government funding. The premiums for this insurance are mandatory, and the insurance pays until death. Even investments can be structured simply by 'paid until death'.

Not so in North America. While care insurance available here, for starters, are hardly known, and since not mandatory, not many people are inclined to sign up. When they do at a later age, once the need is recognized and it sets in that perhaps not all of old age care burden is paid by the government, the contributions to that care insurance becomes prohibitively expensive. To make this kind of insurance even more unattractive, the ages that these benefits to be paid out are capped. They are only good up until a certain age, i.e. 80 years. That makes it nearly useless, and not many are interested in signing up. That's the age it is most needed. As usual, insurance companies tend to limit known risks. In this case, they are bound to really shell out once older age is reached, which they are trying to avoid. Still, it would be most important to sign up from the early years of employment on, so that premiums are lowest. But this of course is in stark contrast to the interests of young earners, who have absolutely no inclination to pay for this kind of monthly expense. Hence it should be mandatory or other ways have to be found. Back home, after 40 years of paying into this insurance, when and if the time comes and care expenses are necessary, or even only the cost of living in a retirement home, funds are available. That fact alone makes the option of living in a retirement home in Europe much more attractive and even possible. By and large, it is paid for, even if only partially. While it is still classified as "private paid for homes", it is paid for by an insurance—at least partially, and depending on the degree of care needed.

This is unlike in North America, where all, key word all funding for retirement home living has to be borne privately.

The risk of running out of funds is real, as opposed to this not being possible in most western countries in Europe.

We have, however, a wonderful financial tool in place which addresses this problem—the life annuity. Trouble is, it's not very well known, and can only be applied in some cases.

With this alternative tool one can buy with an available lump sum an annuity with lifelong payments in connection with a life insurance. Depending on the type, this may be built in. Today even banks offering this financial vehicle.

This would do the same. The purchase of an annuity also has a safeguard built in of spending extra, just because the funds are sitting in the account. Discipline is needed not to tap into that account, but leave it for the payments of monthly expenses. Quite often we hear from people, that dipping into the account took place—a one-time spending. For that new car which needed to be bought, or that cruise, and so on.

In North America, annuities are mainly sold and paid out by insurance companies, which partly explains the hesitance of wide acceptance, especially if the recipient is reliant on the payout for the remainder of his/her life. Insurance companies have been known to go under. It is this hesitance to hand over a sizable amount of cash, receiving in return a monthly payment till the end of life. Or the promise to do so. There is an understandable hesitance in public view to part with money for a promise. Promises can be broken. As it is, it is up to other insurance companies to guarantee payments in the event one company fails. I believe that in this case as in many similar, the government has to provide a safeguard—next to education. With this safe guard in place, along with a lot more education, it might be possible for the life annuity to become a well-known tool to pay an additional monthly cheque.

The consumer is assured, however, that the process is very well monitored, even to the point that in the event the insurance company has financial trouble, other ones are catching up to continue making the payments. In todays low interest climate, the annuity hardly pays out any interest earned, which again, does it not make very attractive.

I can only recommend Moske Milesky's work on that subject, called "Life Annuities—An optimal Product for Retirement Income". (E-book only) This explains in great depth how the industry works.

So, education is needed. But who is to advise the old folks? There are financial advisors, but don't hold your breath that older people will seek out those professionals. It's not going to happen. If at all, younger family members are the ones who are receiving advice, and then talking to their parents.

As a result, the current financing model is too complicated to be understood, let alone practised. Alternatives are not present, and larger amounts of money are simply held in the bank account, one step up from under the mattress, and simply used up, hoping that life ends sooner than funds.

Here is the typical scenario: Usually, there may be a couple with no family, and there are many of those, and all of a sudden one spouse dies off. That leaves the remaining partner to stay alone in the house. If the decision is made to leave the home, this house then is being put up on the market and eventually sold. The proceeds of the sale are now as a monetary lump sum available for the future expenses, like that of ongoing retirement home living. While this seems okay for a while, at one point the realization sets in that this lump sum is being eaten up as time goes by, and seems to be eaten up faster all the time. Fear sets in over what will happen once these funds run out.

Over the years, we have seen many of those cases, and it is devastating to see folks in their eighties or older having worries about what will happen to them if they outlive their funds—clearly a terrible picture to paint.

In the retirement home I ran previously, I had an older gentleman living with us who befriended a lady, living in the room next to his. Soon a romance developed. They got married. That made even the headline news in the local paper. However, the marriage was not all just because of romance, as it was portrayed, because that looked good.

The underlying reason was—money.

The guy had only enough money left for less than two years of the cost of the retirement home living. If he decided to live longer, he would have a serious problem. The lady, however, was well off.

So this then, is real life.

As an operator, I wish I could help in those situations, and actually, I do—but this is a personal confession. We have had several cases, but are usually not informed of this kind of 'emergency' until the buck stops dead. We have introduced lowering rents substantially to the extent which is against business interests, but in the end, it's human. We just share the headache with these old folks. Then again, I have to remember that there is the other hat I'm wearing—the other mandate is to run a business. Clearly, this is a situation, being torn between my heart to open and help these cases. How could I possibly kick them on out the street, once and if they run out of money?

The last model I have developed and only applied once is to lower the rent indefinitely by $100/month, till we reach the pension income level. This puts the occupant's mind totally at ease. And it certainly stretches the last available dollars. The lowest threshold would be their pension check only, but that's fine with me. It is reassuring to know that one person on earth has been helped. And I know that this is only one case happening once in a while. So it can be done!

At the same time, there are empty rooms to fill! Banks do not ask where the money for their mortgage is coming from, as long as it does!

These situations, I believe needs to be addressed and prevented with and by government assistance, unless we find better ways without government interference.

Even if this assistance just lies with better education about for instance annuities, or perhaps guarantees of sorts. The mere thought that in our society it is possible for once affluent folks, just because they happen to live longer than expected, to outlive their available funds, and have no other options available to them, makes me cringe.

This principle I believe needs some serious revamping.

CHAPTER 4

The Missing Link

The retirement residence as a 'home'?

In one aspect the retirement home industry has failed, and is increasingly doing so.

It has failed to provide the senior resident not just with a fancy place to live, but to provide a 'home', which can be called home, where people love to move to, love to live, and love to get old—older, that is.

The current trend in the name of economics to build bigger and bigger residences is driving this aspect further and further away. No doubt one of the main reasons an elderly person wants to hang in with their present home is because it is just that—their home, the home in which the family has been raised. And there is no pressing reason to give it all up. The alternative of living in a retirement residence among several hundred or so other residents, is for most not very attractive. And then, there is money, the associated cost. Living at home is considered "free", right or wrong, but the same cannot be said for the ongoing cost in a residence. Then there is the fear of getting personal assistance by strangers. For instance, getting bathed and dressed. This alone is a factor many do not like. The fear of losing one's dignity is a big fear. In larger residences, the turnover of staff is so high that the poor occupant hardly gets to know some of their staff members before they change again. Even with all the fancy amenities and activities provided, it is just not the same. It is not 'home'.

And as long as economic reasons keep shaping the design criteria of these residences, the loss of the 'home' cannot be made undone.

The difference from the States:

The typical prospective tenants, or the residents, are the ones who are willing to give up their 'home' for trading it with what I call an "all year round resort style living". Granted, this is a valid option, and many folks like this idea. And the fact that the age of the senior moving into a retirement home in the States is a staggering 12 years earlier than in Canada, speaks for the popularity of this living option. While this is also not a 'home' in the strict sense, it is more desirable for some folks to live permanently in a resort style living arrangement.

This full time resort living is not even an option in Canada. We don't have them, at least not from what I've seen, or at least not to the same grand scheme.

From this aspect, Canada is lagging way behind. Although solid efforts are made to copy the fancy communities housing more than a thousand residents as they are in the States, this has to date not happened in Canada. When the Canadian senior is presented with all the available options, there really are no options at all. It's all retirement home living, albeit with some different faces, meaning services and amenities. The only options are to investigate the different sizes, services, rates etc. but it is all more or less the same. And then there is the difference in price, depending on the degree of fanciness or size. And the mere aspect and the possibility that nursing care is being paid for in Canada by the government does not trigger any need for Canadian seniors to pay huge entry fees, to move in and to live in a residence, and further to give up their home.

During the last 24 years, I had prospective tenants going through the various residences I operated not just in the hundreds, but low thousands.

The responses of many, many of these prospective tenants or residents are always the same, and can be summed up as follows:

The responses are; "You have a wonderful place here, and I would move here in a second, but (in the order of number of responses):

a) "I'm not ready yet"
b) "I'm too young, but will consider your place first when I get older and need your services"
c) "I'm totally healthy, so I do not need to go into a home, just curious what these places look like"
d) "I can totally cope on my own at home, and there is no immediate reason for me to move".
e) "I am not sick and do not need care"

Given those responses, it becomes painfully clear that after 50 years of marketing retirement home living as an attractive alternative living option has somehow utterly failed. People are not willing to give up their home to trade for a living in a retirement home. People love to stay at home. Whatever life throws at them, they are hell bent to stay at home. If all else fails, there is home care which will look after them, so there is no worry. Staying at home it is.

Well, then the course of action is clear. In order to accommodate this basic wish, the retirement home industry would do well to provide folks with alternative living options which are so attractive that people actually want them. What they want is a place they could call home. This would also entice them to move there much earlier, not just when failing health forces these steps.

However, the industry is not looking in this direction, but rather the opposite. Larger and larger homes and residences let old folks feel more and more estranged, and give residents less and less a feeling that they have indeed a new home which they would love to live in and call their home.

So it can be said that there exists a large gap, and this gap is widening.

Unless this gap closes, not widens, the industry has no chance to survive.

Designers are ignoring this aspect. They are not asking for this. Their design parameters are stemming from different interests altogether. The interests of developers and controlling groups is profitability, nothing else.

Most people have the wrong idea about what retirement homes are, and what they offer. What they do is offer an alternative living option for the healthy and independent ones. They offer an "enriched" living for the ones who can still enjoy what is being offered. And, yes, they do offer "assistance". The trouble is that this word has a different meaning for different folks, especially for the retirement home and for public at large. They are not designed to look after considerable shortfalls health wise, or dementia and a host of other cognitive impairments. Today's homes are not the extended arm of a nursing home, or an old folks home where old folks move in just before they die. Although this is exactly the image people have. And it has not changed in all these years. People in earnest believe that they "have to" come to a residence only once they need care—keyword care, not assistance. Because assistance is what is offered, but not care in the sense of ongoing care. People believe once they have health issues and they really cannot look after themselves anymore, then it's time to move. And no one is admitting this fact. Only once they absolutely cannot cope with living at home any longer, only once the doctor tells them they have to live in a home from here on out. There are many, if not most prospective residents who should have moved to a retirement residence 5 or even 10 years earlier. Then the operator would be able to offer 'enriched living' as we call it. From programs to outings to trips to mingling among others to defy loneliness, there is a host of things to do and experience. Instead of coping at home, watching TV and waiting patiently till family comes and visits, or worse, waiting for the time to come to go into a nursing home. Or, worst of all, to hang in and wait to die. What an outlook!

The retirement home industry, however, is not catering to this very needy client, called prospective resident, simply because it fails to sell this aspect of service. And it cannot sell this service, if it is not wanted. In the meantime the prospective resident stays home.

And so what homes do provide is sadly misunderstood.

Enter the fact that indeed the industry is bound to pick up residents with health issues, as we will investigate further, and are even burdened with keeping them even if they really should be in a nursing home. One can easily see why there is such a vast difference between what the home can do, and offers, and what it does not.

Public awareness differs again in their conception of what the retirement home is, and does, and differs immensely from the truth.

The same is true with the cost, in particular, who pays for it. Not a week goes by but that we get a call where folks want to know where to apply for support of payment to a retirement home. The idea that retirement homes are not subsidized and have to be paid for 100% by the tenant, is not known by many.

So much for the future of that industry.

To sum it up: People do not fully understand what retirement homes are, what they do, especially what they do not do, and who pays for them.

Albeit the industry is working hard to make their prospective tenants understand, there is this wide spread assumption that these homes provide care for the ones in need. Keyword care. And since nobody admits that they need care, nobody sees any reason to move into a retirement residence.

This is the gap mentioned earlier, and this gap is getting wider all the time.

If the retirement home industry is not able to see this gap, and is further not able to close that gap, then the future looks not so rosy. And the exploding senior population will seek out alternative living options.

There is another link, which I propose shall be looked into.

Holistic wellness

The retirement home industry is best equipped to provide an add-on service, which would be essential for North Americans to adapt, but is very little practised; holistic wellness. While holistic wellness is indeed a growing sector, it could be an exploding one. Just ask how many homes actually have a swimming pool. Ask the question to American homes, and then Canadian homes. Then compare the number from the States to the one in Canada. There you have it.

There is a big difference right here. Lacking statistics, I can say that in our jurisdiction of approximately 150 km radius, there are 113 retirement residences. None of them offers a swimming pool. And that is of course only one ingredient of being able to offer holistic wellness. The term includes a whole host of health related treatments, all alternative healing treatments, which at an older age is even more important. Now is the time available, and a greater health consciousness is setting in with folks wanting to do something for their health. And there is a ton of available options to provide just that. It's not only medication which enables our folks to age well, but it's a healthier life style, as well. The beauty with holistic wellness is that it is prescribed. Nobody has to question their discipline in actually following the good intentions. It's being done for you.

From this view point, it is foreseeable that retirement homes could offer short term stays, not unlike the German concept of spas, which is a 3 weeks to 6 months stay in a resort type accommodation. (3 weeks to 1 month for the still working population) But opposed to resorts, the type of health treatment is prescribed. Guests have a strict daily regimen of health related activities, carried out under medical supervision. These wellness treatments can be offered in 2 ways: First, off and on in a rotating fashion for the live-in residents, second, in a compact form, that is, a full day treatment for a prescribed limited time of 3 weeks minimum, and from there on in weekly increments up to half year, always with one week relaxation in between. This is how it is practised back home. So this makes a retirement home suite available to a dozen guests or so all year round. It's not hotel style, but it's not full time living, either.

A typical routine schedule may be this: Wake-up call at 6.00 am, followed by a hay sac treatment. Then yoga time. Breakfast is served afterwards, with a diet tailored to the guest's health requirement, issued by doctor's or dieticians order. The same set-up for all meals. Breakfast is followed by outdoor exercise, which may include a long walk. Lunch is at 12:00, and a nap after lunch. At 3:00 p.m., residents are treated to a one hour swimming in the pool, or perhaps a sauna bath. The next day may include the same activities, or a few may be replaced with some other treatments, such as massage or reflexology sessions, followed by Kneipp's cold water bath treatments. After such a daily routine the residents are likely to be off to bed early.

What do you think of that?

This would go a long way in the today's tooted "Preventive Medicine", rather than fixing illnesses, once developed, by means of medication.

Community

One of the big drawing cards of a retirement home is the aspect of 'community living'; that is, as it is commonly understood, the living among others, especially for those who are lonely, which is no doubt the majority of potential residents. The alternative of living with others, like minded folks, is really attractive.

This becomes so important that homes and larger residences use this term of 'community living' for marketing purposes; they even call themselves a 'Retirement Community'.

Studies have shown that it is community that elderlies are after. It is in community they can still function, because there is a purpose. The purpose is to be part of it, and contribute ones share to the well-being of the community, and their members. So it gives the elderly participant, the member of the community a purpose, and because the community has so many different facets, there is bound to be something to do and to contribute for everyone, who is part of this community.

However, one should be a bit careful with this kind of interpretation. The term 'community' is widely used and very loosely these days, and focusses more on the very fact that it sells.

"Community", really is different. There are a few elements which makes a community. Let's have a look at the elements of true community, and see which ones are actually practised in a retirement home setting;

1) A number of like-minded folks get together, on their own will, for a commonly shared interest (in our case, co-habitation)
2) These like-minded folks practise or participate in the execution of this common shared interest (Yes)
3) These like-minded folks govern themselves (No)
4) These like-minded folks make decisions together, usually not in the form of majority voting, but in the form of consensus (No)

5) These like-minded folks identify themselves as part of something larger than the sum of their individual relationship (No)
6) These like-minded folks commit themselves for the long term to their own well-being, and doing their part to help and assist one another, for the entire group's well-being. (No)

One can easily see, that a top-down management in a retirement home setting cannot, by definition, run or manage a community, because a true community runs itself through its members. Thus it can be seen that the term is used incorrectly, but this is not without intent, because "community" is what attracts people to move in to begin with.

In addition, today's understanding of community is different from the past. Older folks have good vibrations when it comes to community, because this was a good thing, back then. Now, there was a time in the past, when "community" had a sour taste to it. If someone remembers the sixties' and its hippie movement, where everything related to community was downright "bad". But this was short lived. That is forgotten. In general it can be said that the word as well as the concept of "community" is considered by and large very positive, especially in the mind of elderly folks, who grew up with this concept.

Trouble is the spirit of community is not existent any more. Look at urban dwellers, who hardly know their neighbors. And how can they, because statistics say that every 14 months an apartment changes hands? In Nova Scotia, by the way, it is every 8 months! No wonder, then, that community cannot establish itself even for younger folks. Hence "community" only sounds good, like a reaching back into the past, when community was good!

However, it does not look all that bleak—enter Spiritual Awareness.

And this is the other link which is missing.

When you see me sitting quietly, like a sack upon a shelf,
Don't think I need your chattering. I'm listening to myself.
Hold! Stop! Don't pity me! Hold! Stop your sympathy!
Understanding if you got it, otherwise I'll do without it!
When my bones are stiff and aching and my feet won't climb the stair,
I will only ask one favor: Don't bring me no rocking chair.
When you see me walking, stumbling, don't study and get it wrong.
'Cause tired don't mean lazy and every goodbye ain't gone.
I'm the same person I was back then, a little less hair, a little less chin,
A lot less lungs and much less wind.
But aint I lucky I can still breathe in.

~Maya Angelou

CHAPTER 5

The Retirement Home and Growing Spiritual Awareness

As we grow to a higher level of awareness, which is currently taking place, we will recognize that it simply is not acceptable any longer to charge older people for someone else, someone younger, to look after them. Especially it is not right to strip them from their life savings in a few short years. Until we reach that final stage of awareness, however, there will be baby steps along the way.

These are recognisable by the insight of yes perhaps a charge, but not a charge through the nose.

As it is today, in most cases retirement home living is eating up most, if not all, of the senior's life savings, and these are the remaining tangible results of a lifelong work. Of course, there are exceptions, especially for the lucky ones who gain the proceeds of real estate appreciation, which is part of their life savings, as mentioned earlier, or the plain wealthy ones. But it must be seen as it transpires today. Our senior population is asked to shell out their life savings for the benefit of someone taking care of them in the last remaining portion of their lives.

For a spiritually evolving, thinking mind, there is something profoundly wrong with this approach.

Alternative solutions have to be found. These are, at this point in time, hardly available, because everyone involved in senior care wants to make not just a living, but big bucks. Not just retirement residences. From a paid companion, who believes her work is indispensable and therefore must be rewarded in dollars, to PSW's, who, after taking a course to become one, now believes she is on the ladder for a senior related job career promising high wages, and to nurses, hospital staff, doctors, and not the least, the pharmaceutical industry. All taken together, it is no wonder that taking care of senior population is a profitable undertaking. With the silver tsunami on its way, it will be increasingly difficult to pay for all this. But even within the context of this book, looking at housing options, we would do well to investigate other, meaning less costly alternatives. Looking at Europe would be a good step in the right direction.

Below mentioned alternative living options are suddenly of interest. Alternative living options do not exhibit maximizing profit as the main driving factor in designing senior living arrangements. With a greater spiritual awareness, there are different parameters at play now, different interests. Maximizing profit is not the main goal anymore. And it shouldn't be, because targeting the care and well-being for the senior population for increased profit is something which should be frowned upon. Whoever is going that route may well be reminded that he himself will be in the same boat one day.

Take for instance the aspect of providing the senior a *home* where she really feels *home* again, and not just being door number 47 in a never ending hallway. So the well-known alternative living options, while not of great interest today, will find more practical application, once more spiritual awareness takes place, sets in and is applied. We will investigate alternative living options in more detail later on.

In practically all northern European countries, it is common to find many family members who are caring for their elder parents, to various degrees—of course not heavy care, but simply assistance. Although this is currently also diminishing, experts are predicting a reverse! Family members may only give enough assistance to get their parents through the day, help with housing chores such as cleaning or looking after the pet, and the occasional errand. Just being there, with the elderly, is helpful and appreciated. Charging money would not enter their minds. This basic knowledge is not new; in fact this is where we all came from, and this is where we all will be heading in the future. This trend will likely continue, in particular with the additional knowing that alternative living options for Mom like retirement home living has turned out to be too expensive. As the somewhat sarcastic saying goes, "Before I save up enough money to live in a retirement home, I will die"! And that is so true.

At the same time, regular family homes are size wise way overbuilt, but certainly not to the extremes of those in North America. All these humongous dwellings and residential houses currently built and overbuilt could now have the added benefit of being able to house a parent, or perhaps both, along with them. Besides the economics, more and more people believe it is only right to have Mom and Dad living with them. Since the trend in North America is the same, it can be foreseen that here, too, room is available one day to house Mom and Dad. Family members will now also have the insight to say that they raised them, and tended them when they were babies and kids, and they did not charge anything. So they just took care of them. Now it's 'payback' time, free accommodation and looking after them.

Did you know that in Europe care insurances do not only pay for care provided by third parties, but also for family members? As said earlier, back home in Germany care insurances are obligatory. The cost of this insurance is a sizable amount, deducted from each paycheque from the working population. As a result, uncounted family members are taking care of their elderly parents and cashing in on the insurance, claiming care cost for their parents.

Again, from the spiritual viewpoint this practice is questionable at best, and in time will be regarded as what it really is: Get the insurance to pay out earlier made contributions. Of course it can be argued that time spent to look after Mom will cut out time available to go to work and earn a living, and to pay the bills.

If room is available in any regular family home the thought might come up to take in someone else's parents, and cash in on their insurance. No doubt fueled by this thinking, it does not come as a surprise to learn that taking care of elderly is becoming a 'moonlighting' profession. The step of taking care of your own mother or someone else's mother is a conceivably only a step away, and after all, it's paid for. In North America, this is close to our Group Home concept, but not quite the same. For starters, it's not regulated, since private parties are looking after private tenants, so are not considered commercial. Apparently no government interference is necessary here, as opposed to our Group Home concept. At any rate, if this concept were to be applied here, and elderly parents are looked after in this inexpensive way, then all these folks living at someone else's private home are no longer possible candidates as future residents for retirement homes.

This concept may work for some, but many do think differently. Now back to the retirement homes.

Another thought is the concept of retirement homes in terms of their set-up, as practised today. From this view, we house a number of seniors together in a separate building, in the name of feasibility of economic returns the bigger the better, stepping back and believing we have done a good thing; to some, however, this picture does not look right—from the viewpoint of society. Okay, let's phrase that more bluntly. What we as a society are doing, is bunch seniors together in a retirement home, and exclude them from the rest of society, something like outcasts, out of the way, out of mind. Let someone else take care of this issue, and we, the younger ones, move on with our lives.

This is something we do also with other groups of people, as well. Slums come to mind. So do prisons. We do exclude them, because otherwise they would be in the way. And to make matters worse, seniors themselves think this way, too; this is why it is so easy to get away with that practise. Seniors know very well of their diminishing capabilities, and these diminishing capabilities are constantly frowned upon by younger people. This is why they feel inferior. This is why they feel comfortable with other folks of their own fraternity—now, everyone is slow, everyone is clumsy, everyone is hard of hearing, everyone has bad eyesight, is slow to respond, is hard to understand, will not get the punchline in jokes and many more diminishing faculties, up to total non-functioning of some. Among those similar elderly folks, they feel more comfortable than being ridiculed by being among others, younger folks.

As Mom always says "I don't wanna be a bother..."

As an advanced society, we have to seriously look at the situation. And realize that there is indeed something fundamentally wrong with this approach.

What is required, then, is a different view point from all of society, in particular from younger folks. That has to be taught. That is not learned in the cradle. For sure not by means of a computer or the smart phone. Respect for the elderly is the first step. *What's required is understanding. What's required is compassion. What's more, it is required to have older folks living among us as we did in the past, and not isolate them and make them feel useless, superfluous and unnecessary.* The retirement home as a living quarter is totally contrary to this kind of thinking, and cannot, by definition, adapt this approach. Hence is it obvious what will happen to the retirement home industry once a higher spiritual awareness sets in?

Good thing that this is not the case today, otherwise we would not even have any retirement homes. The very concept would not exist!

And maybe, just maybe, younger folks would benefit from intergenerational living, as well. Perhaps it is no accident that in past generations, younger folks would actually learn something from elders. Wisdom is passed on. Where is all this knowledge and wisdom going today? It goes to waste. It dies out.

Wisdom and knowledge is being wasted away, particularly so in retirement homes, because there are no young ones to listen—and learn.

It is for this reason that my concept of alternative living options for seniors include the element of intergenerational living. It is for this reason that I believe we will revert back to this basic concept one day, a concept we all came from. And that the present set-up, that of retirement homes, is just a 50 year long error in thinking, which will be corrected soon. It has to be corrected soon. This cannot be any different.

But only once a few underlying assumption are changed. These are:
- Older folks have to be bunched together in homes which are designed for profit, and live separately from the rest of society.
- They have to be stripped from their life savings in order to pay for all services, to feed younger folks who believe this is the right thing to do in order to make a living.
- Working in retirement homes and for seniors is a rewarding career; in the monetary sense, not in the spiritual sense.
- We do not have to listen to old folks' knowledge and wisdom, as it does not apply today. We don't need it. They have no idea about computers, so what is possible to learn from them?
- They have to be housed, fed, entertained and dealt with in a way management feels is the right thing to do, in conjunction with government rules, which have their own view of how older folks have to be dealt with, and treated by staff of retirement homes.
- They are told retirement home living is the only option to staying home. Advertising to this effect everywhere proves this.
- Individual life style choices cannot be met or continued to keep up in the very set-up of retirement homes; therefore, they have to be abolished or suppressed.

Staffing costs, evidenced in the payroll, represents in our residence, more than half of the monthly rent paid by residents. If this cost could be reduced substantially, theoretically to 'zero', the monthly rent to be paid would be half; that would make retirement home living much more affordable. But how? After all, staff is told from the outset of the training course to become a PSW, that is the career path of the future, and it pays well, too.

Today, yes, but once spiritual awareness takes hold, this view may differ tomorrow. Enter volunteering.

If staff cost could be drastically reduced by integrating volunteers, or volunteers with basic expenses paid, that would change everything. Dramatically.

Actually, we have those now, even today—but only on a very small scale, and not in the care providing sector.

But it requires a shift of thinking to wrap the mind around this. This is something which is today totally impossible to apply. But tomorrow, it will be different. And again, I am not talking professional care giving. This aspect will be here to stay. I am talking unpaid staff to do minor jobs, from running errands to providing companionship, not to mention activities provided, like readings, and music played by volunteers.

This shift of thinking is necessary. Today's attitude is something like "I am willing to clean up your poop, grandpa, but I want to get paid for that, and quite a bit, too, just so you know. It's not pleasant to do that job for you." Or "Of course I will come in and read some stories to you, but it's my time, and therefore, I want to get paid. Otherwise, I have better things to do".

Tomorrow's attitude will be that the care or assistance providing person, herself, recognizes that one day, she, too, will be in need of help to get through the day. When she, herself, would not want to hear what she just has said. And when that realization sets in she will understand that she does simply not have the money to have someone cleaning her up. And on that day she will realize that, her response to the *same circumstance*, will be different. She will clean up, forget it and move on, and no thoughts of pay will enter her mind. That will be the shift in thinking. It sounds like a pie in the sky, but really, it is not. The change of our society's spiritual thinking is well underway. And it might not be much longer until a vast change of thinking on all levels will take place. The above mentioned change of thinking represents only one of many. (If you want more, stay tuned for the release of my book "*Spiritual Awareness—applied to daily life*").

But there is more. The idea of having volunteers "employed" is maybe not as unthinkable as it seems. Consider this: As we all know, giving and serving is a basic instinct in all of us. But it's mainly obscured, especially in earlier years, in an effort to make a living, in an effort to raise a family, in an effort to get ahead in life, in an effort to get as much enjoyment out of life, you fill in the blanks. One day, however, it's all done.

On that day, however, once it's realized that all this is out of the way, the basic instincts surface. And one of them is to serve the one in need. This may be an animal in need, it may be inhabitants of parts of the world of the underprivileged, it may be the homeless and jobless in our country—or, one day, it may be to help an old person in need. These volunteers are in retirement age themselves. They have their income, and do not need every cent for every hour worked. What they do need, is, to be needed. They want to serve. They want to be useful, not being stacked up upon that heap of others, older, now 'useless' elders. They want to be productive and helpful to society. They want to do their share, and they want to do that before they grow into the segment which cannot be useful any longer. And they know that.

It is foreseeable that in the future, barring unforeseen events, we will have a large number of older persons in need of assistance. This group simply does not have the money to pay for their own assistance needed, and later on, the LTC's. Home care is serving this niche, but the future of the home care industry is questionable at best. After all, their budget is stretched to the limit now, how can they serve when they load not just increases, but multiplies? This is the segment of our population which will emerge, and hugely, too. We will have a lot of older people which are still quite capable of being useful—and who are eager to serve, and eager to provide, and eager to have purpose.

If retirement homes keep catering only to the ones who have money, they may have a difficult time in years ahead, once this market shrinks. At the same time the supply of homes is growing, and, if not checked, will continue to grow. The outcome is obvious. Supply exceeds demand. So then, one solution is to charge less rent, to be more competitive. Another is to broaden the available base of tenants, i.e. residents. But how to do that? How to cater less expensively? How to keep up today's services with less rent being charged? A lot less rent being charged? The answer is: With the help of volunteers, it's that simple. Except, of course, this is a picture too rosy to paint, and runs counter with todays regulations.

But as I said, there is more. There is the fact, that not only people in their second half of their lives are willing to give, and serve, and with no or little compensation, there is also the fact that there will be many of them available. So, there will be a glut of older people who are not old enough to be in need of care or assistance themselves, but well enough to be wanting to be useful for something. And that something might just as well be to serve in retirement homes. One does not have to volunteer to the extent of a full time job. There may be 3 or 4 or 10 people filling that full time job. By the way, this is called 'job sharing' and is also a growing concept, except in our context with volunteers. By doing so, and with the underlying assumption that a higher level of spiritual awareness of the operator is given, this would result in the operation passing on the savings to their future tenants, and their future market they will cater to.

Rent charges could be halved. Now, all of a sudden, retirement home living becomes affordable. Perhaps even to the point that regular receivers of old age pension with a slight additional income would be able to afford this kind of living. A little bit of math would reveal that this could well be possible. Except today's fancy homes are too fancy, read expensive, to make them available to this segment of the population. But they may downsize again, for instance because this is what the resident, the senior, the older person, really wants. I envision this kind of set-up to become a reality during my life time—because I believe it is the logical sequence of things to come. Then, and only then, all this talk about how to pay for expensive homes, and how to house our old folks, will be simply solved by the awakening of spiritual awareness—and its application.

Once a growing spiritual awareness sets in, care givers are often viewed from outsiders as being selflessly devoting themselves to giving care. While this may be true, in many cases the person *giving* quite often does not see it this way. Instead, the care giver sees her role as being honored to be able to look after an elderly person in times of his needs, in times of his frailty, in times of his requirement of being surrounded by someone close to him, and finally, to be with him at the time he needs it most—at the time of his transition to go home to his Creator. At this point, the elderly just wishes to have someone they love with them; they do not want to be in a hospital, and certainly do not want to pass while hooked up to some machinery, with no human being in sight. They are all busy and buzzing around somewhere. What a terrible outlook, if you just dare to put yourself there.

As said above, remember that there is a vast difference between lending a helping hand, what we call assistance, and actually care provided. Full time care, that is. It's not just a job. Here, things are different. Here we are entering care services as provided in what used to be called nursing homes. (LTC, Long Term Care is the new term). Now real challenges begin. The job of these full time and dedicated care providers will in the foreseeable future remain a well-paid occupation, simply because the care giving person is indeed giving a lot, in the real sense of the word, giving of themselves, that is. Overload and exhaustion are hall marks of the care givers in today's nursing homes environments. Stress levels are high. And indeed the occupation is not very pleasant, requiring a certain mind set to get through the day. With the huge care load looming on the horizon—the silver tsunami—I cannot see anything that will lessen the tasks and burdens for care staff. Only spiritually minded people would be able to fill these growing requirements.

Of course, not all elders are living long enough to enter this stage.

A note on palliative care

Most people, I assume have not the opportunity, or even the inclination, to be with someone who is finished with life and is expecting the transition, expecting to go home to their Creator.

But one thing is for certain; If you have had such an experience, it surely brought you as close to God as possible. And with this being said, it is a very deep emotional feeling. As an operator, we do have such opportunities quite often. And when I tell you that staff members come in, on their own time, and rotate their given time and arrange "shifts" on their own, you know that something is right with humans, after all. We are wired this way, but as usual, have found many ways and excuses to avoid and so not to display our most basic instincts.

Max Lucado says it beautifully in his writing:

What Will Matter Then

My dear girl, the day you see I'm getting old. I ask you to please be patient, but most of all, try to understand what I'm going through. If when we talk, I repeat the same thing a thousand times, don't interrupt to say: "You said the same thing a minute ago." Just listen, please.

Try to remember when you were little and I would read the same story night after night, until you would fall asleep. When I don't want to take a bath, don't' be mad and don't embarrass me. Remember when I had to run after you making excuses and trying to get you to take a shower when you were just a girl? When you see how ignorant I am when it comes to new technology, give me the time to learn and don't look at me that way. Remember, honey, I patiently taught you how to do many things like eating appropriately, getting dressed, combing your hair, and dealing with life's issues every day.

The day you see I'm getting old, I ask you to please be patient, but most of all, try to understand what I'm going through. If I occasionally lose track of what we're talking about, give me the time to remember, and if I can't, don't be nervous, impatient, or arrogant. Just know in your heart that the most important thing for me is to be with you. And when my old, tired legs don't let me move as quickly as before, give me your hand the same way I offered mine to you when you first walked. When those days come, don't feel sad—just be with me, and understand me while I get to the end of my life with love. I'll cherish and thank you for the gift of time and joy we shared. With a big smile and the huge love I've always had for you, I just want to say, I love you, my darling daughter.

"When you are in the final days of your life, what will you want? Will you hug that college degree in the walnut frame? Will you ask to be carried to the garage so you can sit in your car? Will you find comfort in rereading your financial statement?

Of course not.

What will matter then, will be people"

CHAPTER 6

Operational Challenges

Nobody talks about this—I do. If one were to lump together many people of all different walks of life, there would be the perfect recipe for challenges, to use a pleasant term. Reality is much more unpleasant.

You would think that for someone who has been around the block for many decades, a certain level of maturity would reveal itself and show understanding and acceptance towards each other, for the common goal of harmonious living together.

But in many cases, this is just not so.

You might also think that just by the amount of rents being charged, there would be only residents of a certain higher level of society, which in turn should mean a certain level of good manners are expected. Does it?

Yes, for the majority of residents, but in many cases, this is just not so.

It should be thought that affluent folks who reside together very closely understand enough to see the complications of this very fact, and act accordingly, for the common goal of enjoying the togetherness, and perhaps friendships and bonding may develop.

I hate to be the bringer of bad news, but in many cases, this is just not so. Of course it happens, and this is wonderful. This is after all, what makes the home the home it is.

And this is where the enjoyment of staff members comes in, this is what makes our working here fulfilling. For the residents, a harmonious, joyful living together, a sharing of fun, but also pain. And yes, this can be observed, as well.

However, in many cases, this is just not so.

The fact that people who can afford the rent and are affluent is by no means a guarantee of good manners or certain good behaviour. One only thinks that way. Some homes have even a dress code for dining.

Great! I do not know what these places do when certain human traits become obvious, in particular at dining me, the time of public exposure. Add to that elements of dementia, forgetfulness and a host of other illnesses which may prohibit or undermine behaviour patterns otherwise invisible or less apparent; now, at meal time, sadly, they are. And this is highly disturbing for other, cognitively aware residents.

Internet blogs I regular visit tell me that retirement homes are by their very nature breeding grounds for gossip, and residents find lots of reasons for finger pointing and fault finding among each other. It could be assumed that this may be tolerable, and probably it is. But out of finger pointing and faultfinding, more unpleasant and unwanted situations quickly develop. Dislikes and unacceptance among residents is very common, up to the point where intervention is necessary. Swearing and loud voices are common, swinging fists are possible, and downright physical violence is also not unheard of.

"I am not going into the dining room ever again as long as I live, if *she* is in there again. I just can't stand her."

"If *that man* looks at me again in this annoyingly lewd way, I'll move out tonight!"

"I don't know why they don't get rid of *her, she* should have been be in a nursing home years ago!"

"*That* guy surely does not belong here. Why is he not going pounding sand and lives somewhere else"?

And so, the staff is constantly exchanging noted behaviour patterns and remarks of some specific residents towards each other. These exchanges are not taking place to serve further gossip, but to educate each other, to warn each other of situations which could develop into violence of sorts, even if it's only verbal. Tensions—any tensions—are to be nipped in the bud.

Every time we hear some raised voices, we have to run to save the sinking ship, to intervene and bring the situation under control. I call this a constant alertness to keep the ship on an even keel. And this is indeed a job which requires constant alertness. Of course, these comments are just pertaining to a few residents prone to cause trouble, not the majority. But it is these few who do cause trouble, and must be tended to immediately in the interest of a harmonious atmosphere.

A few examples of daily challenges to follow—just for your entertainment:

Speaking of entertainment, we have regular musicians who devote their time to entertaining our residents. This is a very common thing performed by a variety of amateur musicians, and is highly appreciated. It shows that there is indeed some spirit found in serving others, and is often provided by younger people. We are grateful for this, in particular when younger people give their time. We have our regular performers, and sometimes new players who like to practise together. What better "playground" than a retirement home? And these performances are mostly appreciated and enjoyed by our residents, breaking up their day with the music offered. Keyword most—not for all.

As it is with humans, and in particular with residents, this is sometimes not appreciated at all, especially if the performers are working people who have to come after hours, in the evening. We strive to have the event take place as soon after supper as possible, and try to wrap everything up before 8:00 p.m. but there are folks who are bothered by all of this. They are bothered by the folks coming, by the commotion going on in the home, by the type of music being played which they can't stand, by the "racket" going on, which refers to the music, and by the fact that it's dragging on half the night, while decent people are trying to get some sleep. And they never tire of telling you.

And so, we can't please everyone, although we try. And again, while the majority of the residents love this kind of entertainment, the ones who don't complain about it in great detail. And all this trouble can be summed up by the fact that residents are housed together, too closely for comfort, with no opportunity to shut out these events.

Often, we offer "movie afternoons". With today's technology, we have stored several hundred movies in one of those magic black boxes. And our folks really do enjoy these. So one should think this is an easy one. Voila, not so! For some, it's way too loud, while others can't hear a darn thing which is being spoken! Now, this seems to be a trivial issue, which can be easily tended to, until 20 minutes into the movie you see them all storming away, behind their walkers, all in different directions! Something went sideways! Probably that *volume* issue again!

We now have two groups, the group with normal hearing, and the ones who do not belong into this group. Those who think they don't need a hearing aid. This group we have now in a separate living room with another 60" TV. This TV has speakers of more volume. Ah, well…

Another hot topic is the public washroom.

When meal times come, folks amble down the hallway, heading for the dining room. No sooner than they sit down, they remember (hopefully, but not always!) that they forgot to use the bathroom. And so they head for the closest one, the public washroom. Chances are they wouldn't make it back all the way to their own washroom anyways, so that's ok.

What's not ok is what happens next, at least with some of them. They leave a mess. The washroom, then, becomes of course, unacceptable to use for the next resident. So we have to be constantly alert to who just returned from the john, and be ready with rag and bucket, while at the same time serving meals. Oh, the fun…

Many solutions to this problem have been tried and tested from all angles; suffice here to say that these small matters are quickly becoming huge challenges, especially if the next resident to use the bathroom is not understanding in these matters. And it all boils down to the very same subject, the very definition of a retirement home; there are many people bunched together, and this close living together under one roof presents real life challenges.

A never ending issue is the temperature of the rooms, or of the entire home for that matter. As opposed to other homes, which offer only one temperature setting for the entire home, set by management, we have individual temperature settings for each room. This is a feature well liked, and we actually have sold rooms just based on that feature. But the price has to paid, oh yes, it does…

As expected, everyone has a different opinion as to what the temperature of the home, not just individual rooms but common rooms as well, should be like.

Keeping in mind these folks have slowed metabolism, and often many of them are just skin and bones, heat has to be provided to make them comfortable. A lot of heat. The question is, how much heat? How much heat is too much? And when is enough, enough? Everybody is constantly complaining that it is too cold, even if individual rooms are showing 80°F+. That's 25°C if you paid attention in Canadian schools after 1984. Sometimes we go into rooms and are greeted by a wall of hot air, and are literally unable to breathe in there, let alone work. And if we're lucky, the residents feels just about right. But it could be a little warmer, though…

So now staff is complaining, too…

Oh the fun…

How beneficial is living in a retirement home for the elderly person?

This question may be considered superfluous, because everyone knows that the very institution has been determined from the beginning of its creation to be beneficial for the elderly person.

Everyone knows that, except those living there.

And this is indeed so, looking from the perspective of an outsider, from one who has the job of assisting the elderly person on his way to increasing frailness, and on her way of further decreasing functionality. From that viewpoint, the very institution is a well thought out solution to problems which otherwise would be difficult to solve, and difficult to handle any other way. Even home care can only do so much, and in the time not covered by home care, the clients are on their own.

Just don't ask the care or assistance receiving residents themselves. Unfortunately, many care receiving residents have a different viewpoint, which makes the job on a sliding scale from not so rewarding to miserable and then downright unbearable to perform. Care staff members must have indeed a certain personality, and a certain level of maturity, a certain level of spiritual awareness to go through their day. Some residents are barking how terrible this place is, how terrible the care they receive is, how terrible the food is, how terrible everything else is, and of course, that they'd rather go home. This is also very demotivating to other residents, who enjoy living where they are. These constant naggers are what poisons the atmosphere. Add to that that some of them are demented enough to repeat that dreaded phrase "I wanna go home" endlessly, and you understand why staff members have the following recipe to deal with these situations:

Say out loud three times: "Dear Lord, now I understand why you gave me so much patience—you knew one day I would need it—like today!"

Even cognitively aware residents frequently overestimate their own abilities, capacities and strength, all borne and stemming from memory, but long gone. Although they understand that they need support all the way from getting up in the morning all day long until it's time to get tucked in at night, they still tell us all day long that they "wanna go home". That home, chances are, has been sold long ago by the family to pay for Mom's stay.

But also, thank the Lord, not just for patience, but also for the type of resident we really like to cater to. The ones who appreciate where and how they live. The ones appreciating the staff, who tirelessly try to please everyone, and try to get everyone safely through just another challenging day, and keep everything on an even keel. Having said all that, it is refreshing to know that one is doing something right, after all. Especially staff members who need recognition are grateful for residents who are grateful. One feeds the other. That's only human, so a little bit of appreciation or praise is for some the reason to work in such an environment to begin with.

It can be witnessed time and again, that, once the resident has settled in, improvement in the health status is a given. In part, this is because of all the elements which have been provided are helping. Not the least and very important is medication management. That is a fancy word for proper medication intake. Actually, it is more than that. Since medication intake is monitored and regularly, the effects are no doubt beneficial. There is a huge difference noticeable between the resident and his or her view of regular medication intake, and the real monitored intake. Now, doctor's orders are really taking effect. But beyond this, since we as operators and staff not only given medication timely, but noting and recording effects, including side effects. These are reported to the doctor and a regular dialogue is taking place, resulting in an immense benefit over the effects just reported by the resident to their doctors themselves. And so, changes required in medication can be and will be implemented by the doctor, based on our observations, often even unbeknownst to the resident. This is a huge advantage over living alone. This is one plus where retirement homes and proper medication management really shines.

Keeping in mind that it is only a small percentage who are willing to trade living at home for living in a retirement home, it may be only assumed that this huge advantage is unknown by the masses—the ones choosing to keep living at home.

There are indeed many residents who say that if they had known how rewarding life in retirement homes can be, they would have come years earlier. They love the companionship, the fun, the enjoyment, activities which were otherwise not to be experienced, and of course, the care and assistance received. Not to mention the meals, because chances are the menu schedule of many an elderly person tends to get, well, just let's say not all that exciting any more. For many, still living at home, the choices in meals usually consist of a peanut butter sandwich or Kraft dinner. So, if our home cooked meals are well received and even loved, that makes us all smile, especially the cook.

And then there are the extremes: Our Joan says: "Whenever I pass on, I will make sure to come back just to get some more of this…"

And you thought retirement home living is only beneficial for the residents? No, also for us, caring for all of them, too.

Okay, *sometimes*.

Every time I see advertising of retirement homes showing this lovely couple in their late sixties, smiling at each other with a glass of wine in their hands, I smile, too. What a wonderful world. It shows perfectly the world to which the retirement home industry wants to cater to. Keyword *wants to*.

Trouble is, this is wishful dreaming. Reality looks quite different. First, such a couple would not move in, because they have their own lives, and that is most definitely outside of a retirement home. They travel and see the world. They see North America in their motorhome, or they fly to the other side of the world to climb mountains in New Zealand.

Try them again 20 years later.

If however, the health situation changes, and one partner loses some of his or her ability or cognitive functionality, then things are suddenly different. The time is on hand for a move-in to be considered. But by then, however, this rosy picture is not quite as rosy anymore.

Or think of the other common advertising picture, the dancing couple. I smile at that, too.

There is the underlying assumption by retirement home operators that some activities are wanted by just everyone, and it cannot be any different. There are no others. Dancing is a good example, because it represents an activity which is enjoyed by many, and by both genders, and is actually doable within a retirement home setting.

From there on, things get a bit more difficult. The list of activities offered by homes is getting longer and longer, and is mostly geared towards the female gender. This is because there is in average only one male resident for every 5+ female residents, based on the difference in life expectancy. So by default, there are many more women than men in a home.

What it really means is, that the men are yawning if female activities are offered, and women are bored stiff, when activities for men are offered.

The very concept of a retirement home just cannot fulfill this basic need for both genders. The mere fact that someone is trying to determine what folks are supposed to enjoy is a task with questionable results. Since pastime is so manifold, the operator can only go by what he or she believes is *most likely* enjoyed by the majority, knowing full well that this is only partially successful.

While women are totally happy with playing bingo, playing euchre or exchanging recipes, perhaps even actually doing some baking themselves, men, by nature, have different interests.

These can, by design, not be met within the constrictions of the entire fabric of a retirement home.

Outdoor activities like fishing and hunting come to mind. But then there are other interests, too, such as trucks, sex, motorcycles, to name a few. Puttering in the garden, or in the garage. Fixing things. How can these interests possibly be offered in the retirement home setting? They can't, of course.

You may have noticed that I put the word 'sex' in there. But I put it in small print, tucked in between, so you wouldn't notice it so much. And so I do exactly what society does. It is not mentioned other than in hushed tones, so nobody notices it much. Preferably the subject is not even mentioned. Heck, prostitution is not even legal. As a basic human trait, sex is treated not unlike crime. Well, folks, I could fill a book about this subject alone. Trouble is, I am not allowed to. Perhaps, one day I will. Chances are by the time I am allowed to talk about it, it might be a very small book, because by then I will have mostly forgotten all the incidents. But deny it or not, it's there. Talk about it or not, it's there.

I just wanted to share with you one example, and I do so because I feel that a common belief may be revisited. The belief that older people have no sex. Even the belief that older people have no inclination, or capabilities, or desires, or wants or needs for it. This belief may apply for many, but certainly not all. And of course it applies to both men and women.

I can tell you, that many years ago, it must have been before current regulations, we had one gentleman who had, once a week, a female visitor. I will not tell you that this chap moved into our residence with his intention mentioned to us, or whether we had a problem with his habit, or even how this situation was handled by us or in retirement homes in general. I also choose not to tell you about the source of his connections with his frequent and changing visitors. All I will tell you is that he wanted to be undisturbed for two hours once every week. So staff put a "do not disturb" sign on his door, and we went back to business as usual. The amusing side effect was the gossip which developed out of this little habit. And amusing it was, to be sure, especially since every week another girl came by. He must have liked variations. But the good news is, age is not necessarily a stumbling block in experiencing the sweetest of human interactions.

But the government and its associated regulating bodies must know that sex in retirement homes exists, because it is regulated. Let that sink in for a minute. The most private, the most sacred act between consenting adults is regulated. Someone actually believes it is, as a governing body of society, necessary to butt in even in actions of private bedrooms. I am not saying that this is right or wrong, at least not here and now. But what I am saying is, that if this is where we are as a society, it is a sad testimony of the long way we still have to go.

I believe this view seriously needs revamping. Among others, this is certainly one reason that men are even more hesitant to give up their home, and their independence. That's why I mentioned the above. Only failing health, and hence, failing interest in typical man-like interests can finally persuade men to become retirement home prospects, and perhaps residents.

So it becomes obvious that not even the basic interests of both woman and men can be met within a retirement home setting, especially if the retirement home's customer base consists mainly of cognitively competent and independent, fully functional residents. Like the smiling couple with their wine glasses. Just in case you have always wondered about this.

There are many other challenges when operating a retirement home. And here we are just talking about the operational difficulties with human interactions, because all these humans live under one roof, all other aspects put aside. And the source of all these difficulties and challenges of human interactions can be traced to the fact that the personal private sphere of the co-habitants cannot be provided. There is a basic underlying assumption that in retirement homes, all residents live together happily as a group. Trouble is, this is not so. At the very least, physical space and private space must be provided. If such space is provided, as in detached, individual buildings, or at least in separate apartments, then the set-up structure becomes a community. But community is self-governed, and not managed top-down by paid management.

There are other challenges.

What if a resident is getting close to dying, but does not want the residence to send them into a hospital?

At one point, the soul is ready to leave its body. In such a situation, the soul just wants to move on, and the person is ready to go home. You know it, because the body of the person tells you so. But we are not 'professionals' and as such, are not supposed to have come to such a conclusion. We can't. We are not allowed to, by Society. Society and their servants tell you straight to your face since you are not a "professional", you know beans all about any of this. Heck, as a "non-professional", I am not even allowed to help lift a person who is on the floor!

We had a 300+ lbs fellow once, who collapsed and fell to the floor. Our nurse took Ben's vitals and we decided it was "911" time. I explained the situation to the nice lady answering the call, and told her the weight of the resident to be dealt with. She understood the situation and assured me that the trained paramedics would handle the situation just fine. So when they came, they exclaimed immediately the two of them could not possibly lift Ben. 300+ lbs looks a lot more intimidating in real life than it sounds on the telephone. It does not sound heavy at all! The call was not interpreted correctly, and something fell through the cracks. And so I offered to help, and lift at Ben's ankles. The 2 paramedics would grab Ben on each side. After all, we only had a 6 or 8 inch lift onto the stretcher.

But no, since I was not deemed a "professional" I was not allowed to do that. Instead, they called for reinforcement from the local fire department, which took about 20 minutes or so for them to arrive. By then we surely had enough man power available! I do not want to tell you how many men they sent, probably all available, but only one guy was actually lifting Ben—by grabbing his ankles!

And here is another one of those errors in our society's thinking:

Our society does not allow any individual in its last hours of life to go home to our Creator, unless society and its doctors say that it's ok. And the rest of us, geared the same way, are supposed to toot into the same horn, and so we are obliged and have to do our part to extend life at all cost. Therefore, in our residence, as we must in such cases, it's call "911" time, ambulance time. Doctors take over.

And not surprisingly, medical professionals are able to stop the natural process, once again and one more time.

Another few weeks of life for the one involved. But is it life worth living? Perhaps by then visiting family members are hardly recognized. Chances are they might never come out of the hospital anymore.

As a society, we should have a serious look into this our commitment.

I believe this needs some serious revamping.

What about terminal illnesses, when the person involved is still capable of making their own decisions?

As a society, we are committed to keeping one's health and one's life as long as humanly possible. That's all there is to it. Can this commitment be questioned? Can the rationale behind this view revisited?

In our residence, all we can legally go by, are DNRs, Do Not Resuscitate forms. These we do have, from some residents, but not all.

With the huge advances in medical procedures, this "as long as possible" takes on a new meaning, because medicine is now able to make previously impossible situations possible, thus, extending life as never before. It is questionable at which point medical assistance may or may not be, should or should not be, provided any longer.

When is "physician assisted end of life" possible?

With more and more professionals taking on a view of deeper discussions and changes to the law, I can only talk from my experience as a retirement operator. No question, it will be a difficult decision to know "when to pull the plug", if you allow me to use this term. For many years and continuing into the present, the discussions continue. But sooner or later these discussions have to come to a conclusion, perhaps when someone has the courage to tally up the cost—something nobody is talking about. Once it is known that there is a real price tag attached, perhaps we will then come to a conclusion a bit sooner. I am convinced as layman member of our society that this has to be done.

For two reasons:

First, the spiritual one. As I said, at one point the human body wants to change form, wants to leave, but our society does not allow this to happen at just any moment. As a society, we somehow have it all backwards. We believe that we have to take over God's job of calling or not calling someone home, or when to let him or her go. Where is this erroneous belief coming from?

And nobody is talking about this, either. That's because nobody wants to talk about dying. Somehow we are conditioned not to talk about dying. It's something which has to be avoided. Worse, it is pictured as being a terrible experience, and so, everyone hushes, even in funeral homes, where everyone talks in low voices. Why? Who told us to do all this?

Death is a celebration for the body involved, and as such, shall be dealt with accordingly—and celebrated. Not just by the one departed, but by the ones left behind, as well. What really is mourned over is not the person departed, but the ones left behind. They are mourning their own loss. So our society has it all backwards!

By our standard, however, celebration is not what dying is all about. This is not the case at all, by far not. That is, because we as a society take a different viewpoint. That's because religions tell us to do so. And so obediently we do and follow their doctrines—no question asked.

And yes, it is extremely difficult to say with certainty when the time of departure has come. Some folks say for ten years things like, "I do not want to live any longer, I do not see any purpose why I am still around…all I want is to die…"—but really, they do not mean it.

Others say nothing, but show suddenly symptoms of their readiness to go home, by rejecting further food intake, for instance. Or some functions of the body simply stall.

Another instance, and I go a bit further into this later on, is the subject of falling.

Despite all discussions of the subject, we will inevitably advance also in our level of spiritual awareness. Once we reach a higher point we will realize, all of us as individuals and as a society, that letting a person die because the soul wants to return to the Creator is the proper way to act for us, and let the course of nature proceed. The only assistance given will be in pain management, to help to increase the level of comfort. The next thing of utmost importance is palliative care, a fancy word for nothing else but being with the departing person. Again and again we witness that departing of someone *alone* must be terrifying. Companionship at this particular time is appreciated by all, and mostly of course, for the one involved. If the person wants to go home, we shall let him or her go. It's the only way we treat another human being humanly.

If we are talking dying with dignity and in peace, this is one area where retirement homes shine.

It is the best setting one can imagine. We had over the years many cases when family members were asking for no further life support, in the event the person was not able anymore to make his own decision. The same holds true for the one who can, and often no further life support measures will be chosen. No hospitals any more. Since we have a registered nurse on staff, we are licensed to apply pain management, in conjunction with the instructions given by the doctor.

We can have staff here for 24 hours a day and be right there with the one departing. At this point it should be noted that in situations like these, we are proud to say, we have staff members who come on their own time with no pay. Here that it is obvious that, after all, we are humans. They have developed a bond with the resident. They wish to just be there during their last hours of the departing human.

The second reason is indeed cost.

Again, nobody talks about it, either. I do!

There is no price tag on saving lives! Really? Well, I disagree. There is.

And in years to come, like it or not, we will all have to look at that very seriously. Why? Because there is not enough money to sustain life at all costs. At all cost means just that. That may seem farfetched today, but consider these two simple facts.

First, we are advancing our medicine constantly further and further, but at the same time, only at astronomical cost. And secondly, we have more and more old people who are prime candidates for life extending measures.

Who should pay for this? Again, dear reader, you may be outraged by these statements, but consider that looking into the future, in a mere 15 years Canada's senior population over 65 years will swell to one out of four Canadians. And if the trend continues unimpeded, and barring any unforeseen global events, in only 35 years there will be one senior for each working person in Canada.

That means everyone working and receiving wages can cut their paycheck in two. One half for the earner, the other half is for the senior to be supported. Actually, this is not quite correct. The senior needs a lot more of that paycheque than just half. This is so by definition, because it is mostly in later years that expensive health care is required. And this will be a real problem, if run-away expenses are not checked. If and when expensive is really going to be expensive. And this is the core of the subject. How much more? It's hard to say. But whatever more than half means, there may be resistance from the one working, from the one whose paycheque is going to be split in two.

I cannot imagine such a world, as it will take out the fun of spending a week at the work place, just to try to make a living, when the majority of the paycheck goes to supporting the bulging senior population. I cannot imagine younger persons being in agreement with perhaps 70% or 75% or 80% of their paycheck being deducted from the government in order to pay for senior care. Can you imagine that? Are there solutions? Something has to give! Perhaps by then, or sooner, the subject of extending life at all cost, keyword *at all cost*, will be revisited.

Just as a closing note, in case you get the wrong impression of the profession I am working in. After reading all of the above, you might erroneously think that I complain. This is not so. I am just stating facts. You might even think I don't like what I am doing. And again, here I have to correct your thinking. I love what I am doing. I am passionate about it. You might even silently consider suggesting to me I should seek a different occupation after all that has been said. And again, here you are totally wrong, because I could not think of any occupation I would rather do. I know because I have been in many. I am particularly fond of dealing with older folks, to serve, and to provide a home which I myself would love to live in. Not just now, which I do, but also at a time when or if I need assistance myself. Driven by this thought, I am treating and caring for my residents in a way which I would like to be treated one day. This always was, still is, and will be my driving motivation. These words, by the way, are part of our mission statement of Golden Pond Retirement Residence.

The joy of operating a retirement home:
The foregoing might lead to the impression that, while yes, operational challenges are many, there is no joy to be experienced. Nothing could be further from the truth. There is a lot of fun, actually more than just fun, there is even fulfillment to be experienced. After all, this is what we all after. Not just staff, but residents as well. The fun can at times grow to belly holding with laughing, or cracking up because of remarks and jokes going around. Quite often we thought of keeping notes of all the remarks, of all the little idiosyncrasies folks have, and the resulting habits and sayings. Perhaps one day I will—hey, another book!.

As I said, there is more than just fun. There is the aspect of fulfillment. I experience great fulfillment in the occupation I have finally chosen. Then there is the aspect of spiritual growth. I have experienced more spiritual growth in the last 10 or 15 years than in my entire earlier years. Quite a few accumulated views and goals are coming to full circle. Growing awareness means also increasing understanding, and becoming compassionate. Even being allowed to be close to someone who is departing is a special moment, which can be not described, only experienced. It also points to our own mortality. One conclusion of this is to enjoy the moment, to live in the now.

Therefore, be grateful for the day, because this day is a gift. Enjoy the moment before it becomes memory.

By the way, if you want more of this, I refer you to my other book (under construction) *"Spiritual awareness—applied to daily life"*, (I think I mentioned that).

In the meantime, however, I do want to assure the reader that it is the most fulfilling occupation, but then again, it's a small path. Next to it on either side is frustration and despair. It needs indeed a special breed of people to take care of elderly folks. Not just in care giving to our elderly residents, but also in running the entire home and operation. Not everyone can, as many of the family members assure us, once they "hand over" their loved ones to our care. At that time, we usually get quite a comprehensive "how to do" list, or better termed, "How-to-deal-with-our-mom" instructions. Later on, we develop our own...

The list of all "thank you" cards we receive from family members we *like to* keep in a binder. It's quite comprehensive. It has a special place in that book shelf.

The list of all written complaints we *have to* keep in a binder—by law. It's one of those policies. But that binder is a lot smaller, if I remember correctly ...now, where is that binder again?

Care Component in Retirement Homes versus LTCs

Many people think that once their loved ones are placed in a retirement home, the home will from now on provide care to no end. All care staff is just waiting for Mom to come in and pamper her all day long. And if this proves not to be sufficient, then for sure the next level—the nursing home—takes over and provide care to no end.

Unfortunately, this is not so. If family members have chosen to perform the tedious task of selflessly looking after Mom themselves, and Mom's care requirement exceeds the care capacity of the family members, I have to be the bearer of bad news, it would exceed the capacity of the retirement home just the same. Don't even try to place them. Again and again, we are faced with the results of pre-assessments before move-in, indicating that the care level expected is way beyond that of what we or any retirement home can provide. Nursing home time it is.

And again and again, I feel sorry for the family members in these unfortunate cases. The only comment I have is that it's a shame this person did not come years earlier; they would have enjoyed their stay with us– now it's too late. If you have a family member considering a move, I feel an urge to tell you to evaluate and consider a stay in a retirement home early on, actually, much sooner than that...

In some Canadian provinces, just like in the States, there are many retirement residences, particularly larger ones, which incorporate higher care levels to the extent of nursing homes. For different reasons: In Canada, for instance in New Brunswick and Nova Scotia, there are no separate licensing arrangements for level 1 or 2 care, but is all covered under the Ministry's "Special Care Home" license, which includes level 3 as nursing home care, as well. Now, they even have level 4. So any retirement home is obliged to obtain the "Special Care Home" license might as well operate as an LTC just the same. In the States it is somewhat different, because since nursing home care has to be paid privately, they can be incorporated also within a retirement home setting. This is very desirable. In Canada, this practise is also present, but a lot less frequent. And this is so for logistic reasons. Retirement homes are privately paid for. LTC's are paid for by the government, with contributions by the resident, which is, they government pension minus some allowance. That being said, these are two different worlds. Since LTCs are strictly governed by tight regulations which differ from the private sector retirement home considerably, it is difficult to incorporate these two different entities within one complex, let alone under one roof. Yet it is offered. Moreover, when assessing the care needs as beyond what retirement homes can offer, it is then when the approval for a move into an LTC is given. But from there on, there is no turning back.

It is here where some improvement is in order. Again and again we see people's conditions are improving once they move into an LTC, but the return into a retirement home is not possible. LTC means last stay. Conversely, we often have cases which were better off in LTC's, but the waiting period can be many months, sometimes even a year or more until an opening becomes available. Here, retirement homes are strained to the limit to provide sufficient care. Therefore, I recommend for authorities and officials to work on a model which is helping both entities; and by doing so serving the resident's needs best, and most importantly, do away with the strict division of the two entities.

This is possible by first acknowledging that both entities exist. As it is, LTCs exist outside of the retirement home world, and vice versa. It is, in the interest of all, necessary that a method can be found to communicate with each other, and to refer residents to each other. At the present set-up, this is not possible.

But even more importantly, these two entities should work together on a sliding scale, so that in the event that the condition of a particular resident improves, they can move back to the retirement home they just came from. This new opening would make room for someone else, perhaps in need of heavier care. It would perhaps be the best idea if an LTC worked more like a hospital, where the stay may be (or not) only temporarily, until the crisis is over, and health improves.

It sounds complicated, but it is really common sense. Except the way we have it constructed is complicated. By such application, all parties involved, both kinds of institutions, and most of all, the older person, would benefit.

This, I believe needs some serious revamping.

How long do people stay in retirement homes?

One of the reasons folks fight tooth and nails not to move into a retirement home is that they believe this is the last place, the last move, end of life in sight. Along with it the fear of signing a lease which, because it is a yearly term, prohibits anyone from moving out. A year at the end of life might be an awful long time. Locked in for life. That's the common perception.

Well, this is simply not so. It may need some clarifications here. First of all, while lease contracts are indeed yearly, and are indeed intimidating in volume to say the least, they can be terminated with a 30 day notice. So, if one doesn't like where one lives, they can move. This is in stark contrast of common understanding. It is also commonly practiced, because once one lives in a retirement home, it is usually known that this possibility exist. Because by law, we have to lay out details of the contract, the lease, at the time they move in, so they understand. But in general, public does not know this earlier on. About 17% of all residents move to another home during the course of their stay. In the last few years we experienced more than usual people coming to us from other homes, because they are not happy there. One of the reasons seem to be the newly exercised method of adding extra charges to the monthly rent bill, which is highly undesirably for folks, and rightly so.

For instance, the practise of charging extra $30.00–80.00 for the weekly bath, or charging $38.00 extra for every time the call bell is used, just doesn't sit well with people. So they look for alternate living options, or another retirement home in all probability.

Approximately 32% of retirement residents are moving to an LTC, Long-Term-Care home or nursing home. This move is usually not intentional. The common way how this is being practised is that if and when the care requirement is beyond the capability of the retirement home, a transfer to an LTC is applied for. Once a bed becomes available, this opening MUST be occupied within 24 hours, or else the opening is forfeited, and the applicant moves down to the bottom of the waiting list. Not something anyone wants to miss, so the immediate move is what usually occurs.

This is not easy to swallow, neither for the landlord nor for the tenant, and certainly not user friendly, if you allow me to use this term in this context. Most of our residents, forced into such circumstances, would love to stay and not move. Just a little longer. They are used to all other residents, their friends and staff members, and understandable do not want to move.

But it is totally in line with governments' interest of having no vacancies in LTCs to see a maximum of occupancy. It is also totally against their own rules enforced by another government body, the Tenancy Board, because it does not allow for the retirement home operator to have the usual 30 days' notice of termination in any rental situation.

But it is most distressing for the elderly person, who, practically is torn out of her familiar home surrounding and placed in another one which is new, strange, and certainly not wanted. No further questions asked. So there, it's now or never.

In real life, folks who had their breakfast with us will have their lunch somewhere else—in that dreaded nursing home.

Both these numbers account for about half or all residents. The remaining half of all residents would indeed pass away, either in the home (their choice) or in a hospital.

As for when this happens, there are quite a number of confusing if not conflicting data available, but it is safe to say that the average stay in a retirement home is about 2.4 years, while in a LTC it is 1.4 years. In our home, we sometimes have to witness the unbearable, that newly placed residents pass away within weeks after move-in. This enforces the view what has been said numerous times—that most people are waiting too long to consider a move and to come. They are so forfeiting their chance of living a good life in their remaining time. Instead, they feel it's so much better at home. Familiarity does not replace having a still comfortable and enjoyable time left. On the other end of the spectrum, we have folks who live with us way longer than above cited averages. At the time of this writing, our resident being with us for the longest time holds the record at 13 years. A few are with us for around 10 years.

The cost, of course, is the monthly charge times the average stay, which represents quite a substantial figure. For some people, who stay in retirement homes a number of years, this number is indeed remarkable high. That's why I refer to it as 'life savings' .Sometimes it is nothing short of staggering.

And then, there are remarkable exceptions.

We had an inquiry the other day, where a fellow, who suffered a car accident in his later years, was awarded $1 Million in compensation, paid out by the insurance. He needed assistance for the rest of his life, so he moved into a retirement home. The residence is charging (currently) about $5,000 a month. The fellow is in his seventies now, and in all probability may enjoy good many more years. However, the reason for the inquiry was that the time has come, in the opinion of his power of attorney, to look into a less expensive residence, because it is foreseeable that he uses up the rest of his compensation, and there exists a real risk of running out of funds. So far, he lived in a retirement home for 14 years. In other words, this resident will spend a million dollars for housing in a retirement home.

Even at a more modest rate of the average $3,000/month, this person will spend nearly half a million dollars in a 14 year residency. As mentioned earlier, in the States the figure of a million dollars in retirement home stay is much more likely, since people move in in average 10 years younger, so there is a much higher length of stay possible.

When Residents require care beyond the ability of the retirement home to provide adequately

As it stands, Long-Term-Care homes (LTC's) are filled to the brim. Also formerly known as nursing homes, their role is still the same, and quite untouched from the fast paced development of the retirement home industry.

For the older and frail ones, the ones in need of medical assistance exceeding one hour of care a day, which is the untold threshold of retirement homes, for those in which care requirements exceed home care services which can be reasonably supplied, meaning financially sensibly, the LTC home is the solution. And then, of course, there is the huge sector of those who cannot afford retirement home living.

But there is one grey area—in some cases suddenly care requirements develop for residents living in retirement homes. And they have to be tended to. This is when things get a bit awkward. These situations, all of a sudden, are disturbing to other residents, who are cognitively quite aware of what's going on. Perhaps we have a situation for instance in the dining room where some residents are having meals, together with one who loses some of his functional abilities. This situation is unacceptable for the healthy ones, to see someone whose ability to eat properly has been lost. He may be drooling or vomiting, and even though he will be removed from the dining room table in a hurry, the damage is done. It's amazing to see different folks having responses to such situations. Sure, there are some who compassionately feel with them or say this could have happened to me, too. And then there are some who are quite upset and don't understand at all. Some might say "I came here to get well, not to get sick!"

Anyone witnessing such situations can easily understand the difficulties involved. Consequently, the operator has to make efforts to divide the healthy ones from the others. This calls for different dining rooms, additional staff, and perhaps different times of serving meals.

This is also the reason that in larger homes it makes sense to divide the actual homes into wings or tracks. Residential retirement tracks and nursing home tracks may be side by side. At the same time, it is just as helpful to have dining rooms divided up. This is just one more reason that larger homes are becoming larger, and smaller homes cannot provide these requirements.

There are no easy solutions for these situations, which could become even more challenging. Since nursing home candidates are assessed according to the severity of the situation and the amount of immediate care needed, the waiting list is accordingly fairly short for the ones in greater need than for the ones who can do a bit longer on their own.

Enter retirement homes. Knowing that care is provided, since resources are on hand, it is therefore true that LTC candidates living in retirement homes are sliding down on the priority list. This makes sense for the government, since it is the retirement home industry which picks up the tab. While quite convenient from their viewpoint, it is difficult for the retirement home operator, because of the added load. And, even if the additional care can be provided, this added service is not paid for, neither from the government nor from the resident, who argues rightly that this is the reason he signed up to come here! But a quick calculation shows that it does not take much of a care requirement to cause that cost quickly to skyrocket. This cost is not allowed for in any calculation. So it is the retirement home which has to pick up the shortfall, not just in terms of additional work, but in terms of unpaid services, as well! On a brighter note, now the government recognizes this imbalance, and in some cases—not in general and not in all provinces—provides paid for home care services for the ones who need it most. Even if they live in retirement homes. And this move is greatly welcome.

But the hammer really hits if a sudden illness, like a stroke, happens, and the resident's care requirement changes overnight to a level the home is simply unable to provide. A logical consequence for the retirement home operator would be, since these are privately owned operations, to call it quits and give the resident his or her notice.

However, where would he or she go? The resident needs not only alternative living, but alternative living by a home or institution which is able to provide the extra care needed. And this would be the LTC.

Considering this, is the government taking over?

Not so. Unfortunately this is not the case. The government's policy of assessing the case and assigning it to the waiting list is the procedure. There are no exceptions. That's good news for the tenant or resident, whose living arrangement is now guaranteed. It's the law. It must be obeyed. It's not optional. But it's not good news for the retirement operator, who now has the duty to handle a difficult situation adequately. So then, in a way it is quite risky to take on *any resident at all*. Who knows, this one may be a costly burden one day. But it's a day to day risk. If fate happens, and it does to some unfortunate residents, the once happy resident who was enjoying living in a retirement home is suddenly struck by illness, to such an extent that the home cannot look after him properly, then the home has an insurmountable problem on its hand.

The tenant cannot be given the notice, and the nursing homes are full. One thing is for sure—the tenant is there to stay.

To add insult to injury, the Tenancy Board, the government body in charge of landlord-tenant relationships, came up with a ruling which says:

If the retirement home is unable to look after the wellbeing of the resident due to changing conditions in his or her health, this does not release the landlord from his duty to fulfill the earlier made obligation to look after the wellbeing of the tenant. If such a case occurs, then it is the responsibility of the home to look for alternative accommodation, one which is able to care for the tenant properly. If such accommodation is found, in no way can the tenant be expected to pay for additional cost, if such occurs. If additional charges do occur, they have to be borne by the referring residence or operator, the one which is arranging for the alternative living option.

So there.

But there is a way out: The retirement residence usually has a clause in its lease for back-out, that is, if care requirements exceed the allowable limit provided, there is the possibility of additional charges in the event that residents require care beyond the amount allowed for in the rent. What that is, is actually well laid out to avoid any misunderstanding. In our experience, however, this practise always leaves a bad taste with the family and in many cases will not or cannot be paid.

Ownership

Who owns retirement homes?

In the olden days, there were mom and pop operations. That has changed, as has the entire landscape of mom and pop businesses in any business sector. The small business operator cannot possibly compete with larger corporations. Just like in many if not all other sectors, larger corporations have taken over and run the show. Here too. Larger corporations own today's retirement homes. How large? Actually, very large. And the trend continues to go this very direction.

Currently, the unbridled thirst of US businesses to take over Canadian businesses does not stop at the retirement home industry: as in many other business sectors, more and more retirement residences, even entire chains, are being gobbled up by the States. Whether this move is desired or not, good or bad, beneficial or not for Canada, is at best debatable. There are many aspects involved, which will not be further discussed here. It should be pointed out though, and it may spark the beginning of discussions, whether or not this move is good for Canadians. I for one would have to add a thing or two. Funny, by and large, nobody talks about this. Then again, the same can be said for other industries.

But one thing is for sure; once ownership changes, bets are on there will be sooner than later major renovations taking place. And after completion, bets are on, the rental rates will become noticeably higher than before.

It can be argued that the entire life savings of elderly Canadians are spend on retirement home living in a few short last years of their lives. Like it or not, this is just so. Bad as this aspect is in itself, it's even worse to think that, if an American owned retirement residence is chosen as the future residence, all this capital saved up in a working life will now flow quickly into American hands.

But there are other views, as well. For instance, be it as it may, the now American owned business is providing jobs—Canadian jobs, that is. And that renovation work has not been done during the time of former ownership.

It's up to the discretion of the reader.

By the same token, it's not just the retirement home industry. It's the same in countless other business sectors, for instance in building supply chains.

Walking with Grandma
(Source unknown)

I like walking with Grandma,
Her steps are short like mine.
She doesn't say "now hurry up"
She always takes her time.

I like to walk with Grandma,
Her eyes see things like mine do,
Wee pebbles bright, a funny cloud,
Half hidden drops of dew.

Most people have to hurry,
They do not stop to see.
I'm glad that God made Grandma
Unrushed and young like me!

CHAPTER 7

Where Does Home Care Fit In?

As said earlier on, in North America the "invention" of home care services in the late 80's early 90's was a big thing. Authorities saw a chance to get out from under the load and cost of nursing home cases. In addition, people wanted to stay at home anyways, so it was a win-win situation all along. Everyone who wanted to stay home—that means by far the greatest majority—was now offered a tool to do just that. They received the much needed attention and could stay in their home just the same. It just may be noted here, that in Germany for instance, the development of home care, called "travelling nurses" was already underway in the late fifties. And incidentally, a travelling nurse in North America is a different kettle of fish. And so, home care services are, at least in Canada, paid for by the government, as an extended service of what nursing homes should have done.

It is indeed a great relief for the ones who want to stay at home, and do not want to leave. And do not want to pursue any other living option, or simply cannot afford it.

As it is, home care services are here to stay. This is the common view.

Practical application of a client, as they are called, involves an initial assessment, on a case to case basis, and to determine what kind of service is required, and the frequency. So far so good.

Over the years, however, it became painfully clear that even this set-up has proven to be too expensive, although, in comparison, it shines. For instance, while not directly to be compared with, but the statistics do so, a typical hospital stay costs between $800–1,200 a day, a nursing home stay is presently fixed at $126/day, while home care comes in at $42/day. That's pretty obvious which scenario wins. However, this would be comparing apples with oranges. One service vehicle is by far not equivalent to the other. Care in the hospital is not the same as in a nursing home, and home care is just a small band-aid compared to the other two. So why is this comparison used to begin with? One has to be careful in simply observing and comparing those numbers, because home care services at a cost of $42/day does not mean that the care requirement is actually met. As opposed to a 24 hour hospital stay, where we can assume that it is. Assessments tend to be on the low side of care required, and should be taken with a grain of salt. To make things worse, these intentionally low care assessments are then cut back even further as times go by, and then some, in the interest of saving money.

As a result, many seniors accessing care service from the government are hiring additional privately paid for home care providers to fill the gap and make up the shortfall. Provided, of course, they can afford it. And here the bills rack up quite quickly.

A typical scenario is an assessed care-giving requirement of 2 hours daily, for assistance in the morning with toileting, washing, dressing, preparing breakfast etc.

However, CCAC (Community Care Access Centre) as the body assessing and assigning the home care services, picks up that tab for every second day. Nobody asks what happens in the days in between. It is not unusual in these cases where this support will be cut further to twice or even only once a week. Now the senior has to stick it out during the non-served days, or turns to private home care companies. Doing the math, these 2 hours for the missing 5 days a week will cost in excess of $1,000 in privately paid funds, in addition to the time the government pays for care.

But, of course, cutting back is also only part of the solution, simply because the day is longer than 2 hours. What happens if service is needed during the other 22 hours in a day? A question many seniors asked themselves. And many find out the answer the hard way, so to speak. Even with more home care hours paid for, this is only a band-aid solution for a larger problem looming.

This will explain why there are, in addition to the about 5–8 home care companies who are under contract with the government, there are presently 172 privately operated home care companies in Ontario alone. These are picking up the shortfall to government provided home care services, in other words, the difference between what's provided for versus what's needed. And of course, these are the home care companies which will provide service to all the folks who have income greater than the maximum threshold specified. Only people with lower income are eligible to receive home care services paid for by the government.

So if people think that our government fully pays for home care services which are *adequately* looking after their needs, key word *adequately*, they would do well to think otherwise. And so it is no surprise that the actual care provided by home care proves in many cases to be insufficient. Period. Further, over time the care requirement is likely to increase, but is only revisited and reassessed upon application for increased service.

By and large, we are talking here care or assistance. To be technical, it is assistance with ADL, activities of daily living. There are many situations where this assignment becomes a must for the older person. But there are other needs. Shopping for groceries for instance. Or that famous issue of cleaning the house. Then there is simply companionship, for folks who put themselves in danger and at risk, especially if dementia is becoming an issue. All these services must be viewed with a critical eye, though. While it is true that the demand is there, it is questionable if there could not better solutions to be found. Providing care—yes. Providing shopping and cleaning services, or even only companionship, well, there is a very hesitant 'yes' to follow. Keeping in mind that all these services come with a hefty price tag. It is for these reasons that assignments for these services are the first ones to be axed, if services are to be cut. In Nova Scotia, for instance, house cleaning performed by PSW's has been cut out altogether 20 years ago. Ontario followed suit, but only in recent years.

There is another element to consider, which is exactly the opposite of the foregoing. It is no secret that in many cases, too many according to home care workers, the persons involved in obtaining home care *simply do not want to function on their own with no services provided any more*, in order to prove to the world, and to the home care workers in particular, that the *service provided is actually needed*. The motive for this is that the client fears cutbacks in their services provided, so they *purposefully pretend incapability*, just to make sure. This becomes obvious when the persons involved can do very well the task at hand on their own, outside of the time frame of home care services. This becomes a dangerous concept which encourages people to willfully pretend needing services which really they don't. And the more the assessment shows no further services are needed, or worse, cut backs of services are in sight, the more the person pretends the opposite.

And how does the living location of the client factor into all of this?

I asked CCAC what happens if a person requiring home care is located in isolated areas. What happens if that person lives, let's say 100 km from the last known hamlet which still has a name and is a dot on the map. At which point is a person needing home care just too far away to be looked after?

Think of it this way. In Ontario, 85% of the population lives within 15% of Ontario's land mass. 15% of the population lives within 85% of its landmass. No matter which way you look at it, there are folks living out there who are a long way from any populated area. What if those folks need service?

Well, as one can imagine, for reasons of equality and discrimination, service has to be provided to all residents of Ontario just the same, no matter where they live. At the same token, I just assume that the same holds true for all of Canada's provinces. However, the logistics here become a little bit more challenging, if not downright out of focus. It can hardly be expected for anyone to be looked after by home care services if excessive travelling is involved. Now, what's the definition of excessive? Can services be denied just because the distance is too far? Perhaps it is okay for the government to pay for excessive travel time, but what about the wasted fuel? Or is it not wasted? And moreover, what if, even at the far distance of whatever we are determining being too far to be, there is no trained health care worker available? Let alone a second one who picks up the off time of the other worker? From which point on is this whole concept questionable? From which point on is it just outside of any justification to perform?

I have not received satisfying answers to any of these questions, other than I have been assured that in the final analysis, everyone will be looked after properly.

That answer, however, also begs the question whether this whole concept—granted in only extreme cases like these ones—really makes sense in its basic set-up, to be performed as a society, regardless of the price to be paid.

In Ontario, PSW's or Personal Support Workers, is the designation of choice for anyone involved in the industry.

Surprisingly, this industry is presently not even regulated, although registered, so all colleges which turn out "certified" PSW's are really using self-appointed accreditation because there is no governing body. In the olden days, there were a number of different names out there, such as home support worker or health aide worker. These are all the same.

But statistics are available, since being recognized under one umbrella:

In Ontario, approximately 100,000 PSW's are registered, of which roughly one third work in government associated home care companies. The others are mainly in various institutions, hospitals, and to some degrees, in private home care companies.

While this seems a lot, we have in Ontario about 1.56 million seniors. That means one PSW for 15, 6 seniors. And it proves that indeed older folks take advantage of that service, since about 400,000 seniors have received care. (This number allows for the fact that not all home care services are provided to seniors alone, but folks of all ages, as well) This means one out of 4 seniors over 65 years of age have received care, paid for care. All told, CCAC reports for 2013 a total of 38 million house calls/hours, of which 73% are for seniors. Sounds like a lot at first sight. But it results into a meager 1.3 hours per week per client of service. That's not much by any stretch of the imagination. That's why, as said above, it will be necessary in most cases to top up the government provided home care with private home care—if it can be afforded.

For the care giver, the much-touted job opportunity of the future is really not all that bright. Given these statistics, it means that every PSW in Ontario has worked in average only 1,137 hours in that year; only 22 hours per week. They had better have another job on the side, which by the way, is very common, but difficult to actually perform since the hours are not steady nor in the same time frame.

Typically if two jobs are held down, sooner or later frictions with one job or the other will follow. After that, undoubtedly, there will be frictions with the employers. That is to be expected. Good luck. It won't work in the long run. So the care giver is better off to budget for half time employment.

As a PSW, so much for being in the career path of the future.

The main shortfall of the home care set-up, of course, is the need to travel. This is so by its definition. While today this represents a minor problem, it will become a major problem tomorrow, perhaps an insurmountable one. The writing is on the wall. We are talking simply increased cost of travel by the home care giver, which, at one point, cannot be absorbed any longer. Neither by the home care worker, nor the client, nor the government. The first few ripples are already noticeable. In Nova Scotia, for instance, since the beginning of time, that is, since the beginning of home care time, staff was paid travel expenses per kilometer driven. That was fine, until the time came for cut backs, first on the rates, then on the methods of how the mileage is actually calculated. Then it was simply scrapped (by at least 2 companies), and staff was told that increase in salary is from now on to be viewed as including travel expenses. Since many pay cheques show more dollars earned in mileage than actual wages, it should be obvious that if mileage is to be included, that pay cheque should show more than double of the actual earnings. However, someone got the math wrong, because this is not the case. By far not. Moreover, travel costs are bound to increase more than salaries, so in the long run it's the care giver who's carrying the larger burden of the travel expenses. Chances are that wages will not reflect the same increases. So at the moment it may look fine, but in the long run the buck is passed on to the salaried staff, and it is just a matter of time till some sort of reaction of the affected employees will take place—and they will bark.

Then there are the logistics. In our home, for instance, we have a morning requirement of perhaps 6–8 residents to be serviced by home care workers. They need assistance in getting up, washing and dressing. We have seen as many as 5 care givers coming and going to do that work load. Why on earth is it not possible to contract the work load out so that only 2 care givers are coming? Well, we have discussed this matter at great length with the folks at CCAC in charge, and obviously, there are different interests and different reasons overriding my concern, which is that of saving gas and time and trying to be reasonable with the employment of care givers, and their time and money. Whatever CCAC's reasons are, they must take priority over sensible reasons. But that's only a minor issue compared to this:

In Ontario it is now also possible to obtain home care for 24/7 straight, for isolated cases, and only temporarily, maximum 3 months, that is. Here the cost to the tax payer is indeed staggering! It amounts to approximately $26,000 per month, per client. For a maximum allowable service of 3 months, this amount will become $78,000. Still for that same one client, not for servicing the whole neighborhood. That's close to insanity. It is highly questionable if this arrangement, touted as a big step ahead in providing *all-encompassing* home care services, is really such an improvement at all. The question comes to mind whether there are no less costly arrangements for that kind of care possible than that.

What a price tag to keep a person at home. At all costs so to speak. And they mean it!

Speaking of insanity—in the end, it is just not feasible for someone to travel 40, 50 km or more for clients to be serviced in outlying areas, or whatever distance is required to get to the client in need. This client may need only assistance to get out of bed, dressed, and ready for breakfast. But the care giver has to drive half an hour or more to get there, and is a salaried staff person. That picture is even worse in the evening. The care giver has to travel back and forth the same 40 or 50 km or half an hour each way, for the client now needs to be "tucked in", which requires all of 20 minutes. And then it's the trip home. Someone has to travel to and fro. And while this practice is bordering on sanity today, it's positively outside of sanity tomorrow.

It's not just the wasted care givers' time. It's much more.

Once we realize that we really need our remaining resources of oil for better things than travelling to and fro old folks in order to "tuck them in", then we need to seek other alternatives.

Perhaps it might be a good idea to start looking for these alternatives now. In fact, right now! There is absolute urgency in the air for us as a society to look seriously how to use our remaining oil reserves in the most beneficial way. Although the present low oil or gas prices let's us rest back comfortable, the fact is that every drop of oil burned is gone, done with, not coming back, as in *not sustainable* resources. From that view point alone, it is safe to say that one day in the future, somebody, like our own grandchildren, will all look back and say, "Look at those idiots of back then in 2016! They actually burned gas to drive to their own grandparents to tuck them in. Just look at that!"

They may even add: "No wonder we don't have any gas left today for us to go to work…"

Again from that view point, it is highly questionable that the practice of home care will survive long term. Key word long term.

Just for fun, here is one quick calculation of what the actual gas consumption is like: In Ontario, as said above, there are roughly 30,000 PSW's on their way to go to their clients every day. Short of statistics, I have asked every PSW I ran into in the last few years how many job related kilometers they drive.

From that admittedly rather poor source of data, I have found that each PSW drives approximately 20,000 km/year, about half of that job related. That's 10,000 km to keep it simple. Multiply that by 30,000 to get 300,000,000 kilometers a year. In words, that's 300 million kilometers a year. If that number is not big enough for you then let's extrapolate that for entire North America. Which assumes, of course, that home care services are on the same level provided as in Ontario, in all provinces, and for good measure, in all States in the US. This may be farfetched, since there are definitely differences, but just to demonstrate what this means.

Now, since Ontario has 10 million people, and all of North America roughly 330 million, (let me cut a few off, to make my math easier!), we do not need experts to come up with that figure. It's times 33. It's a lot of 'zeros'. In words, roughly 10 billion kilometers are driven.

Thanks to the metric system, I can tell you that this relates to a total fuel consumption of 1 billion litres of fuel, assuming a small car is used, at a consumption rate of 10 litres per 100 kilometers. Which is more than on the conservative side. If the care giver uses a truck to go to work, double that number.

For American readers, I suggest to do your own math. For the above, I did not need a calculator. Try to do that in the imperial system! By the way, it's a lot of gallons!

Now that's each year. Now, we have arrived at a total fuel consumption of 1 billion litres. All that's left to do now is to bring that huge number down into something we can understand. Like, if the gasoline were still in the form of heating oil, you could, at a rate of 2,000 litres of oil usage per house per winter, heat your home for 500,000 years—that's a lot of winters! Or 1,000 homes for 500 winters. And so we can play with all these numbers any way we want to. But all of this is really irrelevant. What is important, is, that it is intrinsically wrong to waste our oil in a way to accelerate the rate of depletion of our worlds resources, just to "tuck in" our grandparents!

Gentle reader, do you still question my earlier remark, that future generations will call us "The idiots from 2016"? (And perhaps a few more years after that, till we get our act straight!)

At one point, we will ask ourselves if it is a wise way of paying home care workers a 'mileage', I don't know the metric term for that, perhaps 'kilometer allowance', to travel to and from clients. As it is, the mileage paid is very high, so that even the expense of that gas guzzling truck borrowed from the husband in order to get to work is covered by that expense allowance. Since there are always people who like to cut expenses, at this point it will be asked what we can do to reduce the cost of that mileage. The answer is obvious: Use a vehicle with less fuel consumption. Today, in North America, we are not even asking this question. In Germany, this question was asked—and answered—25 years ago. The logical next step is to reduce the mileage paid, to reflect the expenses of a small vehicle only. The reasoning behind this is to discourage people from using higher expense or gas guzzling vehicles, because the mileage paid does not cover the cost. But this is only the beginning. As it is in Germany today, no mileage is paid at all. Home Care companies supplying company owned vehicles for their workers. And since these workers have no tools or material to carry for the client, just themselves, they are using small vehicles. And I mean small. If you know the 'Smart' car, this is the size of vehicles these home care workers are driving. All-electric, of course, they do the job with perhaps a 100 mile per gallon or better consumption, (for the American reader), if we compare electrical usage with that of a combustion engine. And they can park crosswise in between two regular vehicles. This is the way the job will be done in the future, assuming that North America will soon follow the trend and develop an electric charging network of stations to charge up the batteries of the vehicles, similar to the network of gas stations. And advanced as this may sound, it is already on its way out. Newer home care models are being tested. All these tiny vehicles, owned by larger home care companies or municipalities, are similar in colour and have printed messages on them. Call it advertising, but it is not. It is sobering. So, if one sees them all day buzzing around in the city, one cannot help and wonder what kind of apparatus is necessary to provide the care of our grandparents. Perhaps younger people will recognize this way, rather than the private vehicles in North America driving undetected of their purpose, that it is really them who are supposed to look after their own grandparents. If they choose not to, then at least it becomes obvious that they must pay the bill to have someone else doing the job.

Despite of all the short comings, and all put together, the home care industry is here to stay. At least for a while. Or so they say, simply, because we don't know how else to handle the care of seniors any other way. That's with today's care load. Worse, we have no idea how to handle the care load of the "silver tsunami" on its way. And with that, not just double, but multiply the number of older folks requiring care. The demand is just so overwhelmingly large that no one has come up with a better solution, so far. Or even any different solution!

However, I sincerely question the validity of that statement. Perhaps for now. Perhaps for a while. But not long term. *We have to find better solutions!*

There is no waiting any longer. We have to look for better solutions now. Starting right now!

Says Cheryl, PSW

I have worked in long term care and retirement residences and the community. I have been a PSW for 5 years now and have enjoyed all aspects of working with the elderly.

I sometimes feel that the bond we share with our clients is like them having a second family...we are there for their complaints/compliments/illnesses and all emotional aspects of a lonely individual.

In chapter 8 you mentioned that housekeeping had been cut out of a PSW' list of tasks in Nova Scotia when working in a clients home. Most agencies today in Ontario have eliminated this task as well as we are hired to do personal care and assisting with meals. Some clients may still have their lines changed and laundered by a PSW. There is now a program offered by the government for housekeeping & shopping which is known as the Smiles program. Most times there is a wait list for this free service.

The agency I work for does pay my mileage, however it does not equal out to the amount I spend on fuel or the repairs or the wear & tear. This being said, I can submit the difference on my income tax and also the repairs and portion of insurance as well.

I had a client who lived in his own home once say to me... "Cheryl, by the time you get to be my age, who will look after you? There will be no money left to pay for the service you provide." I believe he is correct.

You are correct in saying you have to be a special kind to work in these environments. We are the ones who see the resident at his worst (on a bad day). We are the ones that try to find a way to relieve their discomfort or sadness. I have to laugh when a family member comes to visit their parent and when they ask ... How are you Mom? ... and Mom says I am fine ... the family member has no idea how the last week of vomiting/diarrhoea was for their Mom or the caregiver.

In conclusion, at the end of my day, I feel if I have brightened one individuals day, then I have done something right. Whether it is to help them get dressed or put shoes on or wash their back or clean up an accident while on the way to the bathroom.

CHAPTER 8

Looking Ahead Into the Future

Looking ahead into the future, this is what it will look like: The retirement home industry will continue to pursue its goal of providing its residents a high comfort and style of living. Their mandate is first concerned about the wellbeing of their residents. This includes assistance with daily living. This includes lots of activities, and amenities, as well. Their mandate is *not* to be an extended arm of nursing homes. It is *not* their function to provide care. But this is exactly what many people expect knocking on our doors. People have in general the wrong idea about what exactly 'assisted' means, where it starts and in particular, where it ends. More often than not, once we have seen and assessed the health status of prospective residents, we just look at each other and say 'this person should have been here years ago!' Or we say "oh, well, another LTC case!"

The current model will not continue to grow as it does today. It will shrink because of reasons mentioned. Unless the industry is providing also different models, such as holistic wellness, or, and of course, care. Then the function changes from assistance to care, and thus become an extended arm of LTC's. The "assistance" provided is now clearly defined and can be summarized with assistance of the ADL, that is, the "Activities of Daily Living". This is their mandate, and so, retirement homes are here to stay, at least for a while, until the current surplus of real estate appreciation is spent, and new ones fail to come in, simply because appreciation will be noticeably lower in years to come. But while retirement homes in Canada are still struggling to reach the popularity of the US homes, they are already losing momentum. And they will even more, for reasons already mentioned.

Clearly, people are not lined up. So something has to change. But what?

The retirement home industry is the only known industry which consistently tries to sell services which only a few of their customers want. The majority do not. Conversely, because of still lingering misinformation and misconception by the customers, the potential resident expects services which are by and large not provided, at least not to the extent expected.

This is an amazing contradiction. What's more amazing is the fact that this controversy has existed for a long time. Despite tremendous efforts by the industry, this controversy exists since retirement homes have existed.

As explained earlier, the main problem can be summarized in a few words. First, retirement homes are ill designed in that most people do not want to move there—they do not want to leave their homes.

The very fact that more than 92% of all seniors keep living in their homes proves it well. That means only a little more than 7% live in alternative living options, the vast majority of these, but not all, in retirement homes.

A homey atmosphere can simply not be created in the set-up of large style residences. It may look like home, but it isn't. No matter what the advertising tells you, a homey atmosphere in large residences cannot be created. Add to that the significant cost, and this is the recipe for declining attractiveness. The trend in the last number of years is going straight in the wrong direction. The residences are getting bigger and bigger, in the name of profitability, and thus moving more and more away from the "homey" atmosphere. And second, they are getting fancier for a number of reasons and so, are getting more and more expensive. Granted, there are a number of older folks who like this kind of living arrangement, no question. If money is no object, it certainly is nice to be pampered to, and for these folks retirement homes are just wonderful. That's why the concept will stay. But for sure not for most homes. We have happy residents, too. It is those residents who tell us again and again: "If I would have known how beautiful this is, I would have come here much earlier". And that is great to hear. But it doesn't take away the fact that the majority of older folks have different ideas of where to live, once the time comes and a move is envisioned. And if there are no attractive alternatives, then they would rather stay home, and stick it out.

Therefore, it is time that these aspects should be looked into:

First, if the retirement home concept is to survive, it has to change its course, drastically. Not in the short term or immediate future, but long term.

What will happen as in any other business is that retirement homes will have no choice but to look into what their customers really want. What they really want, not what they are being told to want—and to buy into. The industry may not like to hear it, but what will happen is what is silently and marginally tolerated now—they will become the extended arm of nursing homes. But they have to change their set-up in order to be prepared for heavier care loads, among a ton of other logistics involved to change to that new mandate.

Part of this prognosis is based on what happens in the nursing home 'industry'. To sum it up and not to deviate too much from the subject, although there are strict requirements in place by means of assessments in order to qualify as a candidate to move into an LTC, the fact is that there are quite a few residents in nursing homes who just should not be there. They just do not have the funds to pay for private homes, and are beyond what home care can provide. Although conditions in LTCs are improving since a lot of innovations are tried and tested currently, and have done so for years, that does not deviate from the outcome—LTC's are a poor living alternative. And it does not change the fact that LTC's are overloaded today, and this trend will obviously increase in the future, with additional load on its way.

These folks have a dire future ahead, indeed. Simply because if all cognitive facilities are still in place, these are let's just say not the nicest environment to live in. There is a common saying which is: "Before you send me to a nursing home, shoot me!" Drastic, but to the point. But there are no alternatives, unless the government seeks other solutions. Here is one which I am proposing, and one which is already practised in some provinces.

Subsidize the cost of staying in retirement homes.

That would bring fresh air into the retirement industry. It would also mean that finally the government and private sector are working together to alleviate or at least attempt to minimize the problem of seniors requiring more or less care, which may be changing. Perhaps if and when subsidizes are paid to the homes, part of the workloads could be taken over by retirement homes, and to shorten the endless nursing home waiting lists. Today, LTC's and private homes are both existing on separate islands—there is absolutely no cooperation taking place. At first sight, and logistics put aside for a moment, it just does not make any sense at all that LTC's have endless waiting lists, and retirement homes have unfilled vacancies. Why is no one looking into this? It could obviously mean a win-win situation for all involved, in particular for the senior, who, if such a cooperation would work, could move into a retirement vacancy tomorrow! No long waiting lists. And with the earlier mentioned increasing vacancies in homes, it can only be hoped that someone is taking the initiative to bring those two elements together. With today's legal structure, however, this cannot happen. Because the government believes that care is a matter of government inspected long term care homes, and retirement homes and their inspecting bodies are just not the same, and do not qualify in this. Still, these matters are being discussed as long as I can remember. This is proof how much work still has to be done to get all wrinkles ironed out. The private retirement home industry and nursing homes are just two different worlds.

I believe this approach needs serious revamping.

However, even folks who do have the money, and are in need of care, have few alternatives for future living options to choose from. Because of their monetary situation, they do not qualify to be admitted to a nursing home, but retirement homes do not provide the level of care they require. Hence this is the area where change should be on its way. This no doubt also contributes to keeping the vast majority of people living at home. And they are looked after by home care services only.

And once retirement homes do cater to residents requiring care, it is then, finally, when the industry will provide what their customer, the resident, really wants. At least for the ones who can afford it.

The beginning of this trend can be seen in homes that are introducing care packages in the event that the usual "assistance" is not sufficient any longer. This way they keep the back door open for extra expenses not covered in their basic service. If additional charges are agreed on by both parties, then the situation is quite different than when in additional care is unexpectedly and suddenly required.

But here the dollar clock starts to tick very soon and very loudly. A mere 20 minutes of extra care, 4 times a day, which is by no means a lot, spells out an additional $1,000 charges per month. If the care requirement doubles, well, then the extra cost is $2,000 in addition to the $2,500 or $3,000 rent the resident pays already. Hence this model reaches its monetary limit very soon, at least for the majority of residents.

In addition, chances are that the resident of the future will have even less money to spend than today.

Nevertheless, it's being offered. Another example is that of extreme. Again, the beginning of that can be seen in the current trend of larger residences to cater to specific care cases, for instance, 'memory care', which is a nice term for folks with dementia.

This is great news, because private industry, can very well cater to the needs of those residents. Probably much better, because extra staff can spend more time than nursing home staff can. Of course, extra staffing hours means extra dollars. The only inhibiting factor is money. And if money is no object, then care can be provided 24/7.

And as long as we as a society tell care givers that their profession is a high income career path, coupled with perhaps a unionized environment, the resident who has to foot the bill must be ready to pay for those services. And they must have deep pockets, too.

If for instance dementia is progressed to the point where one-to-one attention is required, the highest level of care, pockets must be very deep, indeed. See for yourself: After all, just PSW's in a unionized environment earn in the tune of $18–20/hour. Add to that the employers cost, sick time, vacation, training and a host of other paid time but not productive time, multiplied by 720 hours/month and the bill to be charged to the resident for the care portion alone is now $16–18,000/month. That's the care portion only. Add to that the price of accommodation, meals and add-on services, medication administration and nursing supervisory services, which is the basic rent of $3,000 and up, and the cost would spiral to more than $20,000/month. Is this possible? Are these amounts really charged? The answer is yes. In the States I have seen those. There are also homes with 'regular' charges of $10,000/month.

That's the rent per month, not buying shares in the company. In general, though, even one-to-one care is usually not charged 100%, with the underlying assumption that the care giver indeed is not at the bedside for 24 hours or, alternatively, does do other chores as well, i.e. folding laundry etc. while attending to the resident. It is also assumed that this level of care is not provided from day one of the tenancy.

Again, this is drastic. Statistics show that homes in Canada, even the ones providing high level of care, for instance Alzheimer's and other dementia care, are charging a maximum of about $7–8,000/month.

But this drastic sample shows what is possible. And since money talks, it is possible to buy those services.

If you really want your loved one to stay home and he or she requires this high level of care, there is another option: *Hire a live-in-caregiver.*

To hire a live-in-caregiver

Now, we are really talking money. There is a host of foreign would-be-employees waiting to be hired by you. Yes, they are qualified. There are agencies out there specializing in this kind of service. It's just that this is not an inexpensive proposition, either. The agency wants $3,000 or so for the service of finding and screening a suitable person and processing the paperwork, which is assumingly quite comprehensive. Fine. But the buck does not stop here. The charges then approach $2,000 per week, (I still have not figured out why this amount is what it is) for a 44 hour work week provided by the care giver. That amounts to $45.45/hour. First, since the week has 164 hours, and 44 hours are actually worked per week, the majority of the weekly hours, a whopping 120 hours, is still not covered with care. Further, this dollar figure is weekly, so times (a little more than) four it results in a labour cost of more than $8,000 per month. In addition and this may be the real challenge here, is that the family or spouse or other family member now must become the employer of that foreign nanny, with all the conditions and legal obligations involved.

Result: This option is really not very attractive, and one must really like it at home a lot to enter into this kind of agreement. Or else, as usual, we must look at dismantling a lot of red tape to make this very option attractive.

Retirement home living becomes a very inexpensive, attractive alternative, all of a sudden.

Alternative living arrangements must be looked into. Presently, these options are hard to find, if at all. But once they are, the application of those will skyrocket. There is plenty of material from abroad, for us to study here, import, try and test, and adapt to North American style.

Not much in this respect is available presently in North America.

This will change.

Because of the "silver tsunami" on its way, there will indeed be a flood of older folks looking in different directions, other directions than the present dominating model of retirement home living. And cost will be an important issue. As there are no one-size-fits-all living arrangements, a number of new alternatives will be popping up in the years to come. And because it's overdue, and because of the power of the computer, these alternative living arrangements will be introduced in the very near future, and I also predict quite a variety of different living arrangements and options. The first step is to introduce or reintroduce the proven concepts from around the world, and see if they can be adapted to North American Style.

CHAPTER 9

Rules, Regulations and Permits

Too many rules and regulations?

Too many rules and regulations are killing inventive minds of otherwise feasible alternative senior living solutions. Rules and regulations of retirement homes will tighten the industry further, driving up costs considerably, and this makes it actually more and more unattractive for seniors to move into.

Granted, the very introduction of these rules are geared and directed to protect the elderly citizen, the residents, from abuse, from undue hardship and cost cutting measures by operators, which may impact the treatment of residents negatively. They are also geared towards treating the resident right and fairly, and in a professional manner, with professional staff employed. All noble intentions.

It's just, reality looks different.

First, there is cost.

One would think, well, how much could it be to adapt a few rules and regulations?

To answer that, let's just say, a lot.

It is only a short few years ago that Ontario decided to give birth to its own retirement home governing body. It is understandable that things got off to a poor start. The governing body became busy first with coming up with all these rules, and then with enforcing them. Inventing them must have been a challenge because that was the first time in history we had cared for elderlies in a way retirement homes are set up. Fine. It's just that nobody really knew where to find those rules which we as operators have to comply with. At the same time, there was already fear of inspections and the consequences instilled. As a result, and not knowing what to do, we reluctantly turned to consultants, who somehow knew more than the rest of us, and hired those to lead us through the jungle of rules. I remember paying $8,800 for the first one of these consultation services. That was to implement "phase one", there were 5 phases to be implemented. It took a few months until we were finally ready to adapt those rules of phase 1. By then, they were available on the internet by the governing body. To date, our policy binder contains close to four hundred pages. If I include the policies of other governing bodies, like "Health and Safety" and "Fire Safety Plan", it'll be much more. Then there are the "Employment Standards Act" and the "Retirement Home Standards Act". The establishing and initiating of all these rules and regulations took about 2 years of the equivalent of a full time employee, which we hired, after the contracting out to consultants proved to be too expensive. This in our small home. Another strike against smaller operators, who are facing hurdles which are much easier to overcome by larger homes or operations, due to higher financial momentum. All this is just designed to make retirement homes provide care in the right way. I wonder if the governing body cares about the well-being of the homes themselves as much as the well-being of the inhabitants—probably not, as it appears.

The interesting part is that these rules are now actually available to us, so, it's all so easy now. We just have to adopt them, whether we like them or not.

Just like that. What, however, if these rules are not in alignment with the way we would like to handle our affairs? Well, I asked that question. Not a good question to ask. And the answer was that of course, we are not obliged to adopt them. Oh, yes, we have that choice; after all, we live in a free country. We can choose not to adopt them, or adopt them differently, in whichever form we choose. We have total freedom here. There is only one problem, we are not getting the license. So much for free choice.

It reminds me of the sign at airports, at the waiting area just before the screening procedure of the passengers, which reads if I remember right, something to this effect: *No individual person is obliged to participate in the following safety and control measures, unless that individual wants to enter the aircraft and assume the intended travel.*

Then there is ongoing cost, in terms of monthly fees per room, regardless if the room is occupied or not. Then there are constant changes to the rules, and amendments, and new rules, to ensure continued employment of the employees of the governing body. After all, we do not want this body to discontinue after all rules are established, do we? So a method has to be found to avoid this, and from what I can see, the body just does a beautiful job in that.

There is not a situation in the day to day operation of our home when we are not confronted with limiting our way of doing things.

Often it is quite frustrating. There is a constant uncertainty by staff members in the air, not quite sure if the situation on hand is being dealt with in the right way, sensibly or according to rules? Sometimes it is even obvious to the residents, in ending a conversation by saying the usual, "Sorry, we are not allowed to…do this or to do that…", or, "Sorry, we can't do this".

A personal note on governing bodies in general—the foregoing is true in many aspects and industries of our society, not just the retirement industry.

Why is there such an urge to regulate free enterprise and small businesses to death?

It appears to me that with farming out the production of all our consumable products to countries across the globe, we as a society, have less and less actual production to do for ourselves. This could be viewed as a blessing, for our dollars are now supporting workers in foreign countries. And we are able to buy goods cheaper, because local workers could produce the same item only at higher cost. But it means that a lot of folks in our country, who were employed in production before, have suddenly lost their jobs—and have nothing to do. But there is a price to pay, which is much higher than the cost of unemployment support. It appears that all people formerly employed in production have now moved to government jobs in search of the now much needed employment. Since, however there is only so much the government can absorb, it came up with the great idea of giving its blessing to have bodies of other natures form themselves, and govern themselves, and make them pay for themselves. Keywords "pay for themselves." So instead of the workers being supported by government assistance in whichever form and shape, they pass the buck to let industry support them. For instance, allowing governing bodies to create rules and regulations for the different industries. Manufacturing industry comes to mind. Construction industry comes to mind. Retirement industry comes to mind. Fine.

Except those bodies are coming up with and continuing to come up with all sorts of rules and regulations and measures which have the effect of hampering the industry in its attempt to exist and thus, to feed the very bodies in order for them to exist, as well. This fact should be remembered by those who are inventing all these rules and regulations. There are, all of a sudden, plenty of those, where there have been none before, which are neither needed nor required, but have to be paid for by the remaining portion of productive society.

This statement goes for all of industry affected, which is, as far as I can see, just about everything under the sun.

And as in any industry, there are also "black sheep" among operators of retirement homes, those who think they can cut corners in order to increase profit. Cutting corners to the detriment of the resident. Or ones who do all kinds of nasty things to the residents, or let nasty things happen without or not enough interference. Abuse is one frequently discussed subject.

And as in any industry, the government tries to regulate, in order to stop those events from happening, or at least to minimize the occurrence. Or bodies sanctioned by the government, same thing. Noble as it is in its intent, as in many other industries, it backfires more than it helps.

Gun registration law is a good example. When the law was introduced back then, all hell broke loose. The honest gun owner felt restricted if not penalised, and the lawless gun owner disregarded the law anyways, and found ways around it. In the meantime, a huge amount of money had to be paid by all involved to introduce and enforce gun law. To the detriment of all, for the benefit of a few, if that can be actually detected.

It's quite similar with the retirement home industry. The majority of owners and operators take pride in what they do, because this is why they have chosen to be in this business. Limiting the majority of operators in their way of doing their job is a serious impediment of freedom. Not all of the wisdom of the regulations enforced may be in alignment with the way operators want to handle the care for their residents. Restriction of the freedom in the very country we came here to begin with, for freedom.

The "black sheep" in the industry, as proven in other industries, most likely will not be eliminated and they will find ways to circumvent law. Still, it looks good on the government to introduce these laws, regardless of consequences. And a huge part of that consequence is cost.

As an operator, however, one can sometimes question the law makers. One feels the pressure of regulations breathing down one's neck. That takes the enjoyment out of the profession. Again, this may not have been the intent by the lawmaker, but is certainly the result.

A case in point is the Fall Prevention Policy.

Again, and I do not want to instill a false impression, it is noble, the intent to prevent unnecessary falls by elderly people. In the view of the regulating body, all falls are unnecessary and hence preventable. Now, how to go about prevent them? Actually, as it turns out, it becomes quite a challenge to attempt to prevent all falls.

The initial fall prevention lies in the design details of the home. For instance, all steps of even minor sizes of perhaps only ¼" or about half a centimeter have to be prevented. That's okay. For someone who shuffles instead of walking and hardly lifting their feet, such a minor step is indeed a major obstacle. Or the installation of handrails. We have 384 ft of them in the home. That's okay, too.

Or the installation of handles in bathrooms. We have about 60 of them in our bathrooms, sometimes two or more per bathroom. That's okay, too.

But what's not okay is that, once a fall occurs, it has to be documented and reported. A commissioner then has the right to come and investigate why this fall has occurred, and what can be done to prevent it in the future. Usually, the professional recommendation is the installation of yet another handle or handrail. By the way, since the governing body has to look after their own finances, they have the right to bill the home for their investigation.

Trouble is, of course, by then the child has fallen into the well already, no pun intended.

And sometimes it goes further than this, as the following case demonstrates. If this handle in the bathroom would have been just an inch more to the right, (or perhaps to the left), or a bit higher (or perhaps a bit lower), then this fall could have been prevented. Or better, yet, another handle around the corner. Of course, it needs a professional's opinions, like OT's (Occupational therapists), who tell us the solution to the problem.

Regular mortals would not know.

I am especially edgy about the so called support poles. Similar to the spring loaded shower curtain rods, they are installed between the floors and ceiling in just about the same fashion, but they are a bit beefier. So is the spring. This way they are designed to not mark the floor or ceiling. The purpose is to provide a hand hold for someone who is getting up from the toilet. And similar to curtain rods, they usually hold. Trouble is, usual, but not always. It's just, if they fail, a person falls down, too, not just the shower curtain. For this reason I used to install them fixed, so this mishap cannot happen. Fixed means fixed. Now they are installed and really solid, screwed to floor and ceiling. Never mind the holes in the ceiling or floor. Safety first. But, of course, that's against the law. Because they are not designed that way. And, of course, they are never in the right place. Worse, they are usually in the way of someone who wants to use the toilet. And if, as is often the case, people with walkers want to use the toilet, they are now really in the way. And so they become not just a nuisance, but a real risk if not a hazard instead. Hence our policy is *not* to install them any more. Alas, until one of those OT's orders them to be installed, so that's it.

That's the law. So there.

Regarding the number of incidents on falls: I dug out statistics from (documented) falls, that is in nursing homes in the City of New York, (It can be reasonably assumed that this statistic could be applied everywhere, because folks living in nursing homes may be considered in similar circumstances as in other States or Canada, as well). The statistics says that there are about 2 people falling a day, per nursing home. Again, these are documented falls. And the average of all nursing homes, disregarding the size. The grey number of undocumented falls is likely much higher. So then, bodies such as investigation commissioners visiting homes in order to determine what can be done to prevent falls might get a bit busier in the future, if they intend to follow up on their mission. Alternatively, they can always hire more staff who will perform this self-appointed work.

Did I mention who pays for the investigation?

A final word on falls: Unlike what society thinks, which is to prevent falls at all cost, I believe that not every fall is an accident. I also believe not every fall is preventable. I also believe not all falls should be made preventable. Instead, I believe that falls have a reason, even though we are not able to see or recognize those.

Yes, many of them can be classified as accidents, and many are and should be prevented. And since we are hell bent to prevent accidents, we are therefore inclined if not obliged to do everything that can be done to prevent them.

Yet, in some instances, it is the soul speaking, and this speaking has to be heard by someone. As mentioned elsewhere, in these cases this fall may be just the beginning of the intention of the person to go home. How else it can be explained, that all of a sudden the person involved suffers not only a fall, but perhaps other health related problems, even other accidents, which are all pointing in the same direction? All at around the same time?

Usually, however, no one thinks along those lines. The first response is the usual "911" call, which is our first action of duty, if a serious fall occurs. This is the law.

I may mention here that this fall prevention policy is one of many which need to be addressed—and revisited. I am certain that once, as a society, we reach a higher level of spiritual awareness, it will be then when we will collectively look into and re-evaluate not only the aspect of fall prevention, but many other here unmentioned issues, as well.

Another good example of regulations getting out of touch with reality—stair lifts

As a retirement home, we are considered "commercial".

As such, we have to have a "commercial" stair lift. We have four rooms upstairs.

What's the difference between a commercial stair lift and a residential stair lift? At first glance, not much. The commercial version features more safety equipment. Why people transported in a commercial residence must be protected more, I am not sure. At any rate, it is not important. There are 3 more micro switches which shut the stair lift down if an obstruction is detected. Like, in case a person sticks out his feet which might result in an injury. Again, why this situation is not protected in residential type stair lift I do not know. And then there is that yellow flashing light. I do not understand the reasoning for that. Perhaps that everyone gets out of the way? Well, as it is, the stair lift is flipped open when in use, and requires the entire width of a staircase. There *is simply no room* for anyone else, so this requirement of a flashing yellow light is unnecessary, and rather annoying for anyone using the lift. Speaking of annoying, when the lift is in use, there is also a horn blaring, for all neighbors to know when our lift is in use. And here I am not exaggerating. All are aware in our home, as well. Even in the furthest distant corner. Now that silly safety feature I am not allowed to silence—you know why, so I won't tell you.

It's the law to have the horn blaring, so that's why. It's probably invented from the same people who think that once the driver's door of a car is open, some horn or buzzer must announce that. Otherwise the car could be moved, with the door open. So here again, I do not understand rules, especially the ones which do not make sense at all.

The price is something worth mentioning. While a residential stair lift unit is in the tune of $ 3,200, the commercial version is, hang on to your hat, $ 14,000. That difference surely must pay for the 3 additional safety switches and the yellow strobe light. And of course, that horn. Perhaps this is why it is nerve shatteringly loud, to justify that huge price difference.

Fact is that we cannot allow any residents to move up or down after bed time, which is somewhat restrictive to the point that I feel sorry for the resident, who might just want to come down for an late evening snack or night cap. But then, the noise of that lift cannot be accepted, because the whole house would be awake if that thing is moved. I wonder if the manufacturer or its engineer have ever slept in a retirement home, with the contraption, designed from his desk, in operation.

But the silliness does not end here. Because the lift is commercial, I believe I mentioned this, there is another government body on the plan. The TSSA, the safety folks appointed by the government. Another self-appointed safety body who have their own rules and regulations. Actually, plenty of them. They make sure the lift is working properly. Of course, they don't check this themselves that would be too easy. They want a licensed elevator and lift company to inspect the lift, twice a year, and put that famous stamp on the maintenance report. Then TSSA comes and checks if that stamp is there. For this visit, of course, they charge a fee, $100 per visit. Also, there is the maintenance of the elevator, the charge by the Lift Company. Trouble is, these guys are few and far between. In fact, the closest one I initially found is located in Toronto, a mere 2 hour drive. Actually all 4 big names of elevator companies you all know of are located in Toronto. We called the first company, and they instantly bent over backwards to have our stair lift on their maintenance contract. After all, they just waited to maintain my lift, right after they finished fixing and maintaining all the shopping mall elevators and high rise elevators in Toronto. Funny, the same interest I found in company 2 and 3, and finally in company 4. They said more or less go pound sand. What must I do? Yes, I want to satisfy regulations, but cannot find anyone who is interested, even remotely, in my contract? And so it is obvious, that none of these companies is interested in taking on the maintenance of my lift, and we are not even talking money! And yes, I did check into their rates. The elevator companies must do or have something magical, because their hourly rates for their servicemen is astronomically high. This is possible because in malls and similar applications, nobody is asking money. The cost is just split up among umpteen stores or tenants, and in these cases the charges are not even obvious. You ready? Their service rates for their mechanics are around $400 per hour. In fact their rates are suspiciously close, in the wide range of between $396 and $404 per hour! So suspiciously close, in fact, that I elected to report suspected price fixing to the government. There is a body who is interested in this kind of set-up. However, I was told that if nobody in public is complaining, they do not act. And I thought I was complaining! I must be not public!

I remember one particular day that my old lift needed service. Trouble is, when I do need service, I mean it. If there is someone upstairs and cannot be transported safely downstairs, that's really bad. After all, I cannot carry the resident up or down. Besides, I am not allowed to. Anyways, I called a company in Toronto, which, to make a long story short, agreed to send out a man. This service tech needed 2 hours to get to us, and a further 2 hours to take the lift apart, and put it back together, but it still did not work. Then the 2 hour trip home. The bill came to 6 hours of $400 each, resulting in $2,400 plus tax. Upon my complaints the company acknowledged the incompetence of their service man, who declared that the lift is too old to have schematics available (12 years), and so, he, the mechanic could not fix it. Because of that, they graciously cut their bill in half, $1,200 + tax. I chose not to tell you the end of this part of the story, but I wanted to mention that this brought me over the edge and I decided to get a new lift installed. Hence I know firsthand about the above mentioned price tag—the one for commercial applications.

Finally, I was able to find a smaller company, a one man outfit and closer nearby. And so, my lift is under contract, at the cost of $1,900 for two visits a year. The mechanic pushes the "up" button, then the "down" button, and applies the stamp. Job done. For a mere $950 per visit.

This simplified demonstration should show what small operators have to face; ridiculous would be the nicest term I could come up with.

On a final note, I have seen times when I only had one tenant upstairs, and I have seen times when I had more, but I have also seen times when none of them required a lift at all—they were able to walk.

There are many more rules and regulations in this business, which defy logic and sense. But I opt to leave it at that. I assume you get the picture.

Chances are that you have your own version of superfluous rules and regulations at your work place, so enough said.

Permits

You may not believe what you will read next.

At a time when everyone and their dog is trying to find alternative living options for seniors, and to be ready for the "silver tsunami", there is a hurdle you would never believe—and a huge one, at that.

You would also not believe that our society could be that backward; but it's true. The hurdle is the issue of permits for alternative and future oriented senior housing models. In short, anything different than retirement homes.

Apparently municipalities have difficulty understanding that there is more between heaven and earth than following established rules.

As soon as something unknown is applied for, and does not fit the categories established, it will be rejected, just to make sure Shelley from Solterra Co-Housing Ltd. tells us her experience with the application of a permit to construct her first 4 unit Co-housing project:

> Shelley reports that Solterra had tremendous difficulty with obtaining permits for the establishment of their first home. Permits were not going to be granted. This experience is in line with mine: as soon as a future oriented but different model is proposed, no permits are granted. It's the unknown that municipalities seem to have problems with. Nobody seems to have the courage to welcome change. Nobody is there to embrace new concepts. After all, Shelley's concept is wonderful and very future oriented, but the set-up of the home as a senior co-housing project is hard if not impossible to classify, and municipalities do not like the fact that there is something they cannot classify. It's not a residential residence because of the variety of folks living under one roof. It's not a condo project, because of the common element, and the type of ownership it entails, and the ownership is 'tenancy in common', not condo.
>
> It's not a rooming house, nor a hotel, nor a retirement home.

CHAPTER 9   Rules, Regulations, and Permits

So, just to make sure, the municipality did not give its blessing in the form of a permit to Shelley's project. That part is not new, really for everyone who tried. What's really outrageous, though, is the fact on *which grounds* the rejection had been based. Are you ready?

It was felt that the co-habitation of the residents is "immoral", since the residents are living under one roof and are not related.

I leave your imagination to go hay wire on that!

All being said, permits have been finally accepted as presented, and from here on out, all senior co-op housing projects are being permitted, but it took Shelley all of 6 years taking on the municipality in a legal battle. The argument that retirement homes are set up really in the same way, did not do much good.

Just a reminder that these permits are approved and issued in this particular municipality only. If you are a developer or builder seeking permits in a different location, be prepared!

And this is where we are today;

As long as we have heavily regulated operational rules and regulations, the implementation and actual day-to-day performance of which is costing a lot of money, the associated cost must be met, as well.

As long as we have heavily regulated requirements such as fire prevention equipment and training, including big-ticket items like sprinkler systems and retro fitted automatic fire doors, pumping systems for emergency use to be powered automatically from generator stand-by systems, to pick just a few rules of many, as long as all of these requirements must be met, the associated cost must be met, as well.

As long as we have heavily regulated requirements such as health and safety, to pick just one of many, as long as all of these requirements must be met, the associated cost must be met, as well.

As long as we have heavily regulated requirements such as drinking water quality, to pick just one of many, as long as all of these requirements must be met, the associated cost must be met, as well.

As long as we have heavily regulated requirements such as protection for staff members through the application of masks to prevent contagious air borne diseases, to pick just one of many, as long as all of these requirements must be met, the associated cost must be met, as well.

As long as we have heavily regulated requirements such as increased level of quality of building homes, increased requirements as spelled out in LEED, to pick just one of many, as long as all of these requirements must be met, the associated cost must be met, as well.

Add to that staff workers who needs to get paid, wants to get paid well, but over and above, expect vacation pay, training time to be paid, off time, sick time, holiday time, vacation time, all of the non-productive time to be paid, the cost of which must be met.

You now have a small taste of my frustrations regarding regulations, while at the same time, seeking frantically alternative housing options which are affordable —clearly trying to make the impossible possible!

CHAPTER 10

Medical Emergencies and Their Cost

As expected when living together with people mostly over 80, medical emergencies are something of a constant companion. Again and again, I am surprised at how the Canadian model is executed, and the development from there. For instance, the "911" call is standard procedure, and the standard response is the ambulance coming. Compliments to a well-oiled system, it usually takes only a few minutes till the ambulance arrives. From there on, however, things get a little out of hand, because it's not just the ambulance. No there is the fire rescue truck, sometimes two, and then come all the firemen on duty. Those who were unable to catch the truck leaving come with their own vehicles. Sometimes even volunteers from the fire department, I suppose for training purposes. Then a bigger fire truck shows up, that's the one which carries the defibrillator, and the assembly is complete. By then our resident is safely strapped in the ambulance vehicle, ready for departure, to where exactly is not known to us at the time, so we cannot inform family members. That's because the destination, as to which hospital is best able to handle the patient, is currently being looked into, and the ambulance is advised on route. In our case, we have 3 hospitals within a 20 minute drive.

After "911" has been initiated, we have counted as many as 12 professionals showing up, but usually 'only' 6–8. As usual, nobody is talking money. But I questioned how much it would cost to round up more than half a dozen people, and their corresponding vehicles, for the given task. Even if there are a few volunteers, I can only imagine the cost being astronomical. Doing a little bit of research on this subject, I did not find anything on the Canadian side, but I found some figures from the States, and some municipalities showed their cost. From what can be gathered from their web pages, the cost per emergency call is in the range of $2,800 and in excess of $5,000 per call. If you ask anyone about what they think it would cost, they will tell you the 40 dollars or so they charge as a service user fee will pay for that call. As can be seen this is just a drop in the bucket of the real cost.

Paramedics employed have salaries of around $50–100k/year. Given these numbers, I wonder what is being done to try to downscale those costs.

I believe this needs some serious revamping.

It's not for lack of trying. We have even a body in place, which monitors and watches other countries on how they handle their health care system, and the related, spiralling cost, which is the same, all over.

Perhaps there will be some improvements, one day.

For what it's worth, here is my suggestion, something which I recently observed first hand from Germany: They, for instance, adopted also the equivalent to the "911" call system, but there is an immediate assessment by the operator that takes place, to determine, if an ambulance is really needed. And so, if the associated cost really must be spent. As such, there is a 3 tier system. The emergency by the caller may be of such nature that an ambulance is really overkill, excuse the pun. It might only be necessary to send out a doctor. Or, tier 3, it might only be necessary to send out an RPN, or the equivalent. Thus the incoming load of health related emergency calls is being handled and looked after on three levels, so cost can be controlled enormously. Plus, it's only one person who shows up in level 2 or 3, not half a dozen or more.

On my recent trip to Germany last February, I had the questionable pleasure of needing medical assistance during that particular night myself.

I experienced severe pain and the source I did not know, painkillers had no effect, so I decided to make this dreaded "911" call.

What transpired was this experience: First, it was determined that a doctor was all that was needed, which was great news for me, since I was sure that because I was not insured, that whatever cost comes my way, I surely had to pay for it. The response time for a doctor to come was given very correctly with 45 minutes to 1 hour, and it was about 45 minutes until the doorbell rang. What I saw coming my way was a tall very attractive looking lady, her fur coat open, showing a mini skirt and black stockinged legs. I would have enjoyed that view much more, if it wasn't for that pain I mentioned. When she reached the door and we exchanged greetings, it wasn't hard to notice, besides her legs, her strong perfume she wore. For a minute I thought perhaps I had dialed the wrong number, and reached an escort service instead. With this thought I was hoping none of the neighbors were still up and watching. But the huge medical suitcase she carried told otherwise.

I suppose I have lived in Canada for too long, and have forgotten that these matters are looked upon in Germany much more openly—at home it would be considered unprofessional and inappropriate for a doctor to show up on a house call in this manner. But professionalism was exposed immediately, and after a quick examination, the doc gave me an injection to calm down the pain. Curious about this tier of the emergency service and the one which is responded to by nurses only, I was trying to ask her some questions—to no avail. She was busy, all right, no time for small talk. All told, she was with me no more than 5 minutes. And the bill I worried about was more than reasonable. About 80 Euro, or $110.00, including the injection. I figure that back home in Canada every handyman would have billed me a minimum of $110 for a housecall.

And no injection.

One little hitch, though. The pain did not ease much, and since I was so desperate I made another call. Not because of the lady doctor, I promise, it was just too much to endure. But alas, I was told in no uncertain terms that the preacher only preaches once. No more doc visits during that night. What the lady on the other end of the phone told me though, was that she could point me to an open drugstore for me to get stronger pain medication.

On her computer system she knew from where I called, she knew which drugstore was open and on night duty. Now there is a good thought. There are drugstores open in a rotating fashion during the night time for just such cases. I thanked her, but despite the pain, I just felt too tired and worn out to go anywhere—and the night was just about over.

One quick afterthought. I believe this is something which could be adapted back home in Canada too. This 3 tier system and sending out only one person must surely be effective.

It must be certainly much cheaper than having a brigade of rescue people and the corresponding rescue vehicles coming.

In our residence, it is quite often obvious that no ambulance is really needed, but we need to take the attitude of better safe than sorry. Fine. But if only a car is dispatched, and all that's needed is a doctor, that's great. And if the doctor decides that more help is needed, it is then the time for the ambulance to be called, especially keeping in mind the quick response time.

Images of Golden Pond's tranquil settings.

This is the "Golden Pond" which the Retirement Home has been named after.

Annual Summerfest enjoyed by all residents and their families.

Resident watches her sunflower grow.

Self-serve buffet for some, served breakfast for others.

We try our hands on growing our own vegetables like parsley or chives.

Plenty of walking trails around the retirement residence and pond.

The story of the creation of the chapel is well known to the residents.

Airshot—Google makes it possible.

The newly constructed gazebo

CHAPTER 11

Outbreaks

Of the 25 years in the retirement home business, I never experienced an outbreak. I always felt this was for other homes only. I never really knew what that meant. That is, for about 23 of those. Then I got educated. In a hurry. And that was good, because no sooner than that, in the couple of years, we experienced not only one, but two outbreaks.

This is really no surprise if one thinks this through. A bunch of people, because of age by definition, are more prone to get infected, and they all are living very closely—family style close. That is a recipe for trouble brewing.

The threshold as to when an outbreak exists is somewhat grey and in the area of 10–20% of the resident load. That means an outbreak exists if a residence has 100 resident beds, and 10–20 of them become infected. An infection could be either bacterial or virus based, and risk of contagious cross infection exists. In our small home the threshold is set at 3 persons. That means, if we have 3 persons coughing and sneezing, the dreaded call has to be made.

"Hello? Is this Department of Health? *Our residence declares an outbreak situation*".

If this happens, all hell breaks loose. Before the hour is up, fully hooded white coated government officials storm into the residence, take samples of residents' saliva, urine, sneezing mucus—you'd be surprised how many bodily fluids there are—and take them back to the laboratories for sampling. No sooner than this is done and confirmed positive, another bunch of government officials show up, cross taping all major entrances with endless red warning tapes, reading:

This facility is under quarantine—no visitors allowed… This facility is under quarantine—no visitors allowed.

Great—Thanks, guys, have a good day, too!

Quite a feeling!

What happens next, of course nobody tells you because you are in and everybody else is out, including the ones you need further instructions from!

So from here on, one spends a good portion of the spare time on the telephone, trying to figure out from officials, answers to the most basic questions, like how do we get food and supplies, (and staff), among others. But internally, in the home, it's nothing short of chaos, because residents, of course, are ordered to stay in their rooms in order to prevent possible cross infection. If you think that's easy, then you try!

Like kids, if they are told one thing, they do the other! Just for spite! On purpose!

Just kidding. Most of the residents of course, don't understand the complications involved. They are just feel the chaos and chime right in—unsure of what's going on and very concerned—about everything, but mostly of their own well-being.

I wonder if officials come up with solutions with the challenges on hand. After all, they are the ones who came up with all this!

Keeping staff under those conditions is another challenge, for obvious reasons. They would rather stay home to avoid the chaos, and this way they do not get exposed to the risk of getting infected themselves. If they do decide to come to work, well they have their hands full—sorry, no pun intended. No wonder, then, they decide to call in sick. They might even *be* sick! So one has to resort to the textbook to see how all the little details are to be handled from here on out.

In times as such, in our small home we took great pride that in all these years we have never had an outbreak. But then again, if we had only as little as 2 residents with symptoms, we took extra care; constant disinfection of handrails and door levers, trays delivered into the rooms, keeping commonly shared bathrooms constantly sanitized and cleaned—it all becomes a constant challenge. Laurie runs a tight ship, and she is constantly concerned about infection in the home, and makes sure everything is sparkling clean. That way only a low risk of infection exists.

So then, having an outbreak is something like a personal downer for us. We have failed somewhere.

But perhaps there are different reasons?

Interestingly enough, but of no consolation, is the fact that at times like this, almost all retirement homes and nursing homes are 'down', as it is called in the officials' language.

And while this is so, one starts to ask questions.

Like I wonder how this is all of a sudden such a big issue. Never had a problem in all those years. Now, there is a tangible problem. And why is it that just about all homes in a particular area are infected?

The common saying goes, ahh well, everyone has the flu…

And what happened to the effect of the flu shot? I have asked doctors who came to our home, and was told there are dozens, if not hundreds, of different viruses responsible for the outbreak of flus. Flu shots, however, protect only against a few. Then, the flu shots being given before the flu season is only a vague guess by the professionals, by whatever means they apply, which type of flu might develop with the greatest probability. And that guess might be right, or perhaps, it might be wrong, as it was the case this last two seasons. I wonder what all that flu shot hype is all about, if the risk being affected by another virus is so great, or in other words, if the protection of the flu shots given, and have to be paid for, is so little.

CHAPTER 12

Considerations for a Future-Oriented Housing Model

From the observations mentioned above, it becomes pretty obvious that there is something fundamentally wrong with the approach to housing seniors in need of assistance in retirement homes. All together, from all walks of life, and it is expected to assure a high quality of living.

At least in some aspects. In other areas, the concept proves great. To combat loneliness, to emphasis mingling with others, companionship and friendships, are all elements which "staying at home" cannot offer. One huge advantage is the almost instant improving of health, which has many reasons, not the least of it the regulated medication intake, and the observing of its effect including side effects, and the subsequent reporting to the doctors. There is no doubt that the current model will stay unaltered, save the add-on services like more emphasis on care, or specialized care such as post-op care, memory care among others. For a few, this is luxurious living at its best. And for those, things will stay pretty much the same. There are always folks who can afford to live in this kind of set-up, even if rates are rising above average.

However, for the majority of the 'silver tsunami' seniors on its way, there must be other housing options available. Besides staying at home, which will be the ultimate choice for many. But as has been pointed out, this is a poor choice at best.

For a society, it is irresponsible and simply wrong, robbing the elderly person of any dignity being housed in homes or residences among similar older persons only, like they all have a common illness to be quarantined from the rest of the population. This might give the impression, in fact it does create the impression, that society rounds up old people, and separates them from the rest of the population, in the name of housing them economically. But as the result shows, it is incredibly expensive. Somehow that approach does not seem quite right, if not downright wrong.

It is therefore essential to curb this practise and instead, create an environment which includes the benefits of the retirement home set-up, and tries to avoid its short comings, in particular its cost.

The first element to be improved is the fact that in retirement homes the rules are created by the management. And this approach does not sit well with many. Instead, what has to be created is community, real community, where the elder person lives among other members of the society, of any age, in a family or community type setting. This is the only form human interaction can be practised, to the benefit of all involved. This may create, among other benefits, also the healthiest approach of living option for the elderly resident, or community resident.

Not only that, but we also tend to isolate and separate various aspects of our lives—work, play, family, friends. Community seeks to heal these separations and bring back together these various aspects of life. A strong sense of family and community provides the foundation that children and adults need to learn and grow. It provides a framework for passing along values and giving and receiving support. And so also to older persons in community, as well. Community also indeed provides a sense of safety and security. Everyone is relying on others. A key element of community is that one is looking out for the well-being of another. A close relationship with friends and neighbors, as well as the land around us can enrich our lives, all our lives beyond any comparison with material wealth and technological advances.

Instead of narrowing our vision, an intimate connection with others can expand our understanding of our relationship with others—and finally, with ourselves. In the end, it is relationships—to other people, to animals, to nature, and the processes of nature—in which we find meaning, purpose and direction. This is meant when I say that younger folks have a lot to learn from elders. Not just in crafts—but in looking for a purpose in their lives. If we look at nature, have you ever seen part of an animal population letting their own elders live on their own? Of course not. Conversely, is it not so that all of adult and older animals teach their offspring? Where did we get the notion that we dismiss this element of passing on knowledge in the name of economical housing?

Relationships, really, are what it is all about, they are the essence of humanity. Lots of people do not recognized how important it is, to live life in community, to value the other. If it were, our relationships we have every day with everyone would look a lot different. The question then becomes how do we handle our relationships, and perhaps there is room for improvement? Not just relationships with one another, but also with animals and in particular, with nature. Divorce, rape, drug abuse, species extinction, overfishing the oceans, deforestation, oil depletion of the earth, burning—by overconsuming—or otherwise destroying all our resources are all evidence of how few healthy relationships we have today with all around us, even with ourselves. It is essential to the healthy functioning of all living things to recognize our place in the larger environment, to see their connection and so see the connection to others as well. This will then broaden our understanding of how we interact with others, especially if this connection is not a quick "hi" and "how are you?" in the hallway of an apartment building, but living with this person in community. We gain security, self-esteem, satisfaction and pride that we are part of community. It helps to bring us closer to a richer understanding of these connections and our vital role—and that of any other older person living in a community. It is in relationships that we define ourselves, create boundaries and overlaps, and gain an understanding of who we really are. For too long, we have defined our basic needs to see others in a deep way, and from the distance. In community, this distance shrinks, and we become close to all relationships within that community. We also feel the sun and the earth beneath us—not in the 3rd floor of some building. Community, more than any other way of life, can enrich and satisfy these needs. Relationships are simultaneous with others, with all others of all age brackets. As we begin to see ourselves connected to all others, and to all of nature we won't ask for any task, and who is to do it, or who is to be paid for it, and any of the monetary assumptions one has as soon as a helping hand is needed. The task at hand will be done, by you, by me, by all others, and nobody will ask for monetary rewards. Community, thus, is healing the erroneous attitude which is so widespread today, especially among younger people—who expect to get paid for every move they make.

Therefore, we have to re-evaluate the practise of housing many seniors under one roof. Interactions are too close for comfort. Dignity is taken away. Initiatives are taken away. Privacy is taken away, at least for the seniors who are cognitively aware. What is desired is closeness, in the sense of safety and in need of assistance, but not to the extent of sacrificing personal privacy. Interaction among consenting adults in for instance practising sex is out of the question in the present set-up. Somehow it is assumed that at that age bracket, sex does not exist anymore. That might be true for some, but not for all. Suffice to say that older folks are deprived of this basic human element simply for the reason that retirement homes have set-up their priorities differently—and the above is clearly not part of it.

Another very large obstacle is the fact that any older person contemplating the thought of moving into a retirement residence has reservations on the grounds of giving up so much. And not only monetary wise. All the stuff which has been accumulated over decades now would have to be discarded overnight to bring remaining possessions in line with available space, even if rented space is added. Usually, people can hardly believe how much stuff their house was able to hold, once they see the movers dragging it all out. This fact is devastating for the one involved, and can be witnessed time and again. The other part is the substantial downsizing of the present house size and square footage to the actual living space awaiting in a retirement home.

After all in Canada we are, behind the States, number 2 on the list of having big houses. Our present average size of newly built homes averages more than 2,400 square feet, only topped by the States with 2,600 square feet (rounded numbers).

So, then, even fancy retirement homes offer only a fraction of this size. In addition, whether one's new place to call home will be an apartment, house or condo, moving in a ton of stuff is simply not doable.

Same with renting additional storage space. How much space? For how long? And why?

And since nobody wants to part with the majority of their accumulated prized possessions, even if it does not make sense of keeping it to anyone but the owner, they simply prefer to stay put. In their own house. That solves that problem, because it never becomes one. Erroneously, they also think that their family/grandchildren will treasure their stuff one day. Needless to say, this is not usually the case.

As a result, the future housing model must first of all offer bigger units, just for the fact that the shock of downsizing is softened. It must be hard for the ones involved to downsize from 2,500 square feet to a 250 square feet room—especially if a major health issue is not forcing this step. It's like moving from a big house, all along with basement, garden, garage and shed, even if most of the space is not used any more, into a hotel room.

In my model henceforth I propose to build individual living units, small enough to make them affordable and comfortable, big enough to soften the downsizing. From here on, a further downsizing is much easier, especially if health is deteriorating to the extent that not much space is required any more. The major step down has been done by giving up the beloved home, the home for 50 years or so.

There are a number of other design elements which I will not disclose at this point, because it is assumed to be not of interest to the reader within the context of this writing. However, for anyone interested, I have developed a Master Plan, which shows in detail how things can be designed. I liken comparing senior housing with baking a cake. The basic ingredients, like water, flour, sugar, milk, eggs, etc., are the same, but it is amazing what diversity can be created out of those basic components by mixing the different elements or components in different amounts.

Same with senior housing. There are a number of basic elements, but how to put them together, is the key to truly enriched living.

Another key element to be achieved is that the persons considering moving is that they must *love* to move there, and then *love* to live there—and not because the doctor orders leaving the house to live in an "assisted living facility". Because this is the case more often than not.

And, above all, community must be created. But there is a bit more to creating community.

Closeness of other members of society is required. Members of society—I picked that term not without reason. That is, people of all ages, not just other seniors. In retirement homes, the main topic of the day is either the weather or their health problems. Closely followed by comments about the temperature in the home and the meals. That's because there is nothing else to talk about—well perhaps gossip. Every function within society has been taken away. It is absolutely essential to find our way back to where we all came from, that is, from community. Real community, not fake community, as in "Retirement Community". How else is it possible for the older person to still see a function for themselves, if everything is handed to them on a silver platter? How else is it possible to still take charge in some aspects of their lives, as far as practicable, as long as it's wanted, and not be stripped of it all overnight—at move-in time in a retirement home? How else is it possible for the younger people to simply interact with older people? If you do not agree here, I suggest you witness any intergenerational interactions between a male teenager and a resident, perhaps his own granddad. It happens every day, when family including the grandson, now a teenager, visits grandpa in the retirement home. It is obvious that this interaction is sometimes most uncomfortable for the young man. There is simply no basis of communication, and partly to blame for this is the isolation of both parties—everyone lives on their own, and in their own world, so to speak. Interaction would be much more enhanced if some model of co-habitation could be found. That could be found in community.

In community it is possible to pass on accumulated knowledge and wisdom, which took a life time to accumulate. How can we, as a society even think for one minute that the concept of retirement homes can be sustained, and totally lacking this most important, basic human need? That basic aspect of society? For eons, elders have lived with family, children and grandchildren. Conversely, younger folks do not believe that this living together is necessary, because all knowledge there is is available at their fingertips, i.e. the smart phone. This might be true, but there is an important element missing: Experience. And Wisdom. This is something which cannot be learned from smart phones. For eons elders have taught younger ones, by interacting and living together. If this is not possible any more, because we feel it is inconvenient and hence believe it is not possible, then at least we should strive to create community in which elders are living together with younger folks—even if it's not their own family. That concept is as old as Moses, but today it's called "intergenerational" living together. This way, elders are not denied being useful, simply by living in community. Community has a life of its own, and the sum is much more than individual input. And elders are quite capable of providing input. The beauty with this concept is that when and if the time comes when an elder person is not able to provide valuable input any longer, this might happen on a sliding scale. As opposed to a move-in into a retirement home, at which point all input to society, or community, or any other opportunity to be useful, is taken away instantly.

To give just a small example, not even a single bird house can be built because of lack of logistics in providing for such a desire within the fabric of a retirement home. Is it any wonder, then, that folks, especially men, are hesitant to move in? And building birdhouses is only one example of many. What if, in community, there are younger folks who are not glued to the smart phone? Look around and see for yourself what young folks do with their time, and with their lives. It is more than obvious that something fundamental is missing in their lives, as well. It is the purpose. Their purpose. But they have no idea what that is, and they have no idea how to go about finding it. That is partly so because they are sheltered from elderlies, and their assistance in this very search. Assistance with becoming.

Assistance with receiving wisdom. We are all together in this. Everyone can contribute according to their ability. Perhaps it is even possible for the young fellow to give the old man a hand? How would that be? How would they know? They have no opportunity to experience, because elderlies are isolated from the younger ones. It would be wonderful to come back to the basics, to come full circle. This way, perhaps this helping hand may not get paid in dollars, but in having a useful conversation. How are they even supposed to know what they are missing? From the wisdom of the smart phone? In the same way, elderlies are sheltered from interacting with younger folks, simply because they happen to live behind retirement home walls. Who came up with this concept anyways? Pretty stark wording, right?

Attempts to look at ways to pay for care—once the senior population explodes

Or How to reduce the cost of labour
Since the inception of the capitalistic system, entrepreneurs have been looking for ways to reduce labour cost.

For the longest time, this motivation was self centered for the purpose of maximizing profit at the expense of the labourer, profit achieved at the sweat of the labourers. This development sparked the creation of labour unions.

However, times have changed. The problem of maximizing profit at the expense of labourers has long been tackled by labour laws, which ensure within their laws, an even playing field. Unions are therefore, not only not needed any longer, but become detrimental to the productivity of the company. In fact, even detrimental to the productivity of the country. Worse, all employees of the union are being paid for by union members, which is in effect sucking blood out from the labour force, while at the same time pretending to look after the labourers interests. What a constrast. Just look at incomes of union representatives, or its leaders. Of course, the wording by the government, who is silently accepting the makings of the unions, is by its very nature quite different. They call it the 'protection' of the rights of labourers. Protection from what—profit greedy entrepreneurs? Well, reality looks a bit different. The protection of the labourers means protection of their rate of earnings. And it means that the consumer, who is buying the product, must be shielded from the opportunity to buy products from other companies, who are, since not unionized, able to offer the same product at sharply lower prices. Case in point is the automobile industry. As consumers and car buying public, we know that a car costs today let's say $20–30,000. We are just conditioned to this number. However, this is only true if we buy this product made in North America, where the car industry's work force is 'protected' by labour unions. In other words, a union driven industry.

As a result, the government makes sure that we are sheltered from the fact that there could be countries knocking on our doors who are able to sell us similar cars, if not better ones, for a price tag which not only is cheaper, but drastically cheaper. We do not know this, because we as a country are also 'protected', call it shielded, and hence not offered such a product. If we were, and would be able to buy a similar car for $8–10,000, this would mean the demise and dismantling of our car industry. Hence as an automobile producing country we cannot allow this to happen. Even if the possibility of such an import of an inexpensive car is discussed, it would be simply quickly dismissed in saying that this car would be of inferior quality anyways because if it is cheap it must mean cheap and so it must be inferior. In no way could it compete with our high quality cars we are building here. Of course, we said the same back in the seventies when the Japanese car industry gave North American car makers a run for their money. The only reason that Japanese cars today cost the same as North American cars is because they are manufactured here. Today, we have to make sure this is not happening again, so we don't even know of that car made in Korea which could be bought for 3,400 Euro in Europe. Could be, but won't. No, we do not know this, and it should stay this way. End of discussion.

However, in the future we may be not able anymore to *afford* locally made cars, and will start to look behind our borders, and see if there are not alternatives. And if we see them, we might want them. And if we want them, we might put enough pressure on the government to allow these cheapies to enter the country. If we were, watch what would happen to our car industry. It is sure to falter, but not overnight. Adjustments will be made. Perhaps all the unnecessary fancy frills of our vehicles will be cut out in an attempt to reduce local car production cost. And unions are perhaps cut out. This is where real competition is looming. If this is continuously not allowed to happen, then the playing field as it is today will not change. The only choice we will have would be to buy a car of any make, and since there would be no competition, it will not matter which make is selected. They are all protected, protected from real competition, that is. And from the buying public.

So then, the conclusion of this discussion is that only if we as a consuming customer who is affluent enough to not care, and to accept inflated prices, and by doing so support local industry, then everything is fine. But if in the future things get a bit tighter, then other alternatives will have to be found.

These comments apply the same for just about any industry, also for the retirement home industry.

As far as industry hourly rates are concerned, there is the possibility that cuts will be made. Perhaps then our standard minimum wage may have to be lowered—not upped, as it is practised today. While I can hear hordes of people screaming, it shall be remembered, that—as it looks today—the future may hold to either work for less money, or not work at all.

Costa Rica, for instance, prides itself in having very little or no unemployment. How do they do that? Well, as it turns out, folks are working there for one US dollar per hour. Giving this scenario, then it is no wonder that they have almost no unemployment.

In an attempt to find solutions for the funding needed to pay for taking care of a lot of older people needing assistance, it may prove difficult to see where the money for the labour force in the future is coming from. It rather seems there will be few choices for younger people finding employment for decent wages. Hence the comment to either work for less money, or not work at all. There may be also the possibility to 'import' people from low income countries to come into North America, in order to provide care services to older folks at discounted wages. However, the way it is structured today, again, this is not possible. These immigrants are, once entered into the country, also entitled to earn minimum wages and hence, the concept of providing labour intensive care to elders by imported workers shows that we are in the same predicament we are into today with our own work force and without foreign workers.

So, in order to provide cheaper labour, something has to give. And it must, because the monies necessary to look after tomorrow's seniors will be huge, just because of sheer numbers. They cannot be much longer provided by the government, because they are screaming today that funding for senior health care is hard to come by, and cost is constantly rising. The best example is the home care industry, where things are getting so tight even today, and necessary savings can only be obtained simply by cutting services. Surely this is not a long term solution. In short, minimum wages are fine because it levels the playing field of the industry, and they all have to go by the same standard. As soon as we have access to a market where the impact of this wage level is not felt, then we see the difference in price. For instance, all we have to do is eat out in a restaurant in Canada, and then travel across the border and do the same in the States. Ah, what a difference in prices can be noticed. And this difference is spelled out because of the much lower staff cost of the States, where, at least as far as waitress wages is concerned, minimum wages are less, actually, a lot less.

And while the concept of a lower level of minimum wages is hard to embrace, here is another example, and that is taking place right here, and we do not have to go far to witness it. Chinese restaurants.

Has anyone thought about this? Has anyone spent a thought on how the buffet style China restaurants are able to provide excellent food, in incredible variety due to the buffet style, for $8.50 per meal? While at the same time, any restaurant around the corner charges twice as much, and an American franchise restaurant three times as much and more?

There must be $8.50 worth in food products alone on the plate, for sure if a second helping is desired. Then, how can it be provided for such a low price? Simple. By low wages paid. That's that simple. The operators of China restaurants deserve the highest respect not only for calculating with a sharp pencil, but also for having family members who are churning out excellent meals with little personal earnings. And yet, we are not appreciating all these facts taking place behind closed doors, and instead, taking this extraordinary approach for granted.

CHAPTER 12 Considerations for a Future-Oriented Housing Model

From this viewpoint, it might be seen that it is the Chinese culture which will point the way. Like it or not, this might just be the way we will be told how to run businesses, including retirement homes. It is only a matter of time, until Chinese immigrants and their low earning family members will run and operate retirement homes. By then, once the same principles are applied as with the restaurant business, the rents of those retirement homes will be a lot less than anyone else's. And one principle applied is low wages—the available work force, family members, who are willing and able to work for less.

Consumer products we are using today are mainly coming from countries half way around the world like China, or other low wage countries for the same reason. We enjoy their products simply because they are much cheaper, and despite long and expensive transportation, is made available to us at much lower prices. Why? Because they are by low wage earners. If they were made locally, they would be a lot more expensive. One logical consequence of that thought would be to have our senior population shipped to China and let their care giving labour force provide care for them, at a much lower hourly wage. This would result in a much lower cost of retirement home living. Trouble is, it's in China—not here at home. Ridiculous thought? As in turns out, there is a growing industry who provides for just that. Immigration into low wage countries for the purpose of obtaining low cost old age care is indeed quite a growing movement presently. In fact, their businesses and related industry is just booming. People recognize what the future will hold here in our part of the world, and seeking out greener pastures, even though it may be far away. Read: Affordable retirement home living including care. Check out www.internationalliving.com, Kathleen Peddicord's web page. Or visit www.retireoverseas.com, Jackie Flynn's web page.

However, for the majority of our elders, there must be a way to take care of them in our own country.

So, let's look at a few numbers for demonstration purposes. I do not project them for the entire senior population, because the numbers become too big and the principal of the situation cannot be grasped. We use one older person only.

Earlier on we spoke of one quarter of our senior population over 65 needing service from home care providers. That number is a bit misleading, because it shows a wide age range. It would be far more accurate to use the number for people over 80 years of age, which is about half of the number of people, but three quarters of the hours provided. The other misleading number which is the earlier mentioned figure of $42.00 per client per day for cost of home care. This amounts to a bit more than $1,200/month. As has been shown, this is the $ figure that the government is providing in services. But what's misleading is, that this number does not mean that the service at this cost is actually sufficient. It only means this is what is being paid for. And I have shown that it is easy to spend perhaps another $1,000/month on private home care to top up the missing hours which are really needed. Combined, the person needs $2,200 in care cost. This is average for services provided at a particular point in time. Trouble is, even this number is only a snap shot, and is bound to increase with every day more lived. Once we have the situation where we have as many seniors as working people, then this amount of $2,200 must come out of the paycheque of the working population by means of taxes. Doing some math, someone must earn in the tune of $6,000/month, has taxes deducted, and pays a further $2,200 in senior care deduction, in order to take home about the same amount as is earned today. With anyone earning less, or much less, there is simply not enough earnings to be taxed, in order to pay for this cost of care. On top, this is the cost of home care services only. But once care requirement increases, we have established a much higher cost. We have seen earlier on that if more care is to be provided the cost can easily soar to $8–10,000 per month. If this dollar amount is to be provided by the working population, we need now several, actually *many* working people whose taxes support *one* of those care requiring persons. This care cost, does not include the rest of the health care cost, such as hospitals and cost medical staff and much more.

However, because of the huge number of seniors coming our way, in such a scenario we would simply run out of working people to be taxed. That's in addition to the taxes already deducted and slated for other purposes. I cannot imagine that such a tax burden be applied even in theory. And any other attempt to cover that shortfall from the working population would result into a tax burden which might well be excess their earnings! Therefore, such a situation is unlikely to happen. But then, what will happen?

Add to this labour cost the increased cost of health care in terms of hospitals, ambulance services and all other related health services which are to provide service to older people, and it is easy to see that the whole concept is just not fundable in the future.

And the situation is growing worse every day by leaps and bounds, by the very situation we are facing.

Therefore, in an attempt to find possible solutions, a reduction of hourly wages below the accepted present level of minimum wages would breathe a sigh of relief into all bodies providing care, be it LTC homes or the home care industry. Although, I don't like to bog you down with the math, which I did, but even by cutting the minimum wages to $5/hour, which is also highly unlikely, even then the cost of caring in the present set-up for the 'silver tsunami' heading our way is not fundable.

But it would be a good start. This proposed solution, however, is contrary to what we have proudly achieved for our labourers, and our health care workers, which is the minimum wage earned. At the same time, it must be said that minimum wages are just that—minimum. Chances are that health care workers earn more, sometimes, especially once they are labour union driven, much more than minimum wages. No question: the higher the earnings, the less fundable the entire care for seniors will become.

If such a large cut in salaries could be envisioned, this is only imaginable in a world which may unfold in a way not thought about today.

There are many scenarios as to what our future will look like once the pinch of diminishing oil resources is felt. If we exclude all possibilities of a world surely beyond our perception, i.e. war to fight for and about the last remaining oil resources, and just for simplicity reasons, assume that everything stays the way it is, it surely will be different. Nonetheless, it will not be business as usual. If we as a society do not step up and reduce our oil consumption drastically, and soon, the decision put off for so long will be made for us. It is not a question any longer whether or not we run short of oil, it is a question of when. *Even so today's low oil prices do not suggest that, even more troublesome, let's us believe we are certainly not running out of oil, so this is no subject requiring immediate attention. This is very dangerous thinking, indeed.*

In picturing such a world, it is then unavoidable that excess oil consumption cannot be enjoyed any longer. At last we finally understand that we need oil for much more important things than burning it in cars or heating our homes. For example, to feed ourselves. But stop burning it we cannot. At best, we can only reduce consumption. By driving less, by flying less, by burning less. And a lot less. It's that simple.

It is then when we will have to look for other means of spending our free time, because travelling will not be part of our vocabulary any more. For the purpose of this book, it is not the intention to instill fear of the future. Moreover, I believe it is something which will be embraced. But our priorities will have to change. Our present way of thinking will have to change. And hence, in such a world it is very well possible to live with less income, and on less. Because there are limited ways of spending free time, once we cut out oil consumption as part of spending free time. I invite you to take stock of what you do with your spare time. You will find that the vast majority of free time spent includes burning oil, starting with driving the car, or flying to distant places. And therefore, in such a world and in such times the possibility of cutting minimum wages may not at all that farfetched.

It is for those reasons that in my proposal I go one step further; and suggest the involvement of *volunteers*. This would be a very quick short cut of labour laws, and how to avoid them. But no income? How can that work? Read on, chapter 15 and 16.

We will be revisiting the elements of volunteers—and other money saving measures.

There are perhaps other opportunities or solutions to the care giving problem on the horizon, which might be considered two steps ahead: The application of care giving robots.

Care giving robots

Human ingenuity will no doubt find ways to replace the human care giver one day. This would be a great development, from the viewpoint of the expected care load to come.

However, is it?

Development is advancing quickly, but more commonly in the medical field. From micro robots called microbots scraping plaques from arteries to automated nursing assistant robots, medical robots changing the face of health care—and will do so much more in the future.

However, at the time of this writing, I cannot imagine any robot which could change diapers. And even for more mundane tasks—I cannot imagine that Mom would take great affection to a machine "tucking" her in comes bed time. Or do other personal care chores. So, what then, are these robots actually doing?

As it turns out, they do quite a number of things, albeit, so far, no personal care. Correction, direct physical interface is already installing robots performing personal assistance, as in giving bed baths. Then there are other models, for instance, that can supervise, like a watchful babysitter.

If Mom fell, the robot would raise an alert and dial any preprogrammed number. Actually, it can do much more. It can help the fallen person to get up, by moving to the person on the floor, who then can in turn hang on to handles, which the robot can raise—and hopefully, Mom along with them. At least, that's the plan. This is only one of many useful ways to employ robots. Here is the link of a Canadian company, which is involved in establishing a platform for the widespread application of robots in health related fields: www.crosswing.com

Here is a short excerpt from the Sarasota Tribune Herald, News Feature, Barbara Peters Smith, posted: Jun 03, 2013

If you are 55 years old, you could wake up 30 years from now to the warm, affectionate voice of your personal care robot, asking what you would like for breakfast and why you slept for only 5.8 hours last night instead of your usual 7.3.

After your mattress takes your morning temperature, pulse and blood pressure readings, you might want to reach for the tablet on your bedside table and tap the touchscreen to turn up your home's heat by a few notches before you throw back the covers. The robot can fetch your slippers.

As you rise and walk into your day, floor sensors might trigger an infrared scan of your gait and balance, relaying the information to a nearby nursing center. If anything seems amiss, a car could be on its way to your home....

This then, might be the future to come. It surely would top earlier proposals of working for less or even for free, as in volunteers. Chances are that the development and even the handling and operation of robots may be handled by folks who are earning a lot more per hour, than the old fashioned "hands-on" care provided today. Wow, what a future to look forward to....

Senior living options agencies

Whatever the chosen name will be, I am certain that a number of agencies will sprout up in the next few years for the different kinds of services seniors are in need of. Some of them will be active in the alternative housing sector. Back in the nineties when I transformed my first 26 unit apartment building into a senior residence, I needed senior tenants, and quickly. After the work was completed, actually long before that, I was on the lookout for paying residents. Marketing strategies were developed. The mortgage clock was ticking. I was looking in vain for rental agencies which I was going to hire to help me fill the building. To no avail. That was back then. Now there are a number of rental agencies in Halifax, as they are all over and everywhere. As the retirement home industry will in the future not have waiting lists any longer, they will feel the crunch of filling their home in years to come. Actually, it is already happening in some areas and some residences already. It is then when they will look for agencies to help them fill their rooms. I predicted years ago, that rental agencies specializing in senior residences will come. It's here. Now a nationwide "agency" is in place, which actually does a lot more than just rent senior spaces. "A Place for Mom" has established itself very well in a very short time all over the States, and is now present in Canada, as well. The set-up is not unlike the well-established real estate industry, and as such, commissions are paid by the homes or residences upon successful placement of tenants. No resident placement—no deal—no commission. In the meantime, their senior consultants take the tenant prospects literally by their hand and guide them through the jungle of what is needed to know to make an educated decision as to which retirement residence is most suitable. This means that there is no pressure at showings, it could be the case that someone is just coming off the street for a viewing and touring a potential residence. This is a great service, and seniors are much more comfortable with contacting someone unbiased rather than the residences directly. From the provider's point of view, these consultants are a tremendous help as well.

    This can be judged immediately, if we have a showing or tour. If the prospect is not coming from the agency, upon entering the residence, introductions of the parties take place. If we were to ask for further information, like contact addresses or email, we get the famous "Don't call me, I'll call you" response, "…In case we continue to be interested".

    Often, it is surprising how little prospective tenants know about retirement homes and their set-up. That is, because the very subject is not very high on people's agenda. Until that day—usually something unexpected happens. Like Mom has a stroke, and has to go into a hospital. From there on, the doctor tells the family that Mom is not going back to her house; its retirement home time. Family then tries to learn everything there is to know about retirement homes before breakfast, and are totally unprepared and overwhelmed by the task at hand. Everyone who has parents over 50 (just kidding) should look into these matters, to be prepared for the unexpected. What are the options if Mom has to move? Are there long term contracts? Who pays for what? Are there subsidies? What is included in the rent? What kind of services and care is provided?

By the referral through the agency "A-Place-For-Mom", we already know a lot about the prospect, not personal information, but information pertaining to the health issues present and past, and so have initially a good idea of what service is required. We know why the move into a home is envisioned, and the urgency involved. This is the way it is supposed to be, and saves a lot of small talk. We also receive information of the financial ability, or inability, which the prospect may not be comfortable with sharing at the time of the showing. These folks at A-Place-For-Mom are doing an excellent job, and I can only congratulate the entire set-up of this enterprise. Just take a look at their web page and see what wealth of information is available. Another one which is big in Canada is Senior Zen, which works very similar to A-Place-For-Mom. I am sure there will be more on the scene soon.

Check www.aplaceformom.com or www.seniorzen.com

At this time, I also predict that agencies for senior co-housing as well as Abbeyfield and similar set-ups will establish themselves—and soon.

As pointed out under the appropriate section, one of the major drawbacks of these kinds of senior living options is the finding and keeping of interested people-committed people.

An agency could be of tremendous help to find interested parties and make them available to the group. Pre-qualification can be performed, saving the group a lot of weeding out before much time is spent.

The typical set-up of a senior co-housing project as described in a later chapter, initially what is needed is what I call a "spark plug", a determined individual who has the intention and vision to set up such a project. This person, or perhaps a group formed already, or a few friends, are then on the look-out for like-minded people, to make this project feasible and to be able to move ahead. This is where the agency would come in, to provide contacts and connections of like-minded folks. Besides the establishing of connections, the service could also include back ground check, financial ability, and the overall personality in order to try to establish a 'fit', all difficult to obtain during an informal information session to show the prospect details of the project. Hence the service could further include the initial weeding out of tire kickers, no doubt saving tons of time for the group to proceed.

Thus with a broader application of these at the moment hardly known agencies, the principle involved would become much more popular, and many more parties would jump in. The agency is the solution (as opposed to pre-building the entire project by a developer, which is the other feasible option) to the most difficult phase of establishing successfully a Senior Co-Housing Project, or an Abbeyfield Project. Or related projects, which use some of the elements of either one of the two.

Richard Carr-Gumm, the founder of Abbeyfield homes, saw this kind of development already in 1956, when his famous saying was: "*I foresee an Abbeyfield House on every street*". Perhaps a bit on the optimistic side, but then again, it may be a possible vision for the future, especially the way Abbeyfield has construed itself. However, at the present time it is safe to say that his vision was a minimum of 60 years ahead of his time, probably a lot more.

Still, this concept may take root—too bad Dick is not around to see it happen. This is what Marjia Babic, Senior Consultant with the agency 'A-Place-For-Mom' has to say:

As I work with adult children and seniors on a daily basis all over Canada, the increased need for more care is evident. Specifically, the rising cases of Senior's being diagnosed with Dementia and Alzheimer's. "Memory Care" is being provided in a select few Retirement Communities. I feel, in the next decade, "Memory Care" Communities will multiply drastically. Seeing a loved one go through the disease is the hardest part. They require much attention, and with the sandwich generation of the Adult Children it's hard for it to be on all shoulders. As I tour newly built Communities, they offer state of the art amenities. This is far from what seniors saw when they were growing up. I feel this will only be more prevalent in the near future, with every level of care in a Community offering the best of the best.

However, with this I also feel the price of Retirement Living will reflect those add-ons.

Are retirement home residents free to leave the home anytime?

Upon signing up the tenancy agreement, Muriel asked the question to the administrator of that big residence if she can leave the home anytime she wants to, and come back anytime she wants to.

And she was assured that Happy Residents Villa is technically well advanced, and does not curb residents leaving at all.

That was good news for Muriel, because she had friends who would pick her up and bring her back.

After some weeks have passed, and the opportunity came up for Muriel to visit her old neighbor, things turned out a bit different. At first Muriel thought she does not have to tell anyone of her absence, remembering the initial conversation with the administrator. But then her friend Glenda thought it might be better to tell someone. Anyone. But nobody was around. They were looking and they were waiting – nobody. Then a good thought came up. The call-bell. That's it. And so the emergency button was pushed. Soon enough staff was here, but not very much amused once the reason for the call was explained. But the care staff told them they have to 'sign out' at the reception.

Okay, fair enough they thought, and proceeded to the entrance foyer.

'Signing out', however, turned out not quite as easy as what the term indicated. A list of questions had to be answered, and punched into the computer, including contact phone numbers of the person who is to be visited, and of course, the expected time of return. The computer also knew Muriel's medication intake, and it was necessary to provide her with some of her meds during her afternoon hours of absence.

No doubt Muriel must have enjoyed her time with Glenda, and the hours flew by. At 6:00 sharp Glenda's phone rang. A distorted, computer generated voice said: *"This is Happy Residents Villa, and we have a resident missing. Her name is Muriel and she has reported being with you. Is she? Please call us immediately of her whereabouts. Please call…I repeat…Thank you"*. Click. So much for freedom.

Then again, it is the mandate of the residence *to know at all times the whereabouts of all residents*. Todays residences house several hundred people and it is not surprising that ways must be found to deal with all these comings and goings. As Muriel was told at the time of admittance, Happy Residents Villa is indeed advanced. Other homes, not quite as advanced and fearful of losing that control, simply curb residents from leaving the home, short of doctors' visits. This obligation to know at all times the whereabouts of all residents is from the operators view indeed hard if not impossible to meet. But since serious accidents happened, and continue to do so, especially by people with dementia, who are wandering off the property undetected (called elopement), some means of control must be introduced. The question then becomes how to do this.

Couples aging gracefully together

Blessed are the couples, who, after 50 or 60 years of marriage, are allowed to grow old together—in harmony.

Blessed indeed are the ones who do so not requiring assistance and are aging together gracefully, and in harmony. The last part is the key, the harmony.

Real life, however, looks different in many cases.

More often than not, one spouse begins to need more attention, the other spouse becomes the care giver. Sooner or later, increasing health care needs begin to deteriorate the heath of the care giver as well.

Husbands have to take care of their wives, in about 1 out of 5 cases. (European Statistic). Obviously the vast majority of women look after their husbands, in 80% of all such situations.

How this care giving is dealt with, is vastly different in the individual situations and reflects all of our human instincts, including the different influences by religious upbringings. For simplicity, all following scenarios are written in the form of wives attending to the needs of their husbands.

Some wives will look after the requirements of their husbands in ways which are commensurable, right up to the degree of selflessly giving care, in the wide spread assumption that this is the way it is and even should be. Their own quality of life is diminishing more and more, as more and more is required of them. But then again, for many this is not regarded as a burden at all, and for some, even viewed as being honourable. Again, views of this vary widely.

For others, such a care giving burden is not to be considered at all, and is not tolerated, because the spouse is unwilling or unable to provide, especially as the care requirement grows. Then, there is home care. To a certain extent and up to a certain degree, home care is the service which lets the couple live longer in their own home. Trouble is, of course, this assistance is only there for a short while, like an hour or two per day, while the other 22 hours are for the spouse to fill the gap. And as the care requirements become more and more, finally when it cannot be provided any longer, other services, like nursing homes, are sought out to give what cannot be provided at home any longer. This will effectively separate the couple in their living arrangements, and now, each one lives on their own.

Quite often, this is what happens in real life.

It is only surprisingly recent, that retirement homes attempt to fill this requirement of housing couples together.

And back in those days, about 10 or 15 years ago or so, the solution offered was that the living quarters became larger, i.e. two rooms, and the standard rate for those seeking out a larger unit, in many cases called suites, was an untold rate of $1,000/month in addition to the basic room rate.

The difficulty lay in the fact that this second person may or may not require assistance herself, but for the operator, this was not an option. Room provided meant service provided, if required or not. Today, this attitude has not changed, only the rates. Suites for two persons, even if only one requires assistance, are very pricey, and are hardly affordable since the cost is almost as if two separate rooms are chosen.

And if a couple has to shell out $4–5,000/month just because they would like to stay together, then the question is really if such a set-up makes much sense, even if the monetary resources are available.

I believe this needs some serious revamping.

Retirement homes are built around certain parameters, of so many square feet are expected to have a certain amount of revenue. If a room is occupied, it must be paid for at regular rents charged which includes services such as assisted living. This explains the above, and shows the out of focus cost for suites housing couples.

It is here that we finally see that providers of retirement homes have maximizing profits on their minds, and it is here that we see things could be different, if it were desired. We must strive to force developers of homes to take into account the wishes and needs of the spouses, who want to be with their partners while not willing to be regarded as just another person filling the necessary revenue numbers required to run the home. There must be in any residence offering suites for couples the allowance built in for this second person to live inexpensively.

As the building cost indicators show us, for instance in apartment buildings, it is quite possible, but perhaps not in the interest of the provider, to build second rooms for the spouse at a much lower rental cost, and allow the non-requiring second resident to stay for a cost reflecting those much lesser costs, even though including, of course, add-on services such as meals. If such parameters are chosen, the second person could move in and live together with their assistance-requiring spouse for a much lesser cost of what is charged today.

Perhaps then the couples who are forced to stay at home today, with the one spouse caring for her ailing husband to the extent of not having any quality of life on her own, destined to do so just because the cost of retirement homes is out of reach for couples, would finally have a chance to move into a retirement residence without being gouged, and at a cost reasonable and affordable.

Hint: Most *alternative senior housing options* introduced further below do not have such cost set-ups, and therefore must be the first choice over retirement home living.

A few thoughts on location of future oriented senior communities: City or Country?

There are as many desired location choices for senior living options as there are folks opting for those. The possibilities are nearly endless. And as we go through life, we have developed our personal preferences as to where we would like to live. Just because we are getting older does not mean we do not have preferences any more. These preferences are very pronounced, as I have found out the hard way. I operated retirement homes both in the country as well as smack in the middle of a city as well as in a town. Hardly anyone is willing to give up their acquired view and change over to the other camp. Country folks could not be persuaded to live in the city, and city folks cannot be dragged out to the country no matter what.

If you were the developer, where would you build? Where would it be? City or Country? When, as a location, let's say the city is chosen, then every potential resident preferring country living would balk at this option. Not even ten horses would get him to the city. Likewise, if the residence is located in the country, every preferred city dweller could not be made to move and live in the boonies. There seems to be no happy medium. Perhaps the suburbs, but municipal regulations take away that option—usually zoning requirements do not allow for a retirement home to be in the suburbs. So we can, for simplicity reasons, classify these two groups very distinctively as city or country.

What to do? Perhaps it can be summarized that it is developer's choice, and whatever his/her interests are. Most often, the developer seeks the city as the location of choice, simply for the reason of closeness to all amenities. That's a fair assumption. But is it really what the residents want? Yes, for all who like the city. And that's great! But what about the country folks?

Well, too bad, they either accept this retirement home located within the city and move in, or they don't. Since the city group seems to be the majority, and as commonly practised, majority wins and the other ones have to go by what the majority has chosen.

A good many thoughts I have spent on this very subject. And it's true, one residence cannot possibly satisfy both preferences. No question, there are far more folks who prefer to live in the city. That's why cities exist. Closeness to all amenities sits high on the list of their requirements. Closeness to shopping opportunities, their preferred church, perhaps even their preferred doctor, and of course, closeness to medical care and hospitals are all high on the wish list. So, city it is.

Yet, all these presumptions lose their importance, once we apply a little bit of common sense: That is, once someone reaches the age and that stage in life where retirement home living is the choice, it's really *only in their mind* that this closeness to all amenities is important. The reality is, in large retirement homes, one is stretching the limits of strength just to reach the end of the hallway and the dining room, never mind walking any distance to shopping centres. This was perhaps once important in the past, but is no more. It's wishful thinking. That part is over. Everything outside the residence, once again, *everything*, can be reached only by vehicle. It's as easy as that. If it's the shopping centre, or the church, or the doctor, it's all too far to walk to. The term 'walking distance' becomes a whole new meaning. Now walking distance is defined as the length of the hallway—or worse, bedroom to bathroom.

What's remembered from the preference of the city is just the fact that *one thinks* all is close, and everything *is imagined* to be within walking distance.

But the reality is, all what's left of this is memory—today, one can sit on the window and count the cars. And if that is a preferred occupation, or pastime, then city living has its merits, after all.

But what's missing with this living in the city approach is *nature*. Closeness to nature. Nature is out of reach in the city, unless the van takes the residents *into* nature, and make a trip, a destination out of it. But this is not very likely, since there is really no tangible purpose for that.

Or is there?

Henry David Thoreau, the philosopher living in the last century, who spent considerable time in the woods of Maine, fending for himself, observed:

"If a man walks in the woods for the love of them half a day each day, he is in danger being regarded as a loafer. But not if he spends his day as a speculator, shearing off those woods and making the earth bald."

And that's the whole point. At the very core of our being, we are wired to be in nature because we are one with nature. Despite all the different conditions we are used to, and have ourselves conditioned with, this is fact. After all, we are part of it all. Hence we yearn to be with nature. But even if city dwellers deny it, and tell you the opposite, denying it they cannot. The Eden Concept, developed by Dr. William

Thompson allows in his approach the re-introduction of nature into nursing homes which can be extended to retirement homes. Within his concept he suggests bringing nature into the home, or, to be more precise, by bringing in the different elements of nature, such as light, water, plants and animals as in pets, right into the residence.

This is indeed a wonderful approach to attempt to satisfy the built in need for all folks, who, due to the city location of the home, or their physical disabilities, are otherwise unable to get back in touch with nature—our very basic instinct. Tell anyone that a retirement home is being located in the country, and the common response is "What? Old folks living in the boonies?" Or worse, "Aren't they scared?"

Fact is we have more reason to be scared in the city than in the country.

But—and here it is—*if transportation is necessary anyways, what stops us from locating the residence in the country to begin with?* Where nature is as close as looking out of the window? Again, it does not matter if a trip to the shopping mall is desired, or a visit to the doctor is necessary, it all can and has to be reached by van—it's just, the trip takes a bit longer—and sometimes not even that. But then, instead of counting cars, nature and animals can be watched. Not trained animals, but as they come, nature unfolds. At Golden Pond, we have regular visitors. Ducks who breed and have ducklings, geese who breed and have goslings, beavers swim in the pond and in fall, they come out every night to gather apples. There are striped painted turtles, which are coming out to seek suitable egg laying places, we have all sorts of birds, including humming birds, blue herons, king fishers. In spring we enjoy the concert of the frogs. We hear coyotes at night, sometimes wolves. We know we have bears around, but have never seen one other than their droppings. Deer are visitors, so are racoons. Many of the regular visitors have been named by our residents, so there is never any shortage of material for conversations. Even former city folks, now due to circumstances moved and planted in the country, completely changed their mind and now love to live here.

It is for those reasons that I am proposing the country.

And by country I mean not totally in the boonies, or in the wilderness, cut off from the rest of society. By country I mean close to all amenities, just not in the middle of it. There are a lot more benefits to living in the country. Nature can be admired by simply soaking it all up, be it by watching it out of the window, or, weather permitting, by being outside. Safety and security is a big issue nowadays, but only in the cities. In the country, however, even today, we are blessed to have no problems with safety and security issues. In the city, locked doors are a must. Perhaps even paid security guards.

Not so in the country. Serenity and watching nature unfold in spring is something city dwellers have chosen to miss out on. Peace is easier to find in the tranquility of nature than in the city. Mingling and socializing among residents is much easier and more profoundly taking place by not being distracted by all kinds of city noise, may it be police sirens, may it be flashing advertising signs or may it be simple traffic noise. And finally, for those who are indeed still able to walk any distance, this is much safer and easier accomplished on trails surrounding the home, than in walking as pedestrians close to the busy city streets.

So then, my conclusion to that basic question is that I believe country living has more to offer than city living. And this is where I would pitch my tent. This is where my personal preference would be. Hence my concept will reflect this location. But it's not just a personal preference—there are some more critical advantages, which go far beyond what has been said so far. Read on, chapter 16

In closing of this chapter, let me share this one with you here:

The Little Boy and Old Man
(By Shel Silverstein)

Said the little boy, "Sometimes I drop my spoon."
Said the old man, "I do that too."
The little boy whispered, "I wet my pants."
"I do too," laughed the old man.
Said the little boy, "I often cry."
The old man nodded. "So do I."
"But worst of all," said the boy,
"It seems grown-ups don't pay attention to me."
And he felt the warmth of a wrinkled old hand.
"I know what you mean," said the old man.
"I sure do"

CHAPTER 13

Alternative Living Options

Several of the concepts in existence in Europe which have been practised and refined for dozens of years, have been introduced in North America, but by and large, with no noticeable impact. This will change.

Europe is much better situated in regards to senior housing. The industry is much more modest in its services provided, and have not reached the "full time resort living style" of North America's retirement homes. And they never will. With this, the cost, while going up as everything else does, is not mushrooming as it is known to do here. Europe features a host of other living options for elderlies, and virtually all of them are unknown in North America.

The first option introduced is really not a living arrangement at all, but it deserves to be mentioned.

The Senior Daycare Centre

The notion is implied that countries in Europe have a different understanding of who is looking after their elders, their parents, and the first choice is the family itself—not paid workers, the very basic concept where we all came from not too long ago.

Mom just moved in with sonny and his family, that's all there is to it. That is, since Dad passed away. Now, over time, Mom just does silly things during the day hours when she is alone. Like forgetting to turn off the range after she heated up her soup. Or re-arranging the house's content—her newly found favorite hobby. Sonny is concerned about this and decides to bring Mom to a senior-day-care centre for the duration of his absence during his working hours.

This concept is very common in Europe, and while known here too, is not very well received. It should be, though, because it is a solution for many problems. However, here the underlying assumption is that the parent lives with the family, and hence, is not very popular. We just don't do these things—anymore. At least not today. Even the granny units, a quickly growing concept which established itself in a very short time back in the seventies and eighties, came just as quickly to a grinding halt, for a number of reasons, not to be further investigated here. The point is, Mom living with family was and is not a very popular option. Just think of all the mother-in-law jokes. Or look back into the statistics quoted earlier, where it is obvious how many old folks are living alone.

One of the problems is distance. Since senior-day-care centres are so few and far between, and mainly in larger cities only, for people who are considering this arrangement for their parents, if a long travel is necessary, the idea is quickly tossed out. And so it is no surprise that this kind of "senior-day-care" is not very popular here. The cost of those centers is around $ 40–100/day, depending on services and/or meals provided.

It is highly recommended to seek out all senior day care options available today in Europe. The internet allows this all. You might be surprised as to what these senior-day-care centres have grown into, quite similar to full-fledged retirement homes without the option of overnight stay.

The next concept I am introducing is what is commonly called Shared Housing arrangement.

It is really not all that well known, as opposed to, for instance, in Germany, where it is and remains very popular.

But the direct translation from "Senioren-Gemeinschafts-Wohnen" may be close to the concept of living in a Senior Shared Housing Arrangement.

Senior Shared Housing Arrangement

This is best understood as in the "Golden Girls" style living.

It simply means that one person—in our context one older person—living alone in the now empty house, opens her doors and takes in 2 or perhaps 3 other seniors, perhaps likeminded friends, who are in the same situation, to share living space, share costs—and have social contact and interactions. And of course, sharing meal times together. It should be noted, that in Germany more than two thirds of the population live in dwellings, apartments and condos, and less than one third own their own home. It is the house owner, who is looking for likeminded roommates, to make better use of the house.

This arrangement makes a lot of sense, although, of course, it is very basic in nature. Care is not provided, other than what the usual home-care service can provide. There is no structure by third parties, no management of sorts, these are just friends living together. So it can hardly be classified as assisted living. And today, it's not just friends. There are agencies out there which bring together likeminded parties, so there may be more to it than finding roommates, and apparently other folks are attracted to this idea as well. With the utilisation of agencies, it indicates that a much higher volume of this kind of living arrangement is becoming popular. It's also easier to implement in the much denser populated Europe. In North America, these agencies are few and far between. Nonetheless, they are in existence. For instance the National Shared House Resource Centre in Vermont, which has been in business since 1981, provides thorough and detailed services for both, the seeker and the provider of shared housing accommodation. Being non-profit, the fees are very reasonable, and even returnable or can be transferred to the next possible candidate, in some instances, if the proposed connection does not work out. They use the nice term, the "geriatric version of a dorm pad".

Since in North America the majority of seniors live in their own house, this results in 2 or 3 or 4 folks giving up their house in order to move in with a friend. This may be a bit harder for individuals to actually do, because there is understandably an inherent resistance in giving up the house, as opposed to giving up a rented apartment. Actually, there is resistance to give up anything. This is just the way it is. On the other hand, we are big on anything related with agencies, and this concept has something to be said for it. For sure this is not for everyone, but should not be overlooked. After all, the agency reports a 30% increase of connections provided since the year 2000. Then again, this is a 15 year time span, and in that sense, is not all that spectacular, a 2% increase per year.

Assumingly, this must be the least expensive way of senior living. Shared cost, shared everything, shared companionship. Period.

Check www. homesharevermont.org.

Senior Co-Housing

A more and more accepted and known model in North America is Senior Co-Housing, also spelled in one word cohousing. In researching numbers, I found a recent U.S. study, which noted about 1,600 of those in the States. However, I know for a fact that this number is not true. This number reflects and includes so called intentional communities, which is totally different. A similar number is quoted by FIC, Fellowship of Intentional Communities, and this pertains to intentional communities. Although in its broadest sense, a cohousing community could be classified as an intentional community. By definition, especially designed and built for seniors in mind, the number of co-housing projects must be much smaller. Also, the majority of intentional communities are not co-housing communities. It also includes all communities, as in all ownership forms, and in all age brackets, which is intergenerational. It only shows that the entire concept is in its infancy stage. By and large, intentional communities are not regulated (not yet) and are very different in nature, and how they are set up. Each one is different from the other, although some common elements can be detected. By contrast, senior co-housing is well established, even though in only small numbers.

Charles Durrett is instrumental in his efforts to bring senior co-housing to North America and to a larger level of public awareness. He just released his new edition of "The Senior-Cohousing Handbook", which is a must read for everyone who likes to learn more or wants to get involved in this kind of housing. In his book he lists more than 300 senior cohousing communities, and that is much more like it. But even if we say 500—which seems quite an impressive number—it is insignificant in context. Typically, there are 10–30 seniors living in one co-housing complex. This results in a total number of give or take 10,000 seniors. However, given the fact that the U.S. has roughly 40 million seniors, this results in only one senior for every 2,500 seniors living in a co-housing community.

Nonetheless, no matter how we look at it, this is indeed a very attractive alternative living option, although quite expensive. I can see nothing short of a much broader application of this concept and of this kind of housing option. It addresses and eliminates many shortfalls of the retirement home living option.

And this is how it works.

In a senior co-housing, each senior or couple occupies one housing unit, which is usually linked, or otherwise clustered close together with others, not unlike link homes. The units are mostly of condominium type ownership, and includes a part of the common elements, such as a common main building. Thus the purchase price of one condo of let's say 18 units would also include one eighteenth of the common elements, which consists at a minimum of the main building. Sometimes there are other common buildings and/or elements offered, as well. The common building is used for getting together, mingling, and enjoying games and activities of a various nature. And then there is the common dining area. It may also house a common laundry. The idea is to live together, and share tasks together, share the duty of cooking in a rotating manner, and finally, share the management of the complex. There is no top-down management or ownership. It is all arranged by the residents themselves. Including providing assistance for living.

But there is a down side. And this is the key: Establishing and building such complexes is based on and done by the future residents themselves. An initial "spark plug" of "someone" is needed, who is looking for like-minded folks to form a group together, and share the same interest in the common goal of establishing such a community. From here on, all likeminded members have regular meetings, and together they share their ideas, and the common goal is getting the project off the ground.

This calls for a lot of meetings, getting to know each other, and along the way are a lot of drop-outs. These voids have to be filled with new recruits, until a core is found of sufficient size which is able, committed and has the financial resources, to be part of that determined group. Then this group discusses possible options for the shared set-up, the location, the planning and design, and finally the input and availability of the financial resources—in the planning stage. This explains some of the difficulties, because it is indeed not quite easy to find those people and proceed to a successful completion of a common goal. This goal, once reached, may be 2 or 3 years down the road before completion. And there are a number of unforeseen pitfalls, which all have to be solved by non-professionals, just a few likeminded but dedicated seniors. Unfortunately, because of these logistic problems, failures are known, and half-finished projects become "pink elephants". These are the ones which make headlines.

There are other disadvantages, as well. As experience shows, the resale value if one unit is up for sale is not as high as it would be with a comparative home. This is because any potential buyer is hesitant to buy into a group, and hence, may consider himself exposed to a certain risk if he does not fit in, or he finds the other co-housing inhabitants not so much to his liking. For this reason, the whole concept must be regarded as a long term relationship with all other co-inhabitants, which is quite a commitment, indeed.

Nevertheless, this concept is very well known and has been practiced in Europe for about 50 years, and was initially introduced and very well spread in the Netherlands—a model which should attract here much more attention than it does. I am convinced that it will do so much more in the near future.

In Canada, the idea of senior co-housing is even more modest, with less than 50 projects which I found on the web, definitely many are currently formed, and also seems to be on the increase. But since we have roughly 10% of the population of the States, the ratio is about the same. Price wise, the very inclusion of a part of the common elements besides the house part does not make this kind of living cheap. Besides, the initial set-up of planning etc. does require financial commitments although no tangible project is built at that stage. But there are indeed a number of benefits offered, and this will make senior co-housing a popular option.

The link is www.cohousing.ca which addresses co-housing in general, and senior co-housing in particular.

Why is it that we do not hear about those projects? Simple, because they are dreamed up, conceived, designed, planned and built by a few private persons. No need for the whole world to know about it. No developer needing marketing efforts. Hence individual projects are not even on the internet, since there is no need either. Unless they start looking for like-minded folks and/or purchasers of their units. Then these projects will appear on the net. Or, alternatively, an agency is involved in matching up purchasers with the project. See below under "agencies". Sometimes these units are also to be found on regular real estate listings, but by the very nature they are very difficult to find, if someone wants to buy a co-housing unit. Realtors are just not geared up (yet) to offer those units in a separate heading or classification. Hence one would have to literally scout through all listings in hope of finding a co-housing unit.

The other option is if the project is developer-planned and purposely built. That paints a different picture. And this is exactly where the future will take hold, because of all the advantages involved. The project can be built just like any other condo project, and then purchasers will be attracted.

In Canada, Ontario, Solterra Housing is just such a company, which owns now quite a few homes.

The concept of Solterra is that their homes are a bit smaller than stated above, with 4–8 residents, but makes just as much sense, nonetheless. These units are for sale, and have their own title, which means they can be mortgaged, sold or willed. In effect, this may mean that the senior may use his or her capital, which can be recovered in the event of a later move-out and sale. Potentially a gain through appreciation may take place. This is the most sensible solution for anyone who has some financial resources. From that view point the capital outlay to be recovered at a later time means house expenses are only the ongoing expenses. In addition, living expenses are drastically reduced as compared with single house residency, since they are paid by all co-owners. In addition, the actual living, because of the community aspect, involves not getting lonely and ongoing social interaction with the other co-owners is conducive to health. In the event assistance and medical attention is required, home care will fill this need, as in any other residential setting. Solterra actually has its own home care company. Because this concept makes so much sense, this is what the future will look like. Some of the units are for sale and offered on their webpage. Prices shown at the time of this writing are well below $100,000 per unit, between $82,000 and $93,000. Considering that 4 of those units buy the whole house, including all common elements, this is indeed a very affordable way to live in a senior co-housing development. It should be stressed again, this set-up does not have any additional services, as in assistance or care, unless extra purchased. So it does not classify as a retirement home, and it does not have to be licensed. By definition, it is a less costly option as opposed to retirement homes. It is therefore intended to be occupied by co-habitants who are still functioning independently.

Shelley Raymond, the founder of Solterra Homes, has this to say:

The Concept:
Solterra Co-housing Ltd. offers an innovative alternative to shared housing options available to seniors. Already practiced in Australia, the concept of "Shared Home Ownership" is growing in popularity, both abroad and throughout North America. At Solterra, we have adapted this concept to the unique requirements of senior citizen.

Today's seniors are re-evaluating their priorities: seeking housing options that balance their wish for independence with an increasing desire or need for day to day support. A Solterra shared housing solution provides support similar to an "Assisted Living Facility", combining personal privacy with the advantages of shared resources and community living. Traditionally, residents share the ownership of the home and all relative cost, rather than paying rent; however, there may be rental opportunities within a shared home.

Owners have their own private bed/sitting room with en suite, and access to the common areas of the home. The shared amenities often include a kitchen and dining room, workshops, guest rooms, home office, arts and crafts area, laundry and more. Each owner has a percentage interest in the home and is registered as a Tenant in Common on the title/deed. However, owners control all aspects of operating the entire home, and each resident contributes to, and is accountable for household decisions.

How it works:
In a Solterra home, owners participate in the planning, design, ongoing management and maintenance of their shared residence. Solterra's Shared Ownership Guiding Principles provide a road map for joint decision making, and regular household meetings are encouraged to ensure active participation of all owners. As members of the residential family, everyone has a voice in the decision-making process. In essence, your percentage interest and private space is a "home within a home". Owners share the ongoing expense for hydro, heat, taxes, water, sewage, propane, insurance and general household costs. In addition, Solterra In-Home Support Service (SSIS) is available for each home. SSIS pre-screens, qualifies and trains staff for food shopping and preparation, housekeeping, administering the household budget, and promoting and maintaining a clean, healthy and safe environment, respectful of each owner's privacy.

Each residential family has its own dynamic. Solterra facilitates the application and selection process to ensure that a new owner chooses the right home based upon his or her support needs and lifestyle choices. Solterra homes are suitable for healthy seniors who no longer want to live alone, or realize that they require more assistance with daily living, but still want privacy and the value of ownership in real property.

Process:
There are specific key elements that are necessary to the success of a Shared Home Ownership solution:

At the beginning of the process, we invite interested applicants to an information session and tour. Potential owners will have an opportunity to meet with the Solterra management team and existing owners. We then require that each applicant complete a detailed questionnaire that outlines his or her preferences. This will assist Solterra in locating a suitable Shared Ownership opportunity in the geographic area of choice. We will then interview the applicant(s) in their own home to begin the LifeStyle Screening process. Solterra has established this process to ensure that individual needs and interests of potential owners are compatible with other members of the selected household. We will also collect medical information at that time, for review by qualified Solterra staff with a goal to identifying support requirements.

Before finalization of the purchase, new owners must agree to an established set of terms and conditions that govern the ownership perimeters within the home. Once a new owner takes up residence, he or she becomes part of the "House Committee" working in cooperation and as an equal voting member with other owners in the household. Working within established, common guidelines, the committee may enhance or modify the house rules to meet the unique interpersonal dynamic within the home. Solterra can provide suggestions and help to facilitate this process if required.

In addition, each applicant must appoint a sponsor before finalizing ownership; a trusted friend or professional adviser who can assist with decisions concerning health or safety, as required.

Why a Solterra Home?
Solterra' Goals:
- Provide an independent living environment respectful of the dignity and quality of life of each individual owner within a shared community of private bedrooms and ensuites.
- Encourage active member participation in the everyday life of the house and facilitate mutual support and respect for individual differences.
- Initiate involvement within the home and in the larger community
- Provide quality assurance practices to maintain the highest standards of care and attention to detail in our homes, properties and services.
- Provide a secure living environment.

Resident Benefits:
- Residents are better able to age at home using home care initiatives as outlined by the Ministry of Health
- Solterra promotes independence and encourages health social interaction to improve overall well-being.
- Co-owners self-govern, self-direct and control all aspects of the ownership model.
- Shared household costs reduce individual expenses resulting in a higher standard of living
- The potential need for subsidized government funding is delayed.

Who are the Co-Owners?
Solterra shared residences are for healthy, independent, sociable seniors, 65 plus. Our homes offer privacy, security, comfort, and peace of mind for seniors who would prefer to live in a quality shared ownership residence, rather than living alone. Perhaps they seek companionship on their own terms and yet want to be able to withdraw and be alone when they need to be. Community living can prevent people from feeling lonely and isolated, and ensure a healthier overall well-being. Our seniors maintain continued control over their environment and finances. By promoting and encouraging their independence, we help to ensure that they continue to enjoy balance in their lives as they age.

About the Home
Solterra owns properties throughout Muskoka: in rural areas, in towns and on one of our beautiful spring fed lakes. Our goal is to locate suitable homes that are within 10–20 minutes of local community amenities, shopping and essential medical services.

All private suites will be 400–600 square feet. In most cases, they will contain a full 4-piece bathroom with roll-in shower, raised toilet, grab bars, rails, sink cupboard and vanity. All units will be set up with optional panic buttons, levered handles and senior assistance gadgets to ensure complete safety.

Co-owners are encouraged to design and decorate their suites to their personal taste, using their own furniture and collectibles. Co-owners' private space can be set up as a single bedroom or double depending on their needs. Newly constructed units have removable walls, which are in fact, moveable cabinets—single or double sided, the placement of which allows unique layouts to suit requirement.

Daily Living
This is your home. Up to 4–8 members share ownership. Each member has his or her own private unit. However, the ownership includes part of the common areas as well. Dining room, living room and kitchen. An excursion into town is another option and owning individual cars is not a necessity. Solterra provides transportation.

Economic Benefits:
1) An investment in real property ensures senior's money stays in their pocket longer & historically real property increases in value over time
2) Rental vs. ownership, rental is wealth diminishing whereas ownership is wealth building
3) Home ownership maintains contribution to the community and to the society in general—continue to pay their fair share of property taxes to a municipality and they employ staff locally
4) Infill into existing stock (meaning a renovation project) using existing home in the community and instead of one person living in the home 4–6 now live there.
5) Delays the entry into Retirement homes & Long Term care facilities—saving the Canadian Taxpayer approx. $40 K per person per year.
6) Cheaper to the Co-owner—instead of paying 100 of the costs of expenses and care they pay only 25% of the costs—living for less!
7) On a broader perspective—individuals (seniors) are taking responsibility for their own needs. The government doesn't have the funds

to give free care to all and in a shared home the seniors are paying more affordable costs and still getting the services they require thereby less impact to the CCAC and the health care system dilemma we are facing in Canada.
8) Multiple shared homes in a community could cluster together pay for one full time PSW or one nurse part-time (sharing the cost for care). Doctors can visit the shared homes and see more than one person, giving better value for their time.

Emotional Benefits:
1) "Age at Home" with dignity, maintains independence and self-respect
2) Self-governed and self-controlled by co-owners
3) Enables the seniors to stay in the community with friends and family
4) Reduces isolation, improves well-being and encourages social interaction
5) Protects capital for use in private care—if and when they move to retirement homes and nursing homes.

On a personal note: (Shelley speaking)
"I know this share-a-home works as my father was one of the co-owners in our model home in Bracebridge and he lived there for 3 years and he was happier in this environment than he had been in his own home after my mom was sent to long-term care.

In his shared home dad had 45 hours of care going into the home weekly, he had someone assisting him to with his shopping, cooking, cleaning, laundry and medication reminders and he paid for only a portion of the costs.

Dad was able to give up his car (thank goodness) and the "house mom" drove him (and the other seniors in the home) anywhere he wanted to go for a mileage charge. Together the seniors organized weekly activities outside the home and interestingly they united as a family. These unrelated people looked after one another and cared about one another. It was wonderful and moving to see him perk back up and love life again.

I would recommend this solution for any independent senior who needs a little support, is lonely and is still financially independent and is determined to keep doing it their way!

In the beginning of my parents health decline I was an overwhelmed caregiver, self-employed and exhausted. I ended up moving in with my mom and dad until we could resolve the health care and housing issues. I committed 3–5 days per week volunteering my time to their caregiving. I used to tell my brother and sister that I was the caregiver by geography; not by choice!

After he sold his single family home and moved to the new shared home with other seniors and staff I was able to visit as his daughter again. I still helped him with some of his day to day banking and explanations of things but, he was in control of his daily activities again and when he needed help or assistance, the "house mom" was there to help.

In the end, my dad lived in his shared home until the last 14 days of his life. When his health declined and he required ongoing meds and nursing care he was hospitalized and after a short stay—he passed, still in control of his life and wishes.

The Solterra concept in a nutshell is about clustering together to share resources, costs and care and live for less! How good is that"?

Thanks, Shelley!

Senior Co-ops

Senior Co-ops are not to be confused with Senior Co-Housing, or Senior Co-op Housing, which are different altogether.

But since we are talking alternative options, this is one, as well.

In a senior co-op, usually one building with a number of apartments is owned by a company or individual, who makes this building available for occupancy to rent. The governing body, however, is not the owner directly, but is a non-profit organization, and usually its members consist of the occupants or tenants, who pay rent. The rent payment reflects all ongoing expenses including management fees divided by the number of tenants, and is so the most cost effective way. Hence this housing model is well sought after, if the housing quality in itself is of good standard.

And this is the catch. This is sometimes not the case. The very nature of being frugal in its operation results in long term deficiencies. Older buildings tend to get obsolete, since the funds for modernization are usually scaled back to only bare bones. Tenants are by the very nature of this set-up reluctant to impose on themselves expenses which they feel should be the owner's responsibility, especially if its long term modernization, or expensive replacement of equipment like heating systems. From the few housing projects I have seen, this is a major problem. Then again, it shouldn't be. Contractual agreements as who pays for what should not be so difficult to establish.

This is why older buildings, which are functionally obsolete but cheap to live in are generally sought after by people of a lower income bracket, perhaps also older seniors.

In terms of permits, Ontario as one province has strict rules as to the governing of such buildings, and have their own Act in this matter. Check www.chfcanada.coop.

In the States, Co-ops are much more common, and also much more popular, at least they were at one point, when this kind of housing was indeed more affordable than the regular housing market. Since its inception more than 100 years ago, this kind of housing was throughout history highly affected by politics and political decisions, and therefore, there is no one size fits all. All kinds of housing complexes have been built, the majority in the 60's and 70's. After that, its popularity diminished, again, mainly for political reasons, which had the effect that the units became more expensive, approaching market rent. In addition, the newly developed concept of condominium ownership took a large chunk out of the co-op market. Still, the US numbers show that a quite respectable 1% of all housing units are available as co-op housing ownership. Check www.coophousing.org.

Abbeyfield House

A further sample of alternative living options I am fond of is the Abbeyfield concept, founded in Great Britain in 1956.

I was lucky enough to have worked alongside Richard Stanton, the executive for Abbeyfield Society in Durham, Ontario, first in the finishing stages of Ontario's model community in Durham and then in the marketing of the Abbeyfield concept as consultant. This role as consultant also touched on marketing of *supportive living of elders in community* and *lifelong lease options*, as well as the concept of *prepaid rents*.

Dick passed away at the age of 94, and was, up to his last days, still pounding the pavement to market Abbeyfield, me in tow. What a fulfilled life this man lived.

I wish I had met him earlier, because there was so much knowledge to tap into. Right up to his death he was sharp as a tack, and we had almost daily email contact. Yes, he was computer literate. The Abbeyfield concept was his life. Dick was very fond of "Community" living for elderlies, although this is a broad term and means different things to different people.

Richard Carr-Gumm founded Abbeyfield Society back in 1956 in the UK. His idea was to use a large home, to have separate rooms for senior residents as in a rooming house style, and have a common dining room, living room, and a kitchen. Meal preparation is done by the able residents or tenants themselves, in a rotating fashion, supported by volunteers if there are voids to be filled. Same for other house chores like cleaning and laundry. So far so good. The concept, although constantly refined, grew exceptionally large and popular in Great Britain in a few short years. It grew outside Britain, but still on European grounds, as well. In 1996, and 40 years in existence, international acceptance was found. In that year, the first Abbeyfield Homes abroad were established. There are many Abbeyfield Homes even in Australia and New Zealand. In fact, more than in Canada.

Despite the tremendous success everywhere, the acceptance in North America and Canada is rather modest. That is today. Again, I believe that the future will develop many more homes operated under the guidelines of this concept. The set-up it is totally different than that of retirement homes, and certainly something to be looked into. The key is the financial aspect, as further explained below.

Internationally and worldwide are about 850 homes run under the umbrella of Abbeyfield. In Great Britain alone, there are close to 300 homes. In comparison, in all of Canada, there are presently a bit more than 20 homes. There are none in the States.

Why is that?

I have spent many a long evening with Dick to discuss the reasons why. And after he has been 'pounding the pavement' for more than 30 years, and devoted his later life entirely to the spread of the concept, there can be hardly anyone more knowledgeable than Dick to listen to about his findings and reasons.

According to him, there is one overriding factor causing the concept to fail here while it is very popular anywhere else in the world; *The cultural difference*. And that's it! That's all.

In North America, we are used to being served. Here, we buy ready built homes. We buy homes, because they are ready to be occupied. Move in tomorrow. Someone else built it. Someone else takes all the responsibility. Someone else serves. All this may come at a price, but that's okay. Serve me, I pay. This is North America. Rare is the buyer who buys a house from a building plan. Rare is the buyer, indeed, who buys and pays into a dream and concept only. Especially if the buyer is an older person. Especially if it's a concept of someone who just like the idea and tries to "sell" it to friends and like-minded people. But that's exactly what's needed to establish an Abbeyfield house. Buying into a concept, buying into a dream, committing financial resources along with a handful of others, hoping for the best that the project will actually be built and ready to be occupied. And all this with no or few professionals on hand.

In this respect it is quite similar to the senior co-housing, in that an Abbeyfield house first has to be established and built from the ground-up by the future residents. Ideally, the building lot may be chosen, so that at least future residents do know where the building is going to be built. Although many Abbeyfield houses are remodeled from existing housing stock, it may be remembered that existing houses are not very well suited for occupancy by older people, who, by definition, have different physical design requirements of the home, i.e. barrier free, to name but one. This is why new construction is preferred. Here again, one "spark plug" is needed to get it all of the ground. So the difficulties involved in finding likeminded people who are willing to go along with the idea, the design, and with financial commitment long before completion is achieved, are the same as in senior co-housing, and is the main reason for the limited acceptance in North America. There are more Abbeyfield houses in Australia than in Canada. So this is something to think about. Alongside with Dick, I have held many an introduction meeting to interested groups, usually, but not exclusively, for church groups who like to know the details of the concept. Although initially everyone was excited, sooner or later the excitement waned. More people dropped out than new ones joined. The logistics proved just too difficult to overcome. In addition, even if like-minded people are found, and the money is pooled together for construction to assume, this project is considered commercial. As such, parameters to build, from the ground up, in order to bring this project to a successful completion with little professional help and just the determination of a few older folks, are very slim indeed.

It is for this reason that I can see an adaption of the Abbeyfield concept only in a way that someone does the building of it, and after completion is then looking for tenants/residents, as it is done by Solterra in the case of senior co-housing, or else, with the assistance of agencies. See below.

In my own concept introduced later in chapter 16, I use some of the Abbeyfield elements, because they do make sense. But that's all. The biggest factor in this concept is the affordability, which is given by the application of very few staff, and a lot of volunteers. Volunteers, or folks who have been around the block more than once, and have recognized in their lives that indeed, giving and serving is the core of human beings. And it is a lot more rewarding than taking. It is volunteers who are in part responsible for the operation of the house. They call it "house", not home and not residence. In my own concept I also use the assistance of volunteers, but for complete different reasons than Abbeyfield.

One of the key requirements of the future occupants of an Abbeyfield House is that they are not in need of any care or assistance. This is indeed a very important component. The concept stresses everywhere that this is not a retirement residence in that no assistance of any sorts is offered or provided. It also prevents the house from being subjected to licensing neither as a boarding house nor as a retirement home. Again, in this kind of set-up it is not possible to include onsite care. Services provided then are limited to common meals, laundry and housekeeping, and most important, of course, socialising. This limits the type of suitable tenants by definition to the ones who are fully functional. This is also necessary since the cooking is done by residents. And this is the key. By this standard, these folks can look after themselves, with very little input from others. The downside, of course is, that in the event more services or care is required, perhaps service beyond the ability of called in home care services, it's time to move—again.

So here are some of the details Abbeyfield has established itself.

A number of likeminded folks, about 10–14, (the concept is very fixed at those numbers, because all of the combinations with more and less have been tried and tested), less than with senior co-housing, establish themselves as being determined to build an Abbeyfield house. None of this converted old house concept any more, although there are many around. This house consists of one large building, housing the individual units, which may consist of two rooms, or at least one individual room per resident. The rooms do not have their own kitchens. The house features a common kitchen as well as a common living area. Then there is the dining area, usually in the centre of the building to minimize travelling distance, but also to emphasize physically the heart of the house. There is an office and a live-in housekeeper suite, as well as a room for overnight stays of visitors. Staffing consist of only one person for preparing lunch and supper only, usually five days per week. Sometimes residents cook for more than 2 days. Hired staff serve meals only on the days the residents won't and fill the gap. She is also doing the cleaning and laundry. They call her affectionately "house mother". Breakfast is prepared and served by residents themselves in all cases. The time where the house mother is in the house is then only very limited hours per day. There are long stretches of time during the 24 hours where no (paid or non-paid) staff members are present in the house.

There are also fees to be paid to Abbeyfield as the umbrella organization, including ongoing annual fees, but these are modest in the range of ½ to 1½ percentage points of revenue.

The management set-up is of interest, since the owning body of the building, a non-profit organization comprised of the residents, will also run and manage the house.

The rent payment then is structured around the actual cost of running the house, including the mortgage payment and all other ongoing cost, divided by the number of occupants. The way to finance the construction of the building is rather unique. A financial commitment for all residents as a onetime payment has to be made, and runs around 50% of the total house construction cost, divided by the number of residents. The remaining 50% of the required capital is provided as a loan, by conveyance of a mortgage, from a conventional lender, usually a credit union. Traditional banks are most likely not hungry for financing of this housing type. This one-time payment from the prospective occupant is structured as a loan to the asset holding non-profit society as mentioned above, which is the managing body as well. If at any time a resident wants to move out, i.e. if care requirement becomes necessary, then the initial one-time payment, that is the loan, will be paid back, but not quite in full; there is an administration fee of 5% applied.

The time frame for the pay-out is one year, to give the society some time to find another resident, whose contribution can then be applied and the departing resident can be paid out.

As an example, if the entire building cost runs at $125/square feet in construction cost, the entire size is let's say 10 resident unit of 250 sqft each, +20% common space, the entire size runs in the range of about 3,000 square feet. Add to that laundry, dining room, apartment for guests for a total of about another 1,000 sqft, times $125/squarefoot, the entire project cost is $500,000. We add to give the project round numbers another $300,000 for the property, as well as site work, parking, paving, water-, wastewater- and power hook-ups for a total of $800,00 for the entire project. At 50% equity contribution, this calls for $400,000 for 10 residents, or $40,000 per resident. That's for new construction. For conversion of existing homes, the numbers may be alot less, but there are Abbeyfields in BC, starting at about $60,000 and even $80,000 for some of the houses I have seen and visited.

It must be noted that this capital input is not structured as in the co-housing set-up. The initial payment does not buy any title to the unit, but is only a loan to the non-profit owners asssociation. Hence there is no way to mortgage or convey anything. This is a loan, and while it is secured, it is in second place only, behind the lender. This is not a very high security at all, in the event something goes sideways.

Interestingly, this loan attracts an interest payment, which varies. In the past and the homes I have visited, this loan attracted 6% interest payment. This interest was applied to lower the rent payment. For example. A $60,000 contribution or loan would lower the rent payment by the 6% interest, or $300/mth. Nothing to sneeze at. But because the mortgage interest rates are now so low, this interest payment is probably much lower now, or may not be offered at all.

So besides the initial cash layout, there is a monthly rent, which consists of all other costs to be paid, as calculated as the cost of running the house, divided by the number of residents. This includes also the mortgage payment of the remaining 50% of the construction cost.

The typical rent payments are in the vicinity of $1,200–1,600/month, per resident. Because of the non-profit aspect, this is indeed a very modest monthly payment. But then again, an initial payment has to be made.

But remember, only minimal services are provided, i.e. no care, or assistance with living as it is called in retirement homes, and not all meals are provided by paid staff members. No structured activities, and no medication management. But for many folks it surely is an attractive alternative to living alone.

Abbeyfield is indeed a very cost effective way for senior living. And a promising way, at that.

As said with the senior co-housing concept, I can see a sharp increase in this kind of set-up in the future, barring the built-in-difficulty in getting it off the ground.

Senior Suite as Condo Unit?

In Germany, they love their "Eigentums-Wohnungen", or as it is known in North America, the condominium apartment.

To understand this fully, it must be explained that after the war years the population was craving for possession of property, as opposed to renting. The housing stock was vastly depleted, meaning destroyed, and so the concept began of having rental units made available on an ownership basis.

This was 70 years ago, and the building market in Germany today is still strong in creating condo apartments, aside, of course, from detached houses. Of course, over time the construction of independent houses surpassed condo apartments. Still, there are at present more than 5.2 million condo-units in Germany.

It is conceivably only a small step away from applying the same concept to senior residences, and even more so, in some alternative housing models, which shall be introduced in a bit.

But the underlying ownership model is that of ownership, which means, the apartment can be purchased, and therefore, financed (if so desired), but also transferred or willed.

From that basic thought, a number of senior oriented housing models have been created, for example the very basic idea of having someone on hand, if a medical emergency occurs. This means that in a multi-unit building of perhaps 12–48 units, there is a nurse on duty, located right in the building, on a 24/7 basis, who can be called if necessary. Otherwise, no further services are provided, and the units are all self-sufficient in that they all have their own kitchens. Quite likely, the design of the apartments are barrier-free, and are designed for seniors only. Apart from the purchase price of the unit, only the cost of the nurse on duty must be paid, borne by all tenants in the building. This is well received for peace of mind of residents fearing being alone, and no one there to help if the need arises. Given the low cost divided up by a number of tenants, this concept is inexpensive and fully sufficient for many.

From this meager beginning, the next step would be the assistance given for toileting and dressing, which now requires more than one person on staff. Again, these care givers are located in the complex and are available if needed. They may or may not live on-site. It must be stressed that similar to our set-up in North America, there is a difference in who pays for what. The above scenario must be paid by the tenant directly, unless the need for assistance is given on a regular basis, which is the dividing feature, and if this is the case then insurance would pay for the service.

The next step from that would be that food service is included, which is practised in a somewhat interesting way: As opposed to our retirement home concept where meals are served in a dining room, these places offer restaurants, which also serve meals to the public at large. In addition, the residents are served, and they may come down for a meal, or the meal is being delivered up to their room. The cost is either directly paid per meal, or the provider offers coupon style payments, with discounts for multiple meal coupons. There are also larger homes which offer bistro style restaurants for their residents only.

If the level of assistance is greater, then the regular retirement set-up is practised. In many residences, units can be rented, the same way as it is practiced in North America. However, there are also retirement residences in which the units can be purchased.

The concept of buying a room in a retirement residence is indeed something we might look into, as well. Now it can be argued that the anticipated length of stay may not warrant the purchase of the unit, and this is indeed so. But here is the kicker. Folks in Germany are purchasing rooms, or suites, or apartments in retirement residences much earlier, perhaps 10 or more years before an actual move-in is envisioned or anticipated. Thus this model in nothing short of an investment, and, since the management by the retirement operator is given by definition, there are no problems with tenants to be expected. Moreover, since the concept is so wide spread, one can literally seek out the suite of their choice, and will know where to go once the need arises.

The units, of course, can be occupied by either one or both of a couple. If something unexpected happens and the suite is not needed at all, it can always be sold, if so desired, by the beneficiaries or family members in case of decease of the owner. All in all this concept is of benefit for all involved.

It is not a big step to realize that the whole idea can be carried even further, and so it is.

From garage spaces in parking garages or underground garages to hotel rooms to rooms in spas or therapy centers, everything can be purchased. And mostly these purchases are regarded strictly as income properties.

For developers, for instance for a retirement home developer, this concept is a blessing as well, since capital can be raised for construction.

On my recent trip to Germany, investigating current trends of senior living options, I spotted an ad for the construction of a new retirement home, featuring 68 rooms. The ad was geared towards selling the rooms. The ad read: 'Only 3 units left', and a little further down, 'construction slated to begin in fall of 2016'. What that says, is, that folks are buying these units right off the plan, or the drawing board so to speak, with the soil not even turned, yet.

Something we certainly would be hesitant to do here.

Speaking of hesitant, there are two overriding reasons why we will not see those principles applied in North America.

First, since we have had condominiums for "only" 25/30 years instead of 70 years, our public perception of condominium ownership somehow lags behind Europe by 40 years, and is not as well accepted as it should be. Somehow we seem to think that apartments are for rent, not to own, as opposed to houses.

The very fact that in many cases, the monthly condo fees are very pricey if not overcharged does not help to make the whole idea more attractive. There are still some concerns, if not downright fears as to the present set-up of condo fees in new developments, and in particular, to future condo fees, and people fear they are left to the discretion of the developer as to future charges – not a pretty picture to paint. Somehow would-be purchasers are also concerned about the value of the unit and will appreciate in value, or if it might actually drop. They are also concerned about the involvement of third parties in managing the complex.

The second reason is the complicated and costly legal set-up of the North American Condominium concept. Too complicated and too costly. No doubt the legal system has made a nice bed for themselves, and they love to lay in it. Everything under the sun is regulated, and the more it is, the less effective it becomes. And as a logical extension, the more grounds for disagreement and even law suits is given. This certainly does not make the whole concept more attractive, save for the legal servants.

In Europe it is very simple, and it is also possible to convert existing housing stock to condominiums. Sometimes in such cases tenants are given the first choice of buying the unit, if such a conversion took place. The tenant then can decide and is given the first choice of refusal. The conversion, by the way, is of legal work only, as opposed to North America, where units themselves differ in construction between tenancy and condo ownership.

Because the concept is so wide spread, even in the case of new construction the legal set-up is much simpler. For instance, if a room in a senior residence of let's say

50 rooms is offered for purchase, then the purchaser buys not just the room, but also 1/50th of the common elements as well as 1/50th of the property. Simple as that.

Here in North America, it must be all measured out and surveyed out, surely no simple task to do, but a costly one. The set-up of the necessary condominium corporation is a difficult task in itself, and everything in it is regulated and to be handled only by expensive professionals, chartered accountants and lawyers, for example.

As has been said elsewhere and repeatedly, there are just too many rules and regulations for this concept to take hold. It must be simplified, and the legal set-up must be simplified, and the cost must come down as a result.

If this does not happen, then I cannot see that this concept has any greater future than the modest spread it has reached today. And yet, it could thrive and could offer a lot of alternative living options for seniors, as can be witnessed by looking overseas. Too bad we are not there, yet.

Shared Intergenerational Community Housing Model

There is another concept, which deserves mentioning; actually, it's no concept at all. But it is the accumulation of a lifelong work and foresight of an architect and his partner, who back in the 90's developed plans and ideas on how to deal with alternative living options of seniors. His ideas are captured in a most outstanding book. This foresight of things to come is most astounding, since Ken Norwood and Kathleen Smith from Berkeley, California developed exactly what is needed today, and more so than ever. I have met Ken in one of his presentations in Toronto in the late 90's, while I was living at the time in Nova Scotia. The travel of more than 2.000 km one way was more than rewarding, and no doubt has contributed and influenced in the establishing of my views as to available and alternative senior housing options. Fact is, I was and still am really excited about his ideas. Ken recognized also the importance of "Community", this time the term and meaning is used correctly. His efforts, being an architect, are mainly focussed on the developing of designs and plans, not so much the construction. Actually, I am not aware of any of his ideas coming to fruition in Canada, but would be most interested to learn, if some of the readers know of any.

Ken's ideas then focus on the housing options of intergenerational occupants. That is, in one building there are senior suites as well as apartments for younger people, be it single or families. Ken recognizes correctly that society's idea of housing seniors and lumping them together in separate buildings is not a sign of a very advanced society. He also points out the waste of time, gas and money for housing projects in the suburbs, the most applied—to type of housing development in the 70's and later. His principals are focussed on community living, and shared living space. That is, while each suite or apartment represents an independent living unit, including a small kitchen only, as in a kitchenette, the emphasis is directed towards a common dining area and common living room. Quite often his plans feature other common elements

CHAPTER 13 Alternative Living Options

THE OUTDOOR SOCIAL COURT

The is the social beehive of the community. The physical form and location of the court, created by the arrangement of buildings, vegetation, pathways, and materials, invites spontaneous interaction and community gathering, aiding the growth of a sustainable community social fabric.

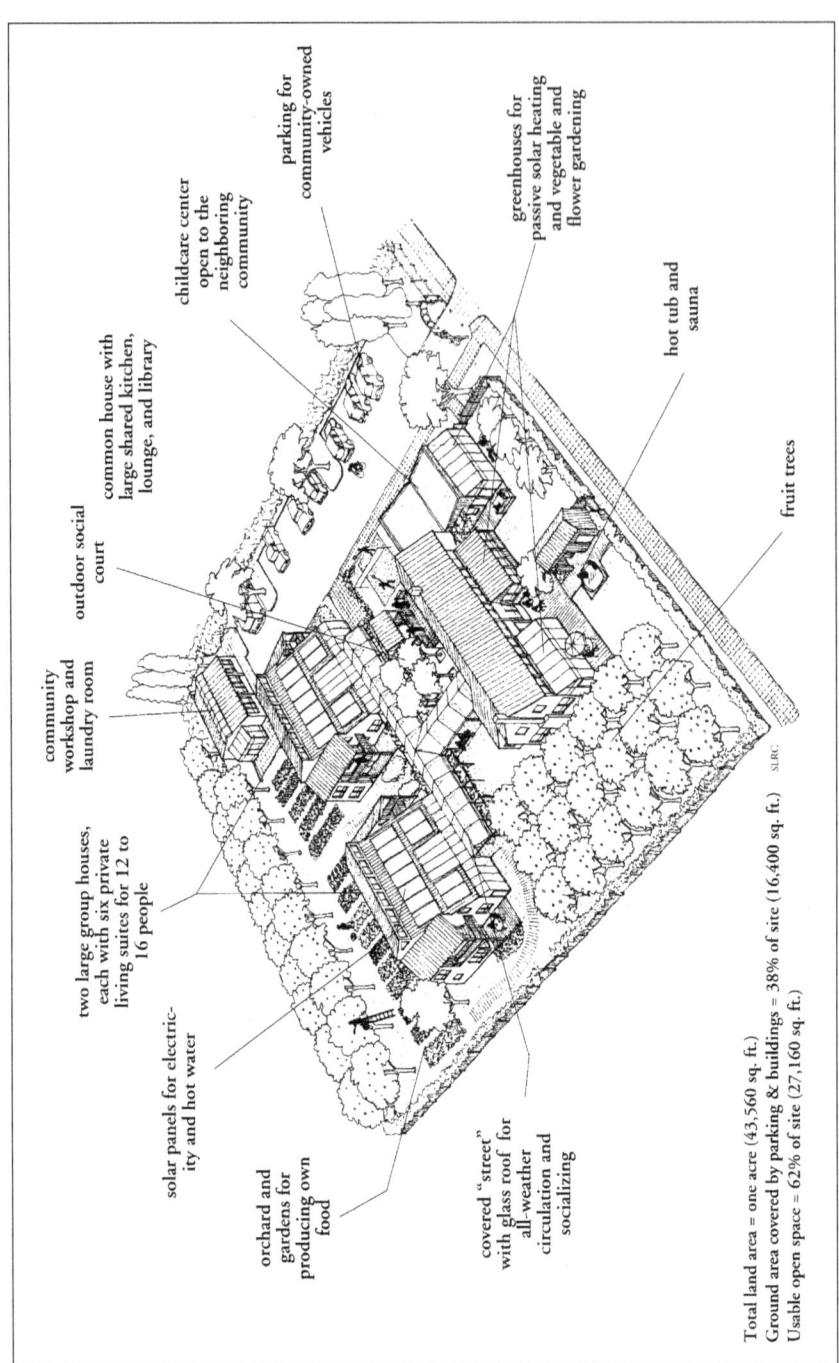

TOMORROW'S COMMUNITY TODAY

In a typical suburban development, one acre of land accommodates only seven single-family house with paved streets and driveways, two-car garages, relatively unusable front and side yards, and postage stamp backyards. At Village Acre, one acre is enough to comfortably house 12 family groups and to provide them with co-ownership control, home childcare, a reduced cost of living, shared resources, open space, mixed-income affordable housing, emotional support, and intergenerational role models This Village Cluster community model is an ecological answer to many of today's quality of life dilemmas.

CHAPTER 14 Alternative Living Options

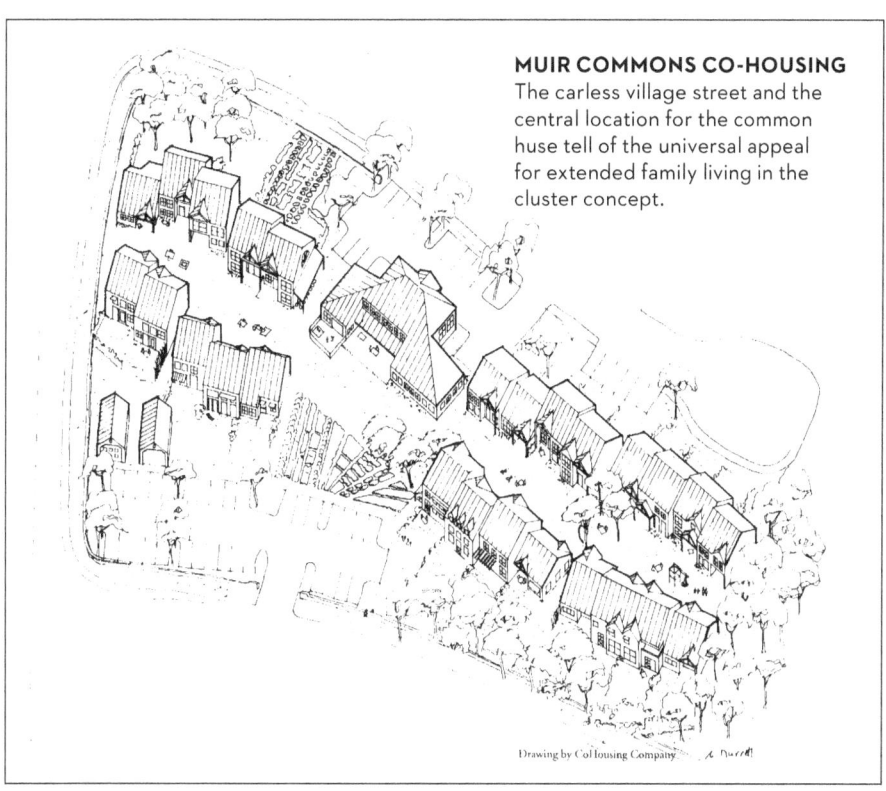

MUIR COMMONS CO-HOUSING
The carless village street and the central location for the common huse tell of the universal appeal for extended family living in the cluster concept.

Drawing by CoHousing Company

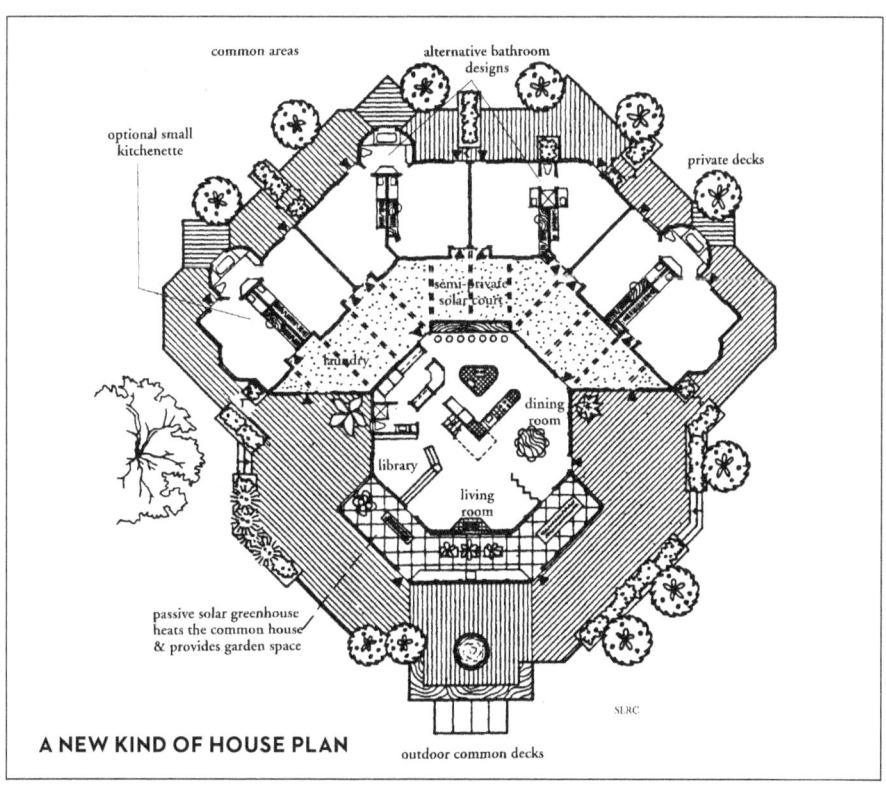

A NEW KIND OF HOUSE PLAN

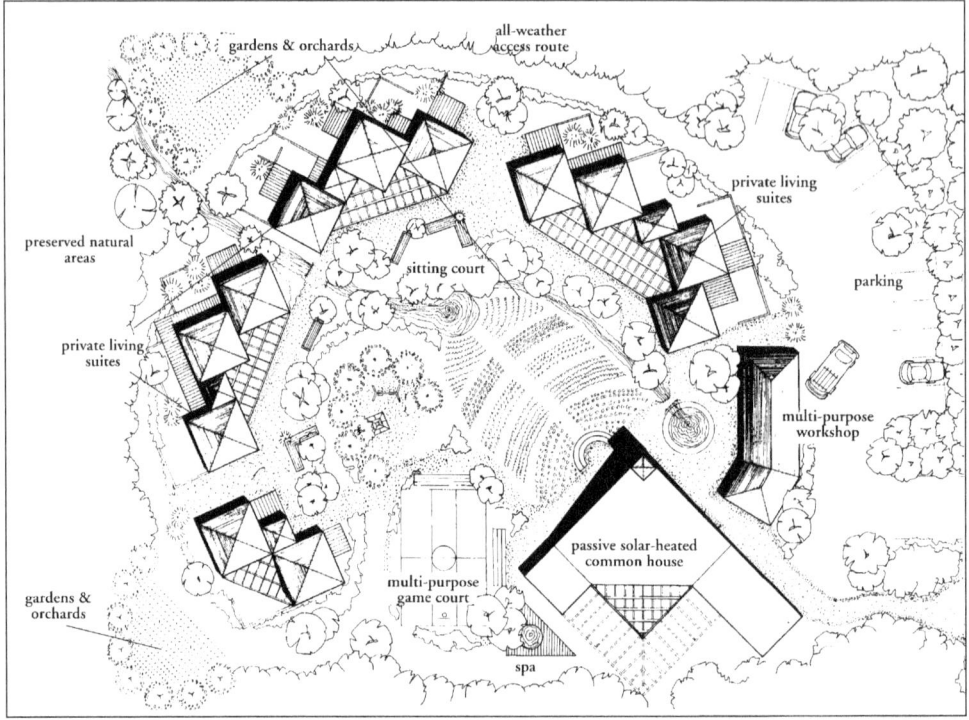

THE 2 ½ ACRE VILLAGE CLUSTER COMMUNITY
This prototype design provides the features needed for a high level of self-reliance, natural energy production, low car dependency, a paradise for children, community-based livelihood, and a sense of belonging.

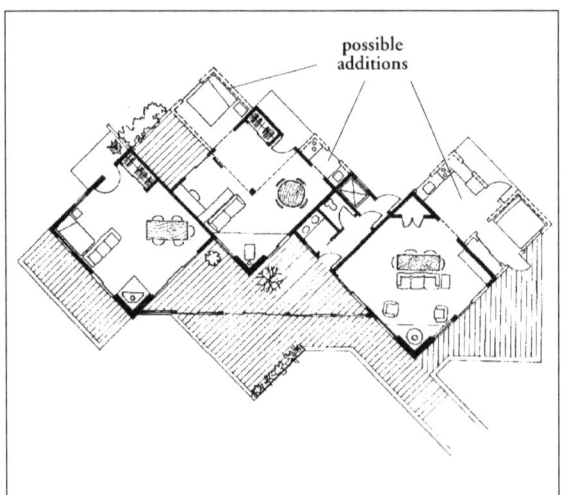

STARTER UNITS
This shows the "starter" living suites with private decks.

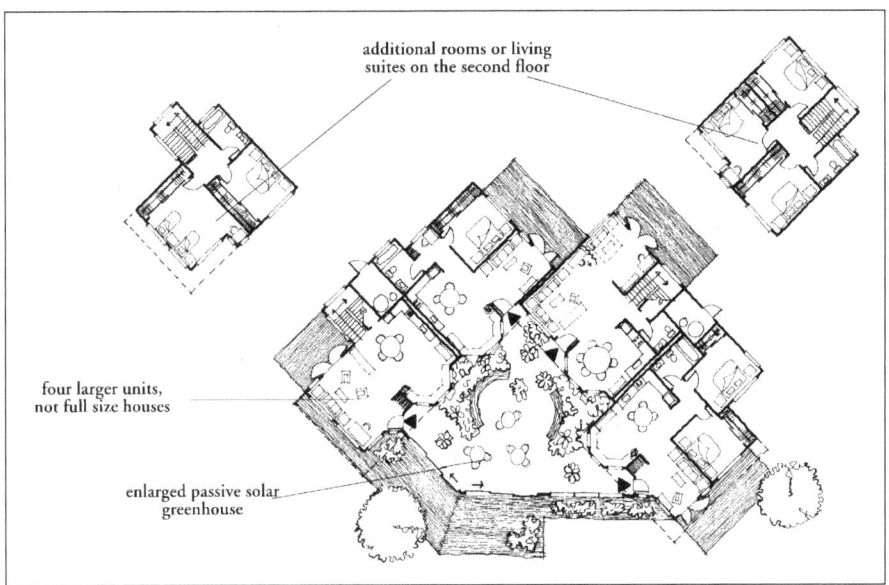

EXPANDED UNITS

The private units shown in the 2-1/2 acre Village Cluster prototype design were envisioned as starter living suites, and were carefully sited to allow for room additions on two to three sides, as well as a second story. Expansion would be optional, occurring when children are expected or other family needs arise. The kitchen of a unit does not need to be full size as in a typical nuclear family tract house, and for some people could even be left out.

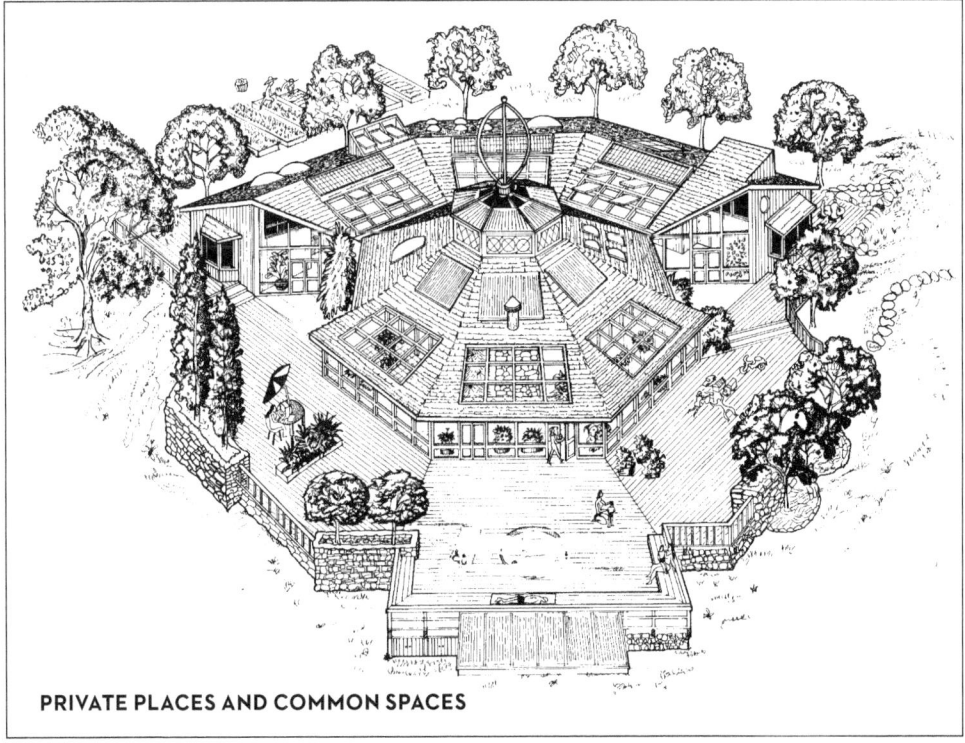

PRIVATE PLACES AND COMMON SPACES

in other designs unheard of, such as a commonly used computer room (Remember we are talking early '90's) and a commonly used baby sitting room. The idea here is for a working Mom to drop off her child right in-house, to be looked after by other residents, i.e. seniors. You also find commonly worked and tended to gardens. That is community living. That is what Ken envisions in his designs and ideas. His book "Rebuilding Community in North America" is a vast pool of knowledge, ideas and concepts on the planning and designs of intergenerational housing units. Ken also emphasises economics and sustainability in his designs, again, an issue which he addressed 25 years ago, and again, is more needed today than ever. Car sharing, commonly shared work and maintenance chores are all the elements which have been discussed and looked into, with the key component being community living.

If these plans were to be implemented, it would solve a ton of today's problems for senior housing options, and I can only encourage anyone who has the funds and the means to look into the actual building of those complexes.

As a final note, I might add that at one point I have been very close in the building and development of such a housing complex, but immediately ran into problems on which I would like to make a few comments.

At one point I was seriously looking to build such a complex. But as I needed financing, the buck stops right here, as they say. There is absolutely no lender out there with the foresight necessary to probe into realms unknown. The risk of building something totally unheard of is indeed a risk, since not even the public at large could picture what is being offered here. Let alone sign the dotted line to occupy and purchase a unit in such a complex. Hence it is necessary to fund such a project privately, and by people who are convinced that this unusual housing model is indeed what people want. The question becomes really, which type of ownership is offered, and with that how to proceed with the marketing. As with any other living option and arrangement, there are a number of occupancy models available, all of them could be applied in this Shared Intergenerational Housing model as well. It all depends what is being envisioned by the developer-builder-lender. Besides the cut and dried rental option, which is a long term relationship with the project, conceivably the units could be made available in a co-ownership, which is called tenant-in-common, as well as co-housing units, as well as condo units, as well as lifelong lease arrangement or prepaid rents arrangement, at least with the units occupied by seniors. All options other than straight forward rent result in a short exit strategy for the lender, a much preferred option for professional lenders. However, again, it might prove difficult to finance, no matter which type ownership is offered. Who is going first?

Community Living in purposefully built Multi-Unit Residences, or Intentional Senior Housing Community

Since today most retirement residences are calling themselves communities, this term now needs a new definition:

It is the Shared Residence Living of several folks in one home, *designed for that purpose for the senior part of the population*. Several folks means all ages, not just seniors. And shared means not just rooms and living space, but cost, as well. It also means management, as in self-governed.

For the senior's units, they are to be senior friendly, a term referring to barrier free. And that's the key point.

Let's back track a bit to Chapter One which discussed the most practised form of living: Keep living at home. That's where Mom still lives, and hangs on.

No one wants to hear it, but it's true; the trusted family home, which served so well for so long, does not serve well any longer. But nobody wants to give it up. Trouble is, this family home is just not designed for old people to live in, least of all to live alone.

And since nobody sees this, it is neglected. At first. Then, some shortfalls become too obvious, and some adjustments on the house have to be made. The arthritis sets in, and door knobs cannot be turned any longer. Big deal. They are changed to lever handles. In no time flat. Once sonny has time to do all that. And that's ok. But this is only the beginning. Soon, as physical abilities change, and physical strength diminishes, more and more things are suddenly wrong with the house. They all have to be changed. Trouble is, all these new developing deficiencies are not coming overnight. They are creeping up. And the needs are more and more frequent, and then more and more complex, and more and more costly. But then again, the expensive cost of retirement home living can be delayed, if not avoided altogether. So money is saved. This is common thinking. At one point, the changes to be made are substantial. Like a stair lift must be installed, rather sooner than later. There is grave danger that Mom might fall on her way up to the bedroom. If she were, this fall might prove fatal. The kitchen has to be ripped out and replaced with a new kitchen featuring only 27″ high countertop. Also, spare room underneath the countertop has to be provided for a wheel chair to slide in. Working on the counter top can only be performed in a sitting position. Perhaps more room for that wheel chair has to be provided. No sooner than the new kitchen is installed, Mom does not feel like cooking any longer. It's now down to heating up the soup in the microwave. High fridges cannot be reached any longer, neither can high cupboards. And the list goes on and on. At one point, family members, who are helping Mom with increasingly changing requirements just for her to stay home and arranging for all these alterations, may come to the correct conclusion that all this has to be changed back to how it was before at the time Mom passes on—when the time comes to sell the house. Now, this is no small feat. Selling the house as it is now with all these alterations done means a good deal for the buyer, because the house is now worth a lot less—the buyer has the job of getting everything back to the way it was, the way "younger" people want to live.

The best way would be to have Mom live somewhere where these changes were already implemented. And could be passed on to the next user, who requires roughly the same. That is, purposefully built by a builder. Enter purposefully built barrier-free living units. That's for one user. In order to create community, we have to grow to create a multi-unit building. So now we have planned multi-unit buildings, in part for the "regular" user or habitant or tenant or co-housing unit owner, or whatever term suits best. Then we have part of the units for the same type user or owner, but these must be suitable for seniors to occupy. These units are barrier-free. Besides the individual units, there are common areas, in particular, but not limited to dining, cooking, and common living room areas. All under one roof. This is planned community living. This is the living option of the future. All you have to do is find those. The hunt is on. Go ahead and look for barrier free apartments or condos in multi-unit buildings. Or as co-housing options. Go right ahead. If you find them, let me know. I can promise you will have a hard time finding those.

As my favorite architect Ken Norman and his partner Kathleen Smith already predicted 20 or more years ago, this kind of living arrangement makes a lot of sense. But only now the time has finally come and their conceptual ideas will finally materialize in the near future. Why now? The glut of older folks to come and who are looking for alternative living options will see to that, and will finally get the ball rolling. They are seeking alternatives to retirement home living.

I predict even in a big way.

Tailor made and barrier-free built units for seniors, but other units as well, occupied by people of all ages. Multigenerational living in a multi-unit building. Fancy wording for something so basic. Normal living together of normal folks of all ages. Old and young together. Each one in their own unit, preserving their own privacy. What's so special about that? Well, if you look around, it may sound strange, but indeed our present ways of living have departed quite a bit from that thought. From the design point, there is a fine line between providing privacy, enough to not feel intruded on, but not to the extent of feeling isolated. Your neighbor becomes your best friend.

In times of need closeness of other people becomes very important.

Just slip for a moment into the shoes of an elderly. Just imagine that for instance, your breathing is not all that well. All of a sudden you feel your chest getting tight. You can't breathe. You are gasping for air. Good thing the neighbor hears you pounding on the floor.

Or your sense of stability is not all that well. One wrong move and the floor is all of a sudden a lot closer. Should've used that walker. It still is there—right where you forgot it. And then, the pain sets in. You realize something went sideways. You went down and fell. You move to get up, but there is the pain, oh gosh, the pain. You can't get up, no matter how hard you try. Good thing your neighbor is close enough to hear you calling for help. Where is that emergency push button again they gave you when you moved in? Ah, you remember now—at a safe place—in that night stand drawer. Trouble is, it's too far. Darn! The pain... the neighbor hears your calling—the neighbor is your best friend.

Now imagine the difference living with common areas like dining and living and other frequently used space all within. Normal living but having dinner together. Younger ones cook for all, in a rotating fashion. Older ones chip in to the extent they can. They may peel potatoes, do the dishes. They may babysit while younger folks go to work. Mingling together. Socializing together. Running the home together, still attending the weekly or so meetings necessary for running the home. Being useful in their still available capacity are accepted, and not pushed aside. They feel needed, and they are. Not being pushed out of the way by the dozens and even hundreds, in retirement home residences which are not designed for their needs but for the needs of the developers in charge. In such purposefully built multi-unit buildings they may still use the abilities they have, of various degrees and to various extents. In contrast, in retirement homes, they are being stripped of all of their still available functions and dignity. In community, they are accepted. And loved. And needed. In retirement homes, especially in big ones, this element is also taken away. This is now really community living. This is now intentional community. No top down management. The residents managing themselves, likely with input of younger people. Services provided in-house to the extent all residents agree on. The ones in need pay the ones who provide, to an extent and as to an amount which is agreed upon—if remuneration is asked for to begin with, because it may not be. Especially if the assistance required is modest.

This is the kind of living which I can visualize will become very popular in the future. It's nothing else but re-living the past, because this is where it all came from, the only difference are now with purposefully built homes or complexes.

There is more. Because of the cost sharing, it is not only an inexpensive proposition for the elderly to live, but for the younger co-habitants as well. Okay, for the younger folks living there, if that wording is better. It's a win-win situation for everyone.

Downside?

It's new. It's not known up to this date. I have not found anything on the web about this kind of housing option, let alone the complex but basic construction of who and how the home is being run. Throw in the different kind of ownership options, or none at all in case of rental units. Who owns the home? Throw in the extent younger folks are helping, or assisting, older community members. Society and municipalities will then step up to the plate in order to not miss the boat on regulations to be implemented. At what point is such a set-up considered a retirement home? Or is it? Then it's getting interesting. If an older community member pays a younger member, is that considered employment? As an employer-employee relationship with all its regulations, and there are plenty? Now, at that point, it's really getting interesting. Time will tell how this is going to unfold. But before I am getting too self-congratulatory, I hasten to add that if and when such set-ups are going to be regulated in whatever fashion and in whatever way, it might become self-destructive. As self-evident in the countless other models which are not even close to the one proposed, and are already categorized. One of them you already have been introduced to. Do I have to mention the retirement home industry?

And most important of all, at this point municipalities and their servants have not discovered this kind of housing, because they have not been approached—yet. As a result, permits will be difficult if not impossible to obtain. If it's new, it's not regulated or categorized. And so, it has to be declined, just to be on the safe side. Because it's not regulated, and because in our society all are so keen on regulating everything, this will undoubtedly follow soon.

And finally, financing for this kind of housing will be also very difficult if not impossible to obtain. It's not proven, because it's new. Hence the hesitation of potential lenders or financing sources as to the potential risk.

For Marie, divorced and living on restricted income, the primary impetus for moving together with others was financial. "My rent", she says, "got to where I couldn't manage it". She considered herself lucky to have found an organization that arranged for her to share a rambling suburban house with four other adults and a child. But after living alone and enjoying her privacy for twenty years, Marie found it difficult to adjust to her new roommate situation, which included adults of different ages, genders, and cultural backgrounds, plus three-year-old Zoe. Only after she fell and broke both wrists did she realize how much of a community her household was. Lois cooked for her, Stephanie bathed her. Mike took her out on drives, and others did errands and laundry. "I was totally astounded," Marie exclaims.

Stephanie, Zoe's mother, cheerfully acknowledges that none of the adult roommates had anything in common before they moved together, and they still mostly lead separate lives. But she loves her huge, U-shaped house (she could not have afforded more than a studio on her own) and here living situation in general. "It started out as an economic necessity, but now we stay together because we're family.

Judy T. and Gary F., by contrast, were financially secure enough to consider buying a home of their own. Yet they had no intention of making that kind of investment—until they went to a meeting of a group considering an urban venture billed as "co-housing". Judy had read about co-housing, an approach to residential living that combines private and shared living spaces, and was curious, but "hadn't really expected to be so taken with the idea. It struck a chord with me—it reminded me of the neighborhood I had growing up in the Midwest, that I had been missing but not really consciously." They committed themselves to the venture right away. Says her husband Gary, "I wasn't too keen about buying anything, but I thought this would be at least socially responsible". Their new dwelling contains their own complete two-bedroom apartment plus extensive common areas shared with several other households. The group spent nearly two years meeting once a week to plan their custom-built community. By this time there was little they did not know about one another. Although Judy and Gary committed not only time, but more than $200,000 to their new home, they feel that what they receive in return is worth the investment.

Between these two extremes is Wes N., a writer who could not afford the cohousing option but liked the idea of shared living. Divorced, with a four-year-old daughter who lived with him half the time, he dreamed of a family-like situation "without the pressure and exclusiveness of the nuclear family". Although he was not actually searching for a group house, when friends told him about one near his ex-wife's neighborhood, he decided it would be convenient for both him and his daughter. After meeting the residents and ascertaining they shared his values, he rented two rooms in the group's stately, eight-bedroom home. He was pleased that his daughter enjoyed the companionship of seven other adults, one toddler, and assorted dogs and cats. When Wes decided, years later, to send his daughter to a high-quality public school in another town, the two of them moved. But when they—Wes in particular—found they missed their intentional family and the twice-a-week communal meals, they returned.

Excerpt from Carolyn R. Shaffer & Kristin Anundsen's: "Creating Community Anywhere"

Says Ken Norwood:

American housing stock is largely designed for the mythical "typical American family," a two-parent household with children and with only one parent employed outside the home.

Reality, however, is more complex; only about 20% of American households fits this "typical" description. Can you imagine a shoe industry making shoes only in one "typical" size? America is a diverse nation and we need alternative housing options.

That statement was made in the early nineties. And in America. See for yourself where we are on this today, 25 years later. What is really different today? Also, what is really different in Canada?

Answer to all of the above? Not a lot.

Community Living designed as Sacred Places

With the *Intentional Community Living in Purposefully Built Multi-Unit Residences* we are now able to create to our hearts content. That is, after the basics have been covered, we can create different versions of the same concept. Unlike retirement residences, which are in its basic set-up fairly consistent—even similar in its design features. Quite often, also with the services provided. Exceptions exist, in particular these super communities in the States housing 1000 or more residents.

Just a quick summary of what will be introduced in these multi-unit residences:
- Larger individual living space, not just a room, but not a full fledged apartment
- Intergenerational, all age set-up, not just seniors living together
- Barrier free design for the senior units
- Affordable as far as possible
- Highly efficient for minimal of heating/cooling requirements, including application of passive solar
- Located just outside city limits, on larger acreages in a country setting
- Integration of active residents taking part in the operation
- Integration of volunteers who take part in the operation. These efforts may be recognized in material or sundry benefits, i.e. occupation of units rent free, having part of the meals and hence, being part of the community. As opposed to strict employment, 8.00–5.00 relationships.
- Commonly run errands and outings with community owned vehicle
- Commonly done meal prep by residents-volunteers and only very limited application of employees
- Separation between owning corporation and operating body, which might be a non-profit organization. The underlying assumption for this is the assumed contradiction and conflict between owning and operating interests.

Tom Bender is an Environmentalist and an Architect. He has composed his "Environmental Design Primer', which goes even further, and shows the possibility of 80% energy savings in his ideas and teachings. And these, along with the findings of Ken Norwood, have been created and introduced 30 years ago. And they are just as important, if not more, today as ever. It's time they are actually applied.

But it shows that his view could be well implemented in such a model community and could become reality in an intentionally planned community for seniors:

Says Tom Bender:

Let us each have a place where we live that is
Free from the stormy and trivial forces of
Everyday life. Free from electricity,
Machines, media, symbolism, economics, and
Pride—free from the flux of coming and
Goings that fill our lives—free from the
Questions, empty words and concepts that
Make and fill our places and minds
Let it grow sound, built of the materials of
nature and the hand of man. Let it speak
of what we love and are. Let it become filled

> with the tranquillity and serenity of
> a peaceful heart.
> let it become sacred in our lives to spend
> time there, free from the noise of culture
> power, growing close again to our roots and
> nourishment which bonds us to all else,
> able once again to hear the subtle and quiet
> voices that speak of deeper and forgotten
> things. Let that place be sacred, for it is so—
> a manifestation of those things that lie
> beneath and before the visible outwashings
> we call our world.

Tom Bender has designed and created a number of future oriented building ideas and energy efficient designs which are worth checking out at www.tombender.org.

Senior Community Living in Tiny Homes

The Tiny Home movement is currently exploding in the States, and takes a strong foothold in Canada, as well. There are definitely reasons for this development.

First, the size or better, smallness, is most appealing to younger people. After all, it is better to own a dorm pad, small as it may be, over a rented apartment, although usually much larger. Defined as 200 square feet per living unit, this is tiny indeed by any standard.

It has been developed originally by young people as an outcry to society, and which incorporates a few very important elements. Designed mainly to oppose the current trend of overbuilding living units, that is residential houses, in terms of wasting resources, be it building materials or energy usage to heat and cool today's large houses—if not monsters. By definition, tiny homes use a lot less material, as well as a lot less energy to heat or cool. Tiny homes also oppose consumerism. While noble in this respect, there is one more overriding element in building small—cost.

It is no secret that one who has not the advantage of any professional education, and therefore, anyone earning around minimum wage, will not be able in his life time to own his own house, build according to the average standard of modern building technology. The cost of housing is outside the reach of a single earners capacity at this income level, and this will not change in the foreseeable future. Many folks are seeing this, and along with it, away go the dreams of owning their own home. The very minimum in that earning capacity is doubling up, as working couples become the norm, in which case home ownership is getting closer although still out of reach, even with both earners working full time. And that is the catch. With today's trend of employers providing part time jobs only, it becomes almost impossible for a working couple to be employed full time. A practical approach then is to juggle 2 part time jobs, perhaps even more, to make a living. If both partners are pursuing the same goal, it is the recipe for a chaotic living arrangement, and the thought might creep up sooner or later whether the whole thing makes sense, and if it's worth it. Add to this that most likely 2 cars are necessary to achieve the above it is then a logical consequence that something is wrong with this entire picture.

The three main pillars of monthly living expenses to be paid for on an ongoing basis are for housing, food and transportation, besides sundry costs of all sorts. Every one of those cost pillars is under scrutiny and corners are cut in every imaginable way.

For instance, food cost can only be cut down by trying to be more self-sufficient and to grow one's own food. This of course requires a list of other necessities one of them is land. For many, food cost is just what it is. Transportation is the next area of expenses to be looked into. Besides the obvious expenses for acquiring and insuring cars, indeed it is very hard to justify someone earning $ 10 an hour to pay for car repairs in order to go to work, when service charges in any repair shop cost close to $ 100 an hour. No matter how hard we try, be it a new car or an old clunker, it costs several hundred dollars a month to have that car. If there is no other way to go the work place other than by car, or if it's not close enough to seek other modes of transportation, this pillar of car expenses is a big one, indeed.

As for sundry costs, such as lawyers, dentists or vets, they charge exponentially more than a repair technician. If those services are required, and must be paid for, there is immediately a huge problem, because monies spent in magnitudes of several hundred dollars per hour can hardly be paid by someone earning minimum wage. Something has to give.

One answer is to tackle the other big pillar of expense: *housing cost*.

This can be reduced by deliberately seeking out the most inexpensive housing option which can be practically applied: for instance, living in tiny spaces.

Because they are affordable, they are on this principle alone becoming popular in an incredibly short time and, thanks to the internet, spreading like wildfire.

All throughout this book, we are seeking out inexpensive living options for seniors, requiring care or at least assistance, thus the aspect of applying the tiny home option shall not be overlooked.

It looks like this is also a solution for lower income earning seniors as an inexpensive, workable alternative living option. But is it?

To find out, I have investigated that option a bit further.

But, alas, sorry to say, at this point in our society, we effectively block out that option, albeit the concept seeks to be applied, as it is so obvious. Yet, the devil is in the detail, as they say.

If we look at the idea a bit closer, we will see that it is simply not possible, at least not today, because of the way we have things structured. As with some of the other ideas and alterative living options investigated, a lot of rules and regulations would have to be adjusted, changed or scrapped in order to introduce tiny homes into intentional communities with care or assisted living provided as an alternative concept. So do the communities where tiny homes can be parked.

Tiny homes in intentional communities with care or assisted living provided
What needs to be done to make this concept feasible?
The first thing we should understand is that the minimum square foot provided within a tiny home concept is less than what we have defined as minimum living area as standard, no matter where we go, in whatever State or Province. So right of the start, these homes are illegal, at least for permanent, full time occupation.

In particular, if someone like a developer is to provide this kind of housing to the public. It is somewhat different if someone on their own decides to live in a tiny home, on their own, and perhaps of their own creation and self-built. That illegality is something which is currently being looked at by municipalities, especially by the ones which are confronted with these issues. I have looked into this in our municipality, and the immediate response was that it is all illegal. However, as I was told, minimum standard living sizes have been taken out of the By-laws, a clear indication that something on that front is brewing.

But because of that, it cannot be taxed, which is great for the ones who are not conforming with the law in the first place, and is a rather a big advantage – until discovered. It can only be assumed that municipalities are not very kind to folks intentionally avoiding orderly set laws in that respect.

To avoid this kind of law breaking, tiny homes living units are simply built on wheels, that is, trailers, and thus, are movable, and therefore do not require a building permit of sorts. And cannot be taxed for the same reason. However, this only helps in one way, because standards do exist as to building movable living units at least with minimum size standards. These laws are then not to be found in municipalities, but to be found in the laws and regulations for manufacturing of mobile homes or manufactured homes. As these are to be obeyed by larger production facilities, the single personal building or production of a tiny home surely cannot be governed and comply with those standards. Or are they? At this time, no. Tiny homes do fall outside those regulations, as well.

As the demand for tiny homes increases, as to be expected, it won't take long for the producers of tiny homes to no longer be able to fly under the radar. As we speak, standards for building of tiny homes are being developed, and some who feel they should have a say in that, have formed associations for making sure these newly created rules will be adhered to by manufacturers, producers, builders and sellers. Ontario for instance has its own association of tiny home builders. It is foreseeable that in the not so long distance the government will jump on the band wagon and will come up with its own ideas as to how to govern this newly emerging concept of living.

At this point, some freedom still exists, and new units can be bought for as little as $20,000 for a 200 square feet unit, fully winterized and suitable for year round living. On the other side of the scale, there are manufactures out there offering tiny homes with purchase prices exceeding $100,000.

At that price, however, the whole concept of cheap living becomes questionable. After all, in this price range of tiny living the square foot price exceeds $500, and as such, equals condo prices in exquisite locations, perhaps in larger cities, waterfront condos etc.—surely outside the initial idea of an inexpensive tiny home.

The basic idea of a tiny home, besides its smallness is to use commonly used building methods for fixed housing and apply those to a trailer, resulting in tiny square footages. They are stick built with the common 2 by 4 construction. The 8' wide tiny home is narrow for the reason of movability, and can be towed on its trailer relatively easy, if not at highway speed, but without a special permit. The size of the unit in terms of square footage is then entirely resting on different lengths, a common one being 24' long for a total area of 200 square feet. There are some individuals out there determined to live in much shorter units, but that small size becomes the size of a walk-in closet of a conventional home.

Design Challenges for Seniors Living in Tiny Homes

As it is today younger people, perhaps chasing jobs in different parts of the country, sometimes use easily movable tiny homes to pursue these options.

It can be said with certainty that once the option of frequent moving is no longer necessary, as is expected with a senior, it is quite possible to enlarge the unit to maybe 12' wide. This now would indeed offer a more comfortable ratio of width to length and a much more appealing living space. And we still have the ability to move the unit, even if it becomes a bit more expensive and is reserved for companies who specialize in these kinds of tasks.

But wait! We are now back to mobile homes, reminding us of a time which many of us went through. We have grown out of mobile homes as an attractive alternative, because buying real houses is for most of us much more appealing, if they can be afforded. Are we now growing back into those kinds of living arrangements?

Actually, tiny homes are very close to that, just smaller.

Then the question becomes, what are seniors actually expecting in terms of the size of the living area? And if we are offering sizes smaller than conventional rooms in other kinds of living arrangements, even retirement homes, it may be argued that we can only go so small, and beyond that, it is simply too small. After all, society has set minimum standard sizes of living not without reason.

As the footprint in a typical tiny home is limited to 8' wide, and roughly 13' high, in order to cram as much living space as possible into the given room, these units offer sort of 1½ stories, or at least, some sort of open high ceiling, with one side closed in with its own floor/ceiling, creating a sleeping loft. These can be accessed by a ladder and other similar space-saving arrangements, which are, by definition, only suitable for younger people. So, for older people this sleeping arrangement is simply out. Other short comings are that the size is simply too small for the application of walkers which are so common today. Similarly, the size of the bathroom door is simply too small for a senior to be accommodated. Not only that, but recommended senior housing design parameters differ considerably from the sizes required by ordinary homes, mostly being larger. Again, tiny homes are even smaller, and thus, cannot accommodate these recommendations. Another problem not easily to be overcome is the access of the tiny home. Since it is located on the trailer, or at least on some sort of running gear, the floor is by definition higher than ground level. This is in stark contrast to the requirement to provide access on even ground, and no steps not even slopes, are desired or acceptable. This problem is not easily overcome. Slopes created by backfill in order to avoid steps are not desired because of the risk of icing up and the risk of falling.

In short, tiny home designs are in contrast to what the design parameters for senior housing units require.

Challenges of the developments providing parks for Tiny Homes and its supporting services

The real challenge, however, is for the developer providing the services necessary in such a development.

Illegal as these tiny homes are to begin with at the time of this writing if provided by third parties, i.e. developers, the challenges do not stop here.

Supporting services as in road ways, supply of water, disposal of waste water and electricity must be provided just the same as in a typical housing development and, of course, the individual lot. Each of those services is to be provided within a well-defined manner, and this manner is costly to the extent that it surely is not feasible within the context of providing inexpensive housing options. Something has to give.

Each one of those service expenses can be tackled, and there may be alternative solutions, but again, the boundaries are very tight for the developer trying to cut corners here-and the result may be in the end not what seniors really want or need.

Zoning is the first one. Which one would it be: Housing development? Surely not, since tiny homes are not regarded as such. Since they are movable, the next logical development permit to be applied for may be a recreational seasonal zoning permit, as in campgrounds. However, this would exclude the necessity of providing housing all year long, since such developments are typically only permitted to provide services seasonally. Besides, all services offered within this context are taxable as in the application of a value added tax, in Canada called GST. Surely this would be counterproductive to the entire concept of providing housing inexpensively.

But some solutions may be workable, if we want to. Then again, we may not.

For instance, the sizable cost of subdividing into lots can be axed and the land can be offered in different ways, and not subdivided at all. But this approach excludes the option of selling individual lots. If the land remains undivided, this then may be called providing a parking space for tiny homes.

The provision of electricity can be axed in lieu of having each unit provide their own electricity, for instance with the application of solar panels, sufficient for each unit on their own.

The provision of energy large enough for perhaps heating and which is beyond the capacity of solar panels may be in the form of propane tanks, again, each unit on their own.

The provision and cost of necessary water supplies or wells and equipment for clean and regulated water supply can be axed by letting each unit having their own water supply, for instance by building catchment systems of rainwater, again, one for each unit, each one on their own. In the country they may even have their own dug well. Expensive as this may seem, the cost pales in comparison to the cost necessary to provide clean water by controlled and regulated water supply systems.

The provision of waste water removal and its associated high cost, be it provided by hook-up to sewer systems or commonly applied mini disposal system, or perhaps also costly on-site systems, one for each unit and its associated large demand in land size may be axed in lieu of provided composting toilets and perhaps grey water disposal systems. Again, each unit on their own.

And roadways built in accordance with highway specs can be axed by making these units not accessible by cars at all, and instead, providing driveways only. The mode of transportation within the development is accomplished by alternative methods, i.e. golf carts. This approach, by the way, may not be compliant with current fire regulations, which require access to each unit by fire trucks, requiring roadways with sufficient carrying capacity. Same for emergency or ambulance vehicles. The question is in how far these rules apply, since tiny homes are not regarded as living units.

Albeit those short cuts may be possible, or at least to some extent possible, the main reason such developments may not take place is simply not to be overcome—tiny homes are illegal as full time residences.

What we may see perhaps is a happy medium to satisfy rules and regulations even though many would have to be altered, as well as providing some sort of inexpensive housing along with supporting services for seniors, the living units in acceptable sizes.

Some samples of that idea may be the application of so-called park models, but only the type for full time, that is, all season living. These units are better insulated and have more powerful heating systems than regular vacation type trailers. Or we may see indeed a re-introduction of mobile homes, but now smaller units suitable for single occupancy by a single person, for instance a senior, but well insulated and energy efficient for full time occupation. About half the size or even less than the current trend of offering units exceeding 1000 square feet of living space.

The developments then must be able to satisfy zoning requirement for full time housing, without the high standard applied which are present today.

With all of these ideas it is necessary to have, in addition to the individual units, a common building which houses the support services necessary for care providing, i.e. staff for assisted living, ready to serve seniors in their units. Home care style without the car travelling involved; staff is available onsite, and perhaps is even living onsite. This building must also be able to prepare and provide meals for common dining, if so desired, as well as common areas and rooms for get-togethers and social interactions, community style.

As a conclusion, tiny homes is just one more approach to create low cost housing.

Building Methods

As with many other alternative building methods or building materials to create inexpensive ways to live, most of them must be set aside back into the experimental stage. Many of them have been tested and tried, some of them are more successful than others. As an example may serve straw bale construction, hempcrete insulating blocks, cordwood construction to name a few, or even living in containers, and many more. But throw into the mix other requirements such as super high efficiency or high efficient heating methods like geo thermal, or the least environmental footprint, or ability to recycle, and there is an immediate clash. These requirements are contradicting the low cost requirement. You can have one or not the other. Unless some medium in between, tending one way or the other, can be found.

Such developments, once all the wrinkles are worked out, and once in alignment with tomorrow's rules and regulations, may indeed offer a feasible approach to provide a supportive living arrangement for older folks.

Today, however, the hurdles are many and almost impossible to meet and overcome, especially in a cost effective, inexpensive way.

Perhaps one day we as a society will see the necessity of such developments, to meet the expected demand of a much larger senior population to come, coupled with diminishing monies available by those seniors who are in need of assistance and in need of inexpensive housing.

On that day we may be finally able to overcome the burdens we have created ourselves. We stumble over our own feet.

One day.

Can't wait to see this day come.

Living Abroad

The final alternative living option I am introducing here consists of the idea of leaving North America for good. Not surprisingly, there are quite a few people who have the vision of our system as it is structured today to not be sustainable in the future. Hence, they are looking for other options outside home territory. It would be outside the scope of this book to get into details here, especially since the subject is of such enormous volume that it would fill a book—or more—by itself. But it should be mentioned that companies specializing in this subject experience a huge growing popularity, which is expected to gain even more momentum in years to come. Anybody interested in the different options, different countries, different immigration rules, different ways of providing for older folks in need of care and a host of other information can be obtained by a number of providers, such as Jackie Flynn's www.internationalliving.com or Kathleen Peddicord's www.liveandinvestoverseas.com.

From the above it can be seen that indeed now we have many more options as shown in this outdated table below.

Overview: Alternative Senior Housing Options
(Compiled: February 2008)

Provides	Owner House	Long Term Care Home	Retirement Residence	Shared Living	Senior Co-Housing	Abbeyfield
Lifestyle Choice	Yes, decreased quality	No	Yes, enriched	Yes	Yes, enriched	Yes
Assistance with Daily Living	No	No	Yes	Somewhat	Somewhat	Somewhat
Social Interactions	No	No	Yes	Yes	Yes	Yes
Providing Meals	No	Yes	Yes	No	Yes	Yes
Care Level 1	No	Yes	Sometimes	Sometimes	No	No
Care Level 2	No	Yes	Sometimes	No	No	No
Care Level 3	No	Yes	No	No	No	No
Laundry Service	No	Yes	Yes	No, but shared	No	Yes
House Keeping Service	No	Yes	Yes	No, but shared	No	Yes
Social Interactions	No	No	Yes	Yes	Yes	Yes
Social Activities	No	No	Yes	Yes	Yes	No
Cost	Low	Med.-High	Med.-High	Low	Med.-High	Low-Med.
Finance Package Available	N/A	No	Sometimes	No	Yes	Yes
Created by	Owner	Developer	Developer	Occupants	Occupants	Occupants
Senior Friendly Design	No	Yes	Sometimes	No	Sometimes	Yes
Barrier Free Design	No	Yes	Sometimes	No	Sometimes	Sometimes

CHAPTER 14

How the Ideas Came About in My Own Experience

I cannot resist sharing with you my own ideas and how they evolved—but before I do so, it is necessary to share with you first the mental development as I have constructed my concept: and so, if you allow, I will tell you my own story:

Just sit back, relax, and start shaking your head. You can start anytime now. I promise you will later on anyways…If you don't feel like it, it's okay, too—just skip this chapter.

My career in senior housing started out of necessity—no noble intention whatsoever, just plain survival.

Rewind to 1990.

At this time, I was at the pinnacle of my real estate career, and my time was more and more consumed with the dozens of income properties and multi-unit properties I had accumulated. And they all had to be looked after.

Usually purchased on a shoe string, or only the mortgage taken over from a distressed seller, and being in real estate as a licensed agent, I was at the fore front of (what I thought of good) deals to be scooped up.

That was at a time when it was still possible to do that. Today licensed realtors are restricted in that practise.

My dealings with "apartment house kings" in Halifax, that is someone with more than 1000 units to call his own, had its effect. At the presentation of a new listing of an apartment building I had gathered a few of those guys at one table, no easy task. At this occasion I had the opportunity offered from one of those guys to acquire a 52 unit apartment building, consisting of 2 buildings of 26 units each, 3 storeys high. Not that he was going to sell them, no, he just mentioned casually in conversation that these buildings were a headache for him, which is a good indication for someone like me at the right time and frame of mind to accumulate properties.

The buildings were indeed in terrible shape. They were located in a rough area, and had known a bad reputation. The tenants were also known to be ruffians, and the occupancy was poor. What was good? The numbers, financial numbers, that is. And if the numbers are good, everything else fades into unimportance. And the numbers were good. For financing, they can be fudged. This was then, not now.

Needless to say, he wanted to get rid of those buildings very badly. That's because the flat roofs were leaking just as badly. He did not want to spend a dime, because, as he puts it, the quality of the tenants wasn't worth a dime.

Me, hungry as I was, saw an opportunity to get into the big boys' game. I figured if the buildings were carrying themselves with the poor occupancy and high bad debt, meaning uncollectable rents, at the same time as the entire 3rd floor was not rentable, that looked good to me. The third floor was not occupied because there were buckets and pans and cans everywhere to catch the rain from that leaking roof, and I saw big profit once I was able to fix the roofs and rent out the entire 3rd floor apartments, 16 in total. The numbers looked good. And so we talked about how to go about it.

The buildings were downright cheap. I remember he only wanted $2 million for them, or less than $40k a door.

What a sweet price!

Trouble was, I had not even quite enough dough in the bank account to pay for the phone bill, which was overdue. Two million dollars was nothing but an awfully big number.

But I knew a thing or two about construction and was sure I could fix that roof, if need be, with duct tape. And I also knew a thing about constructive financing. This was necessary, otherwise there was no chance to get my hands on that nightmare of an apartment building! Actually, two of them.

After a lot of haggling, this is what we came up with: The seller would hold the vast majority of the purchase price himself, as a VTB, vendor-take-back mortgage, and was content with a $400,000 down payment. That could be provided in the form of the equity in 6 residential homes. Since I had plenty of those, and also plenty I wanted to get rid of badly, that obviously took place. I conveyed those to him, knowing very well that he would turn around and sell them for whatever he could get for them, and that was gravy for him anyways.

The whole thing was not unlike the game "Monopoly".

And so the deal was done. By the way, if you want more of that, just follow my book (in preparation) "My Journey". I outline here in detail how I dealt with properties, just like car dealers deal in cars. There was a purchasing and selling, a coming and going. And managing in between—plus a lot of fixing up!

Soon after acquiring the buildings, however, it became painfully clear that managing the tenants became the main problem. Which I really should have known. Although there are buildings with worse tenants, called slums, these ones were bad enough. Although I had a superintendent which took the lot of the headache, there was plenty left for me, and I was always in a state of near burnout. What was also not far away was the local gambling outlet. Gambling machines in a bar. The very first one in Halifax, thanks to the new license issued by the government, after a long time of discussing the pros and cons. The lucky tavern which became licensed attracted a lot of people, including a lot of my tenants. While their rent payment was due and collected on the first of each month, usually the tenant was broke by then. And I was told in no uncertain terms I should have collected last night, before they went to the casino. And so it happened that quite a number of rents became uncollectable on a regular basis.

Then there were a lot of associated problems. You know, like drugs, brawls, drunk tenants, domestic violence, we had it all.

Police were the most seen regular visitors. And the ambulance. All in all, it was a bad scene.

After many sleepless nights, not knowing what to do with this alligator of a building which was eating me alive, one day I had a bright idea! The solution to all the problems: seniors! That's it! What I needed were seniors in these buildings!

No gambling. No brawls! No drugs! No domestic violence! And, perhaps who knows, even rent money?

That was the solution to all my problems. There was only one problem left, how to go about attracting those seniors?

And how to change over the buildings into seniors apartments? What are the logistics? What is required? And even if I found out, how to implement those changes? With no money?

A plan was hatched as to how to go about it. Major remodelling had to be done. But I had to learn first what exactly it was that needed to be done. Then, I had to clear out all existing tenants. While this was no problem, because most tenants were behind with rent payments anyways, paying for the renovation and carrying the additional mortgage was. Again, I tell more of this story in my own biography. What followed was a string of long drawn out thoughts as to turn these buildings over to senior apartments. Thoughts became visions. And how to make those apartments attractive for seniors. Just how?

The point I am getting at is this:

In my mind, looking down the long, 128 ft long hallways in the now vacant building, I thought, who in his right mind would like to live here? The hallways were dim and dingy, only 4 ft wide, and as dull as they can be.

And so I thought what is most necessary is to bring in light. Daylight, that is, not only artificial light. And the next thing is to break up the monotony of the length of the hallways. That could only be achieved by taking out entire walls from apartments adjacent to the hallway, and move them in an alternating fashion in and out.

No easy task. But by doing so sitting corners for socializing could be created. After all, who wants to (or even can?) walk never ending hallways?

The end of the hallways, leading into the stairways, must become the main source of daylight. My visions included breaking out the entire side wall of the building and replacing it with a huge glass area, to bring in daylight.

Fixing of the roof, however, was easily done—in my mind. Never mind fixing it, I simply set new roof frames on that 5 ft pony wall, and so installed a new, 12/12 steep pitched roof on top of the flat roof. This move would in effect create another storey, another 7,200 sqft of additional living space for each building. This gain was nothing to be sneezed at. As it turned out upon application, I was not allowed to create more apartments, but could use the newly created space for much needed common areas. The main room would become a large common gathering room. The gable end of the new roof trusses would become glass only for additional light, and I incorporated a porch with lawn furniture, roofed over to protect from the rain, in the 4th floor, so folks could sit out and watch the traffic from above. They could even sit out in rain, because of the roof, porch like fashion. In addition, and since I had plenty of room, I had planned a nurses station, just in case I got a license as a retirement home, a hair dresser shop, a physiotherapist office, a small gym and storage spaces. None of those actually had been built, but the main common room and a roofed over porch, all on the 4th floor, penthouse style. But I am getting ahead of myself.

Further, my mind attacked that terrible entrance with the bent-all-to-hell mailboxes. My plans included tearing out 2 apartments and creating a nice and roomy entrance foyer, and a roof over the entrance. The main feature in the foyer was lots of large plants. To that date unheard of "solar-lights" were planned to be installed in the outside walls to bring in daylight into the centre of the foyer, besides plenty of artificial lights. In the centre I planned to install a large pond, again with plants around it, along with a built in water fall. The idea was to bring in light, large plants, water with fish in it, a water fall, along with the rushing and calming effect of flowing water. Fancy shopping malls which featured such ponds inspired me to incorporate this aspect and I found this to be really attractive in a private retirement home.

The lots on which the buildings were located were facing the road, while the back of the buildings were facing nature. These were the only lots along the road which featured no developments on the south side. Nothing in the back but nature pure and undeveloped.

I thought it must be nice for the tenants, now residents, to look out to these trees and greens, especially the ones living on the second and third floor. Since this was the wall of the other stairway, it was again necessary to take out a major part of the outside wall and replace it with glass. Structural load was an issue, but I had engineering background, and thought I would not need an engineer to have the static calculated. Actually, there is not much too it. Just imagine this mere thought in today's world. There would be scores of engineering work to be done in such a project, the scope of work would cost a small fortune. But here I had thoughts of actually increasing the foot print of the building by breaking out the walls, creating more room and bringing in some seating areas for seniors to gather and mingle, so seniors could enjoy the view over the nature in their own back yard. The construction of an elevator was planned, in one building only. To house it, it was necessary to construct a separate add on structure.

Ambitious plans, indeed.

Meals had to be served. As for a common dining room, I intended to tear out two more apartments and create a commercial kitchen and dining area.

The back parking lot was split up so high gardens and flower beds could be created, keeping in mind that the parking lot was huge. New requirements were less than one parking spot per apartment. Besides, by ripping out the 4 apartments I had only 48 units of the 52 left. Even with those regulations I had plenty of room to spare. With the high gardens residents could do some of their own gardening to their hearts content, and all that in the middle of the city!

There were also plenty of changes planned in the apartments themselves, to make them more senior friendly. Today they call it barrier free. Since at the time I had no idea what that was, I decided to take a course in "Designing and Building of Senior Living Units" in North Carolina. First time I was introduced to what the new term "barrier-free" meant. This was a half-year, full time course. I will not tell you how I arranged to take that course and look after my business in Halifax at the same time. If I did, you'd think I was nuts. So I don't. Suffice to say that this decision included a lot of travelling, each trip about 2,000 kms. I also should not tell you that I drove once a week, for 2 or perhaps 3 days spent in North Carolina in school, the remainder of the week I skipped school and spent the time to run the business in Halifax. And I will not mention that 2 days every week I was just about useless because of sleep deprivation. And finally, I would never mention to you the complete waste of energy, not only mine, but that of my car, as well.

Today, I would refuse to do this, because I would regard it as a total waste of resources, in this case, gas. And a lot of it, too! But I did finish that course.

Armed with this newly acquired knowledge, I began to plan the remodeling of the apartments themselves. The trouble was that after I had taken the course I realized that it was close to impossible to change existing housing stock into what is now required for barrier free living space for the elderly. But I had to give it my best to get close.

These were then the major components of my intended conversion into a senior retirement building, and the designing of it in the early 1990's.

I do not want to bog you down with details of where I got the more than half a million dollars I needed for doing all this. Suffice to say that I actually started construction in fall of 1991 on the first building. Development and construction according to my design, under my construction and project management and my biggest project done so far was brought to successful completion in 1994, with the majority but by far not all of the planned components mentioned above actually realized. Only one building received this major refit, except the steep 12/12 pitched roof which was installed over both buildings. Imagine just the engineering necessary today to get such a project off the ground. As it was, I was considered the owner, and so by that definition was allowed to do the entire planning and construction by myself. Since I had a construction company anyway for all the renovation work on my buildings, all I had to do is hire a few carpenters, who I have known for years. Only minimal structural engineering drawings had been contracted out. Most had been drawn by me. Even the installation of some specialized areas, like the fire alarm system was done by me. Today, it would be all but impossible to do that magnitude of that project by one person.

You can stop shaking your head now.

Congratulations Dr. Bill Thompson for inventing what he calls "*The Eden Concept*".

I just finished implementing the very same thing, unbeknownst to his concept, applied in my own senior apartment building.

Just a couple of years earlier! But it was Dr. Bill Thompson who carried his idea across the country and spread it around, and it was well received.

The idea then, is to bring nature into the living space of senior housing, in particular nursing homes, which otherwise is not possible for an older resident to enjoy, since he or she is confined to living in a building with no way to get close to nature. Instead of taking seniors out into nature, we bring nature into the building. The real thing, not TV. That was indeed the driving force of my efforts in design and planning.

In my case, the renovation work was a necessity anyways, so it was easier to incorporate.

But there was another component, which also deserves note.

Just in case you, dear reader, are wondering where I am going with this, and where finally the alternative living option comes in—hang on—we are just about there.

As it was, I was determined to initially turn one of the two buildings over into a senior building. Today it would be called a retirement home. But alas, as it turned out, Halifax had a moratorium on licensing new retirement homes, and thus, my building was not able to obtain such a license. I knew that early on, and so devised a plan:

Again, out of necessity, I had to go a different route.

And so this plan was hatched as to how it could work. A home-care company designated to take care of the residents of that building on an ongoing basis was the answer. And since I did not want to experience any more problems than I already had, I thought instead of contracting the job out, I set up my own home care company. But this was a whole new kettle of fish, and fraught with new challenges. Therefore I decided it was perhaps better to become a partner in an existing home-care company.

And so I did. As a result, I could offer rental apartments only, with no assistance provided. Thus this is not a retirement home in its definition. Common meals were provided, but this would not constitute the requirement of licensing as a retirement home. As for care, at the same time, privately paid home care was available, and so, assistance was provided as needed, but by 3rd party. Contracted out! This was a wonderful arrangement. Assistance on site, but not incorporated in the entire housing aspect—hence, this was not classified a retirement home.

To go one step further, since I had plenty of apartments available, especially in the adjacent building not designed for seniors, I could provide housing for support staff. Staff living on-site. And bingo, here was my "retirement residence". Legal and all. The idea of live-in caregivers proved to be a great idea. No commuting was necessary for the care workers, just walking from their apartment to the other apartment—the one of the senior in need of assistance. This is one of the core elements included in the concept introduced in chapter 16.

This idea could be very well applied today for a number of different apartment housing situations, and I am surprised that this idea is not taking hold more than it does. In fact I never heard of any arrangement of that nature practised, but I am sure there must be many. One of them is the earlier mentioned Solterra Concept by Shelley, as introduced under Co-housing. But there is a lot to be said for that kind of set-up. It's not just beneficial for the operator, but for the senior resident involved, as well, and for home-care staff, which lives on their job-site. It is a win-win situation for all parties involved. Mostly, for the senior resident: when no assistance is needed, no cost. The cost is simply the rent for the apartment with add-on services such as meals, laundry and housekeeping. The more expensive clock starts only to tick once care services are actually necessary. And then staff is living right on site! No added travel cost etc. like with today's home care concept.

So there, that's the other option!

Marketing

Marketing of the now available senior units was also done in quite a unique way. Since there were no rental agencies which were established and available in Halifax, I decided to create my own. Since there was an advertising budget calculated in the financial forecast, and knowing from experience that advertising in printed form or even TV and radio ads do not work very well, besides taking too long for an effect, the task must be accomplished differently. Hence I came up with the idea of setting up what I called a "Senior-Drop-In-Centre" in the local shopping mall. A rented space, quite large, actually, was converted into a cozy place something like a coffee shop/bistro/living room style. Here likeminded seniors could spend some time among themselves. Seniors were invited to mingle, play games together, have coffee or tea, and in general, just hang out. This was very well received, since the participation was free, and thus attracted a lot of older folks. They just loved it! From there, it grew constantly. We introduced more and more activities, for instance, we provided health classes, aerobic and exercise classes, checked weight and blood pressure, served hot soups for one dollar, held raffles, sold handmade crafts on consignment produced by other seniors, and finally, provided a private van for outings and bus tours. Where did the marketing come in? Well, we had pictures of my buildings in Mural size plastered on the walls, along with pictures of the apartments, and the nice porch on the 3rd floor. And since the building was nearby, we offered ongoing tours and showings. Every week we would have a few showings, more than advertising would have produced. But of course, running the senior-drop-in-centre was not quite an inexpensive proposition either. The main cost consisted of the rent and one full time manager. But then, we had volunteers who helped to run the show and they did an excellent job! The centre was open the entire open hours of the mall, from 9:00 a.m. to 9:00 p.m. It was hardly necessary for me to oversee details of the centre.

And finally, I have one more card up my sleeve. Since then, and since senior housing is my passion, I redesigned my concept and I am proud to present it below. As mentioned before, just as ingredients of baking, like water, flour, sugar and some spices could create a number of delicious pies and cakes and cookies, so, by applying a number of different components, senior housing could become a delicious experience!

And this is what this book is all about.

Given all the elements which have been introduced, there comes a time when all of this can be mixed together to create a truly attractive and future-oriented senior community.

CHAPTER 15

The Concept Takes Form

And so it becomes painfully clear that the way we house our elderly population today is really everything else but "senior friendly". Worst of all is letting them stay at home and cope with life and with the rest of their lives—on their own. Every day is a challenge, every day brings obstacles they would not have to face, would we have the courage to tell them there are better options out there and available to them. Every day they are alone, facing their own mortality oh so clearly, and yet, we are not able to pull them away, because we believe they "do just fine". Because they tell us that. But they do not, regardless of what they tell you. We must provide them with alternative living options which are offering still quality of life, rather than loneliness and despair.

We owe it to them. It is our duty to provide for them. The time has come to pay back. At one time, early on in our lives, it was them who provided for us. As a helpless toddler, we just expected to be looked after. By Mom and Dad, with their love and compassion. Now, we seem to have forgotten that it is payback time.

But it must be said, that options are indeed few available to even try to offer them a better life than coping at home. And there is another thing with must be said; The proposed concept fits local culture and customs, is non-denominational, and does not discriminate regarding race , gender or ethnic background.

Piecing it all together, what follows is a detailed description of the concept I have developed over the recent years in an attempt to merge the older population's preferences and requirements into a housing model, which will also withstand other elements of expected future challenges and changes. In addition and most importantly, these *needs are to be met in an affordable way.* Affordability in the future will be different than the definition of affordable today. The housing component includes future requirements of sustainability. It is paramount to realize that paid care staff cost must be reduced in order to achieve affordability. It is the largest portion of the rental charges of retirement homes. Cost increases beyond the housing model and staff care cost on the level of general health care must be reduced as well, by means of prevention of illnesses, rather than fixing problems with care and medication, a subject which is beyond this book. However, it must be realized at the same time that exploding health care cost and medical cost for the exploding senior population cannot be paid for by diminishing sources of taxable income, and cannot be paid for by a diminishing number of working people. This is a logical consequence. The question then becomes in which area costs can be cut. Within the scope of this book, we looked at alternative living options for older people, most of them more affordable than retirement home living, and as it has unfolded today. Now we can put some of these elements together and see where they prove not just to be affordable, but also evolve into a more occupant friendly housing model. But in order to achieve and implement those elements properly, a number of present rules and regulations would have to be dismantled and reversed. While this may seem an impossible task, remember we are talking quite a number of years. Not all these older folks coming from the baby boomer generation need alternative housing options and/or care overnight. This is a process drawn out over years; and we know exactly how many. All that which has been said earlier has been implemented, and a number of other elements as well. In addition I have developed a master plan which also includes a number of components which are not mentioned here. The reason I have left them out is that these components are, I believe, not in the interest of the reader—at this point. In addition, some of them are too far future oriented, and may be seen as too farfetched, at this moment in our time. Curious? Okay, I will name a few, but again, will not go into further details:

- Assisted living services provided *for free* by workers who have the desire to look after older people with no compensation at all—Too farfetched? Thought so…
- With growing spiritual awareness, further assuming an increase of unemployment status for many people which is what may be waiting for all of us in the future, especially for the ones who are 50 years and older, many of us we will become aware that making big money by taking care of our seniors is not a concept which can be envisioned any longer. Simply finding work, along with compensation to whatever the extent will be defined at that time, will be possible within the proposed model. Everything needed to live will be provided, except career minded compensation—this is really community style living. Too farfetched? Thought so…
- On-site living units may be for one occupant only. Why do they have to have large apartments on their own? An exploding movement is the Tiny-Home Movement, and such dwellings may be provided for free, in exchange for some working hours. At present, tiny homes are not even allowed for full time occupancy, because they are smaller than what the minimum size of dwelling is regarded as, in other words, our standard of living dictates. Perhaps one day it will. Too farfetched? Thought so!
- Car and vehicle sharing arrangements for staff and residents (who are still able to drive, of course) alike—Too farfetched? Thought so…
- There will be three different sources of heating fuel in this planned senior community, because we may experience *shortages of one or the other fuel* in the foreseeable future—Too farfetched? Thought so!
- The implementation of illness-preventing, health-enhancing alternative healing methods, which ideally could be implemented in the very set-up of such a senior community. Examples may be sauna baths, Kneipp water

treatments, hay sack treatments to mention a few of many—and of course, changes in diet from mainly salt-sweets-fat to a more balanced diet. That again, is a subject on its own. Too farfetched? Thought so.

As it stands, I would like to share with you the conclusion of the concept:

FUTURE ORIENTED SENIOR HOUSING MODEL:

HARMONY SENIOR VILLAGE
Supportive Senior Village Community
I have not found a suitable name, as of yet, at the time of this writing; *(I invite you to write your ideas and comments and contact me).*

Ten components to make housing of seniors a desirable way to live

First component: What the customer, the senior, the future resident really wants

The first requirement of this housing model is recognizing what older folks actually desire. And they desire to stay home. At present, more than 92% of them who decide to continue staying home can't be all wrong. Partly to blame for this huge portion, besides the money aspect, is the lack of alternative living options. Lacking options, the desire is to stay home. But this desire runs contrary to the merging changing housing requirements, and these requirements can only be met by the implementation of the two overriding elements: care or assistance provided has to be done in a housing model which is actually desired by the future occupants, the residents. Not just desired, but seriously wanted. Not just wanted, but finally decided upon to live in—a new home, and one home which is loved and can be called home, a home which replaces the "old home". This is a lofty goal of the highest order, simply because it is impossible to replace the old home filled with all those memories. This is where retirement homes fail. And fail they must, because it is impossible within the very fabric of retirement homes to provide this aspect. However, if the housing model is designed in the most attractive way, then it is second best, and by far superior to any retirement home setting. Home away from home, might be the motto. The very introduction of alternative housing options is perhaps what the future resident really wants.

Second component: Privacy and Access

The second requirement is the basic need to retain independence and privacy. It is challenging to design a housing model with privacy in mind, but to avoid feeling alone. Older folks certainly like to be close to someone, but not too close. This is the challenge. Again, this cannot be achieved within the makings of a retirement home setting. To allow for this component, and in an attempt to reach that critical boundary, it is planned to have independent little living units created. As for the name of those units I propose adobes, or apartment homes. I call them *adorable adobes*. These shall be built in what I call clusters, three to five units in each cluster. The number of clusters can differ. Here just the walking distance to and from the common elements becomes an issue. As a functioning community a minimum of 3–4 clusters are envisioned. Neighboring residents are close, very close, but not too close. Transportation of goods and persons to and from these adobes are to be done by golf carts—not cars. This is the domain of pedestrians—if necessary with walkers—but no car traffic; traffic is to be confined to the common parking lot, save emergency vehicles. For those, and only those, lanes have to be created.

Third component: Unit Size

The third component is size. As laid out earlier, if older persons consider moving, they will envision what they are moving into. The downsize shock from perhaps 2,500 square feet to 250 square feet cannot be tolerated and accepted by many. This shock must be softened at first. It is this huge step downsizing that makes many people prefer to stay at home. They cannot wrap their mind around giving up all this space they occupy now, even if only a portion of it is actually used. They have difficulties to think of parting with their furniture, and accumulated stuff. Hence the proposed size of units varies, and is between 320 and 980 square feet the majority in the 450 to 750 square feet range. Once this size is accepted, folks will grow to love those adobes. At a later time, once the requirement of unit size lessens, a move into a smaller unit may be possible, but only for those units which are rentable, of course. On that note, and keeping in mind the everyday reality as it plays out, I can easily foresee that even units which are purchased might be traded, changed, swapped, bought and sold within the entire project. Many folks feel compelled to trade up or trade down all the time, like changing cars. This aspect has to be allowed for. There are a few reasons for this tendency, one of them to prove that despite the age, they still demonstrate will power, desires, preferences and independence. With the present complicated legal set-up, with owned or condo units, swapping units is difficult to do. But this would be very easily accomplished within our new concept, in terms of legal work, as opposed to condominiums, which require a lot more legal work and associated cost. For that reason, it is proposed to challenge the present legal set-up which is self-serving, but not in the interest of the occupant. As the living option Senior Shared Home Ownership described in chapter 15 shows, it is possible to change ownership easily and with not much legal work required. This is the proposed set up of choice, until the complicated legal set-up changes.

Fourth component: Design

The forth component is the design—and its uniqueness. After evaluating 20,000 design proposals, all found on the internet, I am proposing to use a unique design, which shall be the *hallmark* of these senior housing units or adobes.

That's why I call those units lovingly "Adorable Adobes".

These adorable adobes are very attractive in their design and well distinguished from anything which is built today—a gingerbread type design, not unlike Victorian style, but given its small size, looks almost fairy tale like, to be compared to the Hansel and Gretel adobes. This is the intent. The main distinguishing feature is the steep roof, metal roof covered, that is. Falling in love with such a house can be achieved by designing it to become a home. A small house, a home, is all that is desired. One can feel very comfortable in those. The exploding "This small house" and also the "Tiny House" movement in the States is testimony to this trend. Psychologically this trend is actually explainable by what they call 'womb-effect'. Small spaces are indeed comforting. The ego to own as large as possible is out.

There are a number of other advantages with this design, as well. Not just looks—although, admittedly, looks plays a large part. The reason why this type of dwelling is not seen today in our housing stock is very simple to explain—it is too expensive to build, given all the frills and gingerbread house style embellishments. Expensive labour cost is too precious to waste on embellishments. But this is exactly where the benefits of community comes in, see further below. With the inclusion of younger people eager to learn the tricks of the carpenter trade, older male residents, experienced in the carpenter trade, those who have seen it all and done it all, are now able to pass on their knowledge to the younger generation. And so, talents and craftsmanship acquired over a life time does not go to waste, but instead, is passed on, outside of the carpenter trade-apprentice set-up. And the adobes of the village are the perfect place to apply newly acquired knowledge. Everyone is helped, a win-win situation for all. Now, the 'too expensive to build' is being replaced with extremely useful and beneficial for young workers living on site.

The design further allows for the utilization of the 2nd floor, as additional 'free' living space. Besides their attractive looks, they must fulfill other design parameters. But most importantly, they must fulfill one overriding purpose; they must be loved by the future resident. That's the whole idea. Also, they should be practical for the senior resident. Let's use the word practical, which should serve as a short description of also being barrier free, which encompasses a number of design elements described previously.

For some reason, everyone believes older people have to live on the ground floor only. This is a myth, stemming from the idea that stairclimbing is out of question. This part, of course, is correct. Every realtor brochure contains a few smaller 2 bedroom homes, titled "starter or retirement homes".

However, I do not share that view. All that needs to be done is to incorporate for the second storey a stair lift. But this stair lift shall not be an add-on, as it usually is as an afterthought, but designed into the home from the beginning. This requires room to allow for the width of the lift, and so 4 feet wide stair treads have to be provided for easy use of the lift and the stairs as well. The advantage? It's big. It allows for the otherwise wasted space created by the steep roof, and instead, make use of the 2nd floor. Not just for guest quarters, i.e. family members to visit Mom and have their own privacy, but also, for the resident, who may decide to use the room as a studio to paint, or to write, or to knit a quilt or whatever—a private get-away room. This applies only for the larger adobes.

Fifth component: Sustainability of energy consumption

Here, it would be too complex to go into further design details, but the following considerations shall be noted.

We have technology at our fingertips to build extremely energy efficient, even zero-energy homes. However, there is a cost/benefit consideration. It is the intention to build most energy efficient, using sustainable fuel sources, as long as it is economically feasible. 10 inches wide walls and corresponding insulation is one factor minimizing heating requirements. The units will have a steep roof for the snow to slide off easily.

It is proposed and of utmost importantance to build the adobes or apartment houses with an orientation towards the sun, even if other considerations get the short end of the stick. Passive solar heating is essential. The orientation towards the sun and the installation of a large window area will capture the sun heat, especially in winter time, when the sun is low. That's another reason why the proposal for country living is envisioned. On the proposed larger property it is possible to locate and orient the homes with the effect of the sun in mind, unlike in cities, where the orientation is given by authorities with other considerations in effect. After application of solar gain, then there might be the application of solar powered panels for domestic water heating, but this is only second choice. First choice is introduced further below. What's left is a minimum requirement of heating energy. Again, solar panels for directs water heating may be the preferred option. The cooling requirement can be dealt with by the application of strategically placed roof overhangs and shades. At the same time, it shall be noted that older people do need more heat in their rooms, a fact which is expensive to meet during the heating season, if the home is heated by fossil fuels only. But no matter which way you go about it, and keeping in mind economics, some heating energy is needed. To accomplish this in the most effective way, in-floor heating is the best way to radiate heat in a home. It is also most comfortable, albeit initial installation is not inexpensive. But this is what is proposed in this design.

Furthermore, the adobes shall have three 3 different fuel sources. This is in the event that one or the other fuel becomes scarce in the future. Just a thought. You may not think along those lines, but I have my own view on that, and hence I am proposing this. Why?

Here I might admit that I am a bit pre-conditioned this way: For one thing, I have been raised with the concept of energy consumption, which was of utmost importance in our home, where I grew up in Germany. Never mind the so-called smart meters of today; even back in the 60's, the electrical power supplying corporation had the same problem as they have today. They are obliged to produce and deliver power, sufficient enough for the peak time during the day, when all industries and their electrical machinery is humming. At nighttime, the same generated power is now not being used, and is wasted. In an attempt to make up for this, power corporations offered power at night time at greatly reduced rates. They offered us one rate for daytime consumption, and one for nighttime consumption. Accordingly there were two meters, one for daytime—and one for nighttime consumption. The switchover time in the evening varied according to the load of the supplying generator station, and was given by them by means of a radio signal sometimes in the late evening hours. Industry would respond so such a set-up, and soon offered automatic switch over gear to take advantage of the reduced night time rate. For instance, our water heater would only come on at night time, automatically as soon as the cheaper rate was in effect. The water would heat up slowly during the night, and hot water was available during the day. However, there was a shortfall with this set-up. Unforeseen events, like unexpected showers taken by boys such as myself playing in dirt may have consumed all available hot water. Effectively in such situations, we would run out of hot water. As a result, it was sponge bath time with luke warm water. That was in my father's view okay—the main issue was that expensive power is not used during the day time. This was the energy conscious environment I grew up in. It was also common to have heating systems for homes and dwellings set up in the same way, but we did not have one of those. It comes as no surprise then that I am taken aback seeing and witnessing the waste of energy in North America ever since my arrival in the late 70's and really, not much has changed. Not until most recently The good news is that at least there is a growing awareness of energy waste setting in.

My father installed in our home, the one I grew up in, built in 1960, an oil burning central warm water heating system. This was at the time very future oriented. Central heating was the modern way to go. Even more future oriented was the dual fuel system; the boiler could, besides oil, also be heated by means of a wood burning add-on.

He also devoted a full quarter of the basement of the house to install a huge, 8,000 l custom welded steel oil tank into a separate section of the basement. He then enclosed a fibreglass skin (some of the first attempts at utilizing newly developed fiberglass) on the surrounding walls to catch a possible oil leak, which otherwise would have been a catastrophic oil leak into the ground. All this had been installed at a time when everyone was laughing at this silliness. Well, as it turned out, his silliness proved to be clever foresight, because only 12 years later the oil supply pipelines from the Arabs were closed off, even though only briefly and temporarily. But everyone was waking up to the fact how easy it was—and really, still is, to be too comfortable with the assumption that oil is always and at any time readily available, and in all desired quantities. Looking in the future, this may prove not to be so. Especially in the case the oil is imported. Foreign, oil supplying countries do not have to do any more than close a valve, and the industry of the importing country could come to a grinding halt. And also, the heating source in private homes. My father's huge tank had another 'built in' advantage. Since the stored oil supply lasted 6 or even 7 winters before another fill-up was required, automatically at fill-up he paid the lowest price, because after the next 6 or 7 years the oil was no doubt considerably more expensive.

Now, viewing this from another angle, this practise may be questionable, and might be looked at as hoarding or being selfish, but we shall leave this subject for now untouched. Besides, this approach is not legal in Canada. But the point is that supply should not be assumed as being always available, and hence, it is only prudent to allow for those eventualities—and provide alternative back up plans.

Back to heating in our proposed model community.

By now you have come to know that I am very energy conscious. Born in the country I was, and giving where we are today in our country in terms of energy consumption, it is not surprising that I spend a lot of considerations on a future oriented heating system for our senior housing project.

For example, when I took over the building containing 52 apartments in Halifax in the early nineties, I pretty near fainted when I saw how these buildings, and their heating systems, were designed. Sure, they were designed in 1970, being by then 20+ years old, and needing replacing. Actually this was one of my first tasks. Both oil fired furnaces burned a total of an astonishing 80,000 litres per year. Since the entire 3rd floor was not occupied or heated, this resulted in a consumption of more than 2,000 litres per apartment; about the amount an entire house would burn today, not just a 1 or 2 BR apartment surrounded by other heated units, and only one wall exposed to the weather. Upon further investigations, I noticed that there was not a single thermostat to be found anywhere. The superintendent told me that rental units *do not have* thermostats, since the tenants would have it on one setting only, which is way up. If it's going to be too warm, they'd open the windows. After all, they do not have to pay separately for the heating cost, it's included in the rent. So the common thought was it's free. In other words, there was no regulation or control of any sorts. The only regulation of the furnace's heat output, then, was the operating of a huge 3way valve at the furnace, to be operated by the superintendent, whenever it got colder or milder.

This was unbelievable. In turn, since the superintendent had no intention of having complaints by the tenants of the apartments being too cold, she kept the valve on one setting only—"wide open", just to be on the safe side. So, in effect, there was no control. The furnace heat was either on in winter, or off in summer. No wonder the fuel consumption was astronomical. This, dear reader, is no cruel joke but the sad truth. Needless to say, this was totally unacceptable by my way of thinking and just about the first item on the agenda to be tackled. In one building I installed a Viessman furnace system, imported from Germany. This was their very first system in Halifax, and the installing company had to send a technician to Germany for training purposes. The oil savings turned out to be substantial, about 65%, although not quite as much as calculated by the engineering folks back home. Perhaps our winters here are still a little harsher than their calculations assumed. Or the buildings were less insulated that anticipated. The other building was fitted out with a system made in the States. These systems, of course, were controlled with state of the art controls, including heat output controlled according to outside temperatures.

But this was many years ago. Today, requirements are much stricter. While no doubt the best heating system money can buy is a geo thermal system, cost can be quite high, to the point where payback periods are just too long to justify installation. Although cost is coming down. It is assumed that here we still have a long way to go, and prices for systems continue to come down, and perhaps it will be more feasible in a short while. Perhaps at one point in time the government may decide to implement programs to help with financing, once it becomes obvious that we are running out of alternative options to heat our homes.

For instance, it is absolutely not acceptable any longer to heat with oil. We will soon find out the hard way that oil is way too precious to be burned. We need oil for much more important things than burning it to heat homes. For that matter, it is way too precious to burn it in vehicles, either. But that will likely not change soon, unless we run out faster than we think. As it is today, at least in new home installations, as in the proposed concept of senior community homes, burning oil as a heating source should be totally out of any consideration.

So, if oil is out, because it is getting scarce, and geothermal is out, because it's still too expensive, what's left? Certainly not electricity which is today correctly widely understood as the most expensive form of heating. On top of this, many power plants are fired by oil, so then it's the same, no matter if oil is burned at the point of use, or at the power plant. By the way, have you ever considered how much oil is actually burned in a power plant?

Of course not, because nobody asks this question. Perhaps not many people care. And since all these comparisons are big numbers, we lose the oversight of all this. But let's just say, for demonstration purposes, we use the Lennox power plant in Ontario, which has been burning oil since the '70s. It has been "modernized" a few years back to burn heavy oil and natural gas. I set the word modernized in quotation marks, but know very well, that indeed, we have not many options as to with what fuel to drive power plants—besides nuclear. So then, the plant has a capacity of 2.1 GW (+900 MW expansion), and while this is a big number, it does not matter much how many homes can be supplied with electricity, what I am driving at is this—the consumption of oil. Since we all know what an oil truck looks like, the type which is filling up our home oil tanks, then the question is: How long does it take the Lennox plant to burn the content of such an oil truck? What is your guess?

A month? Less? Perhaps a week? Less? A day? Actually, yes, a lot less. It burns the oil content of one of those trucks in 3 to 4 minutes. Every 4 minutes one oil truck full of oil. In its practical application, trains of uncounted tank wagons supply the oil. Day-in and day-out. Just for you to imagine. And this is one plant only, in one province. Is it any wonder, then, that we run out of oil? Where should it all come from?

So, I propose to use propane. Teeth grinding, granted. Because it has other disadvantages. Lots of them. But the availability is well organized, and, similar to oil, can be supplied by trucks to fill tanks. And since the size of allowable tanks is not as restricted as in oil tanks, at least not today, we can have a good supply of fuel on site, in case it's getting scarce. But pricewise, of course, it's not very cheap either. And also because it is a fossil fuel, it should serve as a backup only. There is another fuel source, which is renewable—wood.

Have you ever heard such a silly proposal? After all, not too long ago, back in the late 70's, governments paid incentives to "modernize" heating systems, to throw out the old wood burning stove and replace with "modern oil burning heating" systems. You noticed these quotation marks again? Oil as a fuel source cannot be regarded as modern any longer. Ah, how things have changed! Today, I am proposing wood heat, besides geo thermal, for a few reasons:

First, the wood burning stove will not be an inefficient stove in every adobe—I cannot see the tenant, the seniors looking after it and filling it up constantly—never mind the risk of fire—but an *outdoor wood furnace*, for burning wood as well as *wood pellets*. Second, while some might say they are inefficient, and some might say they are hard on the environment, studies undertaken have shown that this is not the case. Not any longer. All things considered, modern units do not burn inefficiently or generate excess air pollution. And that outdoor furnace will supply hot water to a low temperature in-floor radiant system, the most efficient of all heat radiation systems. Third, there will be only one outdoor furnace for each cluster, so in effect, each furnace feeds three to five living units. And who is supposed to fill the furnace? Well, here is the kicker—*it shall be fed by the residents themselves*. Not everyone is glued to the couch watching TV. Call it providing a purpose, call it a task to be done, call it whatever; the fact is, that many older male folks, if they are still capable of doing so, would *love to tend a wood furnace*. In particular, if it's not located inside the house, to avoid dirt and the added fire risk, but can be tended to externally, and at large intervals, like once a day. Chances are there is more than one resident who is eager to do that, and so the task of feeding the furnace is not resting on the shoulders of only one person; it's a shared task. Community style. Shared work load and shared responsibilities. The older person has just received a new purpose. It may come as a surprise for you to learn that this is done here at Golden Pond.

This proposal is actually received very well, and not just in theory. The entire set-up is proven by my own outdoor-furnace at Golden Pond, in which the above theory has been tried and tested. However, it must be said in the same breath that things are quite different here: first, we are a retirement home, and as such, have only older residents, most of them in need of assistance—there may be only a few guys—or none—at any given time who are willing and able to chip in. Just age wise they are older than in the proposed senior community, which is composed of younger and more able seniors. Plus, in this proposal as opposed to Golden Pond there are also younger folks living on site. In addition, in our home we go through 30–40 cords of wood a winter, which is an amount I cannot expect or even imagine that any older person, or even 2 or 3, to handle, which is about 2–3,000 lbs a day. Moreover, the heating requirement in the proposed model community is quite different. Because of the *efficiency rates of the adobes are so high, not much heating energy is required*. Also, the heating requirement is much lower due to the small size of the adobes. Hence the proposed heating mode is not only efficient in terms of dollars, but also, will do much to give residents a purpose still in their time—it will also act as a reminiscence of their own time past, which no doubt included filling wood stoves, too! Of course, once the wood furnace is for whatever reason not tended to and the water temperature drops, the heating mode would switch over automatically and immediately to the back-up mode; heating the water by means of natural gas (propane most likely) or wood pellets. Again, this is the case in our home and works well. Except it's not propane which kicks in, but an oil burner, which is, of course, to be avoided in newly built installations as said before.

Pellet stoves are also an excellent way of heating, since it is very effective, and nice to look at. But most important, it uses waste material of wood processing plants for fuel. In addition, it is possible to keep temperature in the outdoor furnace up by a modest amount of pellets, in case there is no resident available to feed the outdoor furnace. So, this is back-up for the back-up. You might think this is overdoing it, but I believe it's not. Plus, for a fairly inexpensive installation it's a good purchase and lets one sleep a little better, knowing that the heating systems design is well looked after.

(I just want to mention here, that due to the number of houses I owned in earlier times, there were lots of problems with frozen pipes and frost damage due to split water pipes, because the heating system was for one reason or another not working—and no back-up had been installed. Typically, back-up heating systems is something which mostly is *not* done in North America).

Other guidelines of sustainability shall be applied, which are much easier to realize in a larger living arrangement like in the proposed village rather than in single family homes. Besides the orientation and use of active and passive solar systems, other measures are planned, as well. Outstanding insulation of the homes, in order to cut down on heat requirements as much as possible, may be future oriented today but will be the common way of building tomorrow. However, it is more expensive to retrofit rather than built it right to begin with. Insulation alone will in the future play a much larger role than today. Reducing waste, reducing power consumption, recycling and composting will be all a matter of fact.

When we introduced composting in our residence back in 2004, most staff members needed training in that, since they had no idea how to go about it. Pre-sorting all garbage was the same story, although already known, but practised very sparingly. All these measures will be applied.

Emergency generator

In the same respect, over time I had enough experience with problems creeping up due to repeated power outages of various lengths. For instance, flooding occurred due to failing sump pumps. In short, I propose to install a generator. Not just a small one for emergency lighting, but one system able to handle the entire load of the complex. The system installed here at Golden Pond shows how well systems can be designed: We have an old 50 hp, 37 kW ships generator installed, which takes over 100% of the residence's load at any given time, with automatic switchover gear. So in case of a power outage, the affectionately called "Genny" will take over, and, within one minute power is back on and nobody notices the difference. In a retirement home setting, this is not luxury, but a must. If there is no generator, when the power goes off and the lights go off, there is panic in the house. Of course, everyone is told by staff members to stay put. But in the panic of the dark, the exact opposite is being done. You tell them one thing, and they do another. Everyone comes out of their rooms in panic and scrambles about—the perfect recipe for trouble. Needless to say, it is then when confusion becomes fear, and people running around in the dark may be at grave danger of falling, which is the last thing we want to deal with in such an emergency. This is why.

Cost to build the Adobes

I have been asked often if the designed adobes or apartment houses are very expensive to build.

Indeed, the technical requirements are quite demanding, and hence, expensive. The response to that is that while some of the elements are expensive, other ways must be found to reduce cost, in order to achieve an all over low cost. Yet, there are a number of elements which are manageable cost wise, as long as we use common sense. For instance, the use of solar gain is not costly at all; just a size wise well defined large glass area and a proper orientation to the sun. Shades and overhangs are really not much more costly to build. The fairly expensive heating system, especially the outdoor furnace, is only one furnace supplying 3–5 units, and so the cost per unit is shared. Kitchens of the adobes are modest by any standard, and are more like kitchenettes. A large and expensive kitchen which was desired by house wives and installed in houses of earlier years, has lost its appeal. Most meals are prepared from the one common kitchen. Most important, however, is that the size of the adobes is purposefully kept small which is a direct response in an attempt to keep costs down. And so we can break down all additional expenses to be expected and will see to that these expenses can be capped and controlled.

Sixth component: Community

The sixth component is a big one. It is envisioned to create a well-functioning model community for the elderly to provide for them an inexpensive yet very attractive place to live. Keyword *community*. This will be real community living. The new home will be a place in the community for them to still see themselves as a function of this community, as a function in society. This is possible because there are also younger people living in this community. All living together. Further it can be seen as an operating group, with input from all residents, who want to get involved in this communal body. If the residents have a say in running the operation, then they will still have a function, and keep active. Not a top-down management only. Not a being told what and what not to do. Not a taking-away of all dignity, and being treated like everyone else. Instead, communal living at its best. The term "intergenerational" living will be used to express that not only older folks, but younger folks will live there, as well. It's a fancy word for what we know all along. Younger and older people living together. Close, but not too close.

This supporting base of younger people shall be available for errands, entertainment and mingling with the seniors—and it might work the other way around, too!

Says Mary, living in a community in Wisconsin:

"Funny, when we just focus on ourselves, our problems seem unsurmountable and our world is so small. Since I live in community, we learn to focus on all our problems; and my problems seem to get smaller, as my world is getting larger. And as our world expands, so does our capacity of care".

As a society, we will have to come sooner or later to the conclusion that taking care of our elders is an honour, not a paid-for-career. This is the concept where we all came from only three generations ago, and we will have to go back to this basic human principle, latest when we run out of money to fund the payrolls of all those career driven care givers.

At the same time, this model community will give the younger generation an opportunity to build their own skills, under guidance of elders who have seen it all and done it all. Older residents will have the opportunity to teach, and younger people the opportunity to learn. Interaction is a given, and even the simple tasks like babysitting can be done by elders, in 'exchange' for getting a favour done, perhaps not now, but when needed. All this is not possible in today's ways of living, be it in a retirement home, an apartment building or single family homes. As a society we have chosen to isolate ourselves, from each other, and thought that was the best or only way to live. Isolated, and each one on their own. Not knowing even the closest neighbour. At the same time, still able seniors are running from one event to the next, from one gathering and meeting to another, which means nothing else but to fulfill the most basic need and instinct—to be with others. The younger people preoccupied with making a living, trying to make a dollar and to pay bills, while older folks getting lonely by living in isolation and feeling useless. They have lost the zest for life.

In a community they have the opportunity to rediscover the sense of purpose in their own lives by passing skills down to the younger generation. This is all lost in today's living arrangements.

In this model community, there are many options for younger people to find employment right on site. The larger the community, the more options. And not just the obvious care, assistance, preparing meals, cleaning and offering activities. There are many more opportunities.

For instance, a wood working shop might be created—and is actually proposed.

This workshop could be fully equipped with wood working tools, and production of finished wood products to different degrees could take place. For one thing, to be able to enhance the buildings of the community, but also to create products for sale to produce income for the community—and its workers, from bird houses to small furniture. The aspects of enhancing the adobes by adding all the frills and embellishments which could be produced in the local shop, and installed at the adobes is an excellent way of providing supervised training to the young students. This is but one way to create income for local, younger residents. And most importantly, senior residents can putter about to their hearts content. The other important task the workshop would offer is simple the opportunity for an older person to show the younger ones the tricks of the trade.

Other than the wood working shop, it is possible to implement other, community oriented occupations. For instance, gardens can be created. From creating a garden with produce to be consumed by the residents it is not a big step to envision also selling produce outside of the community.

There is another aspect of community, when I say it is "future oriented". What is that mean?

As we all know, but deny and don't want to know, is that we will sooner or later run out of oil. Not overnight, of course, but slowly. We had a 200 year oil bonanza. And most of it has been used in the last 50 years. Deny it or not, the party is over. At the present time of this writing, we even enjoy very low oil prices. Nobody is asking why, because we really do not want to know the answer. Just let's use it up while it's cheap. It would be a rude awakening to find out that worldwide all oil production facilities are being run wide open. Let's have it, and let's have it now. Although the Arabs mentioned briefly that it might be prudent to slow down production, to no avail. Majority was for more production. And so we enjoy an abundance, albeit short lived supply of more oil. Experts predict that this will come to a grinding halt soon. They are talking about "Why our world will become a whole lot smaller" (Rubenstein).

If you observe older folks in regard to oil consumption, or gas consumption, it is surprising to see that they follow the pattern of all population. They drive their car from one gathering and one event to the other, just so not to miss anything. And there are a surprising number of events in all parts of the country to go to. If they run out of events, they join groups which regularly meet. They drive to friends and family members far and wide, and do not ask about the cost or the consumption. The main goal is to keep busy, not to miss anything, and drive as long as they have the driver's license. They have a date planner similar to a busy company's manager. No indication here that they intend to save gas by cutting back on car driving.

Now, if we all would have our senses, we would realize this and cut back on our travelling habits. Half the travelling would result in this resource lasting twice as long. Does even one of us do that? No, we don't.

Now, if we would be spiritually a bit more advanced, we would recognize that this travelling to and fro is not even necessary, and rather wastes precious time. Is even one of us aware of it? No, we aren't.

Now, if we would act more responsible, we would see our wasteful consumption habits what it really is: We take away this precious resource from our children and grandchildren, who perhaps one day, want to go to work themselves and make a living. Do we save gas for them? No, we don't.

Unless something drastically changes, nothing will change. Business as usual.

This running from one event to the other is nothing else but seeking company, seeking other people. Once the function or event is over, and the participant is driving home, an empty house is waiting. Loneliness sets in again. And since this cannot be accepted by many, off they go the next day again to somewhere else.

One day, however, when car driving proves too expensive, then the time will come when going out all the time simply cannot be afforded any longer.

This is where community shines. The living together right in one place, so that there is no running to and fro necessary. Surrounded by likeminded folks. And if any particular event really must be attended to, there is the community van, which will take a few residents out at the same time.

If developed properly, and given a certain size of the community, a few jobs are created right within the community, besides the maintenance and repair work necessary for the buildings and care of the grounds. As for maintenance work onsite, this work is not performed by third parties, but it will also be done by local residents, younger, on-site living community residents—hence it is much cheaper than being contracted out to a third party. Opportunities abound.

While this model community is no cure for all of society's s illnesses, or even the shortcomings of retirement homes, it surely will address and avoid many. It would be an alternative living option well worth considering. And here are more of the elements, which could be introduced in a community style living.

Alternative Healing Methods and Prevention of Illness

During my research on services offered by retirement homes, I have hardly come across the notion that it may be beneficial for senior residents to enjoy treatments of alternative healing methods or other treatments geared to prevention of illnesses. Herbal remedies, naturopath's healing, all in its infancy stage. Retirement homes, by and large, although very well suited to offer those services, surprisingly many do not. Actually, I have found hardly any. Only a few retirement homes offer swimming pools. Rare is the home which offers sauna baths, assumingly because of the erroneous belief that older people cannot tolerate the heat and this would be of great health risk, but reality of course is different. While this risk may exist in individual cases, it should not be generalized and accepted as the general rule. As with any applied healing method, the individual must be assessed as to the intended treatment being tolerable, and doctor's orders must be followed.

In the proposed set-up of the intentionally developed senior housing community, I believe the application of those would greatly enhance the enriched living experience of the residents. Details of which ones to introduce and how to go about doing so would be outside of the scope of this book, but it should be just mentioned here that it is very well practicable to include in the scope of services offered treatments like massage therapy, hay sack applications, sauna baths, wellness treatments as for instance hydro therapy and treatments known as Kneipp's hydro treatments, and many others. A fairly well known treatment is reflexology and chair yoga which is offered weekly at Golden Pond.

At the same time, it may prove that the general acceptance of those treatments are not extreme, perhaps because not widely known. On the other hand, alternative healing methods in general, for instance chiropractic, are becoming more and more known and accepted by people of all age groups, while others are fairly unknown to the older generation. For instance, the benefits of walking bare feet in the cool morning dew of the grass, or in winter in the snow. This is called "grounding". (You should be here at Golden Pond and see for yourself our resident's reaction when we try to get a few going!)

Seventh component: Care Providing
If circumstances were created which enable some people to assist other people in going through their day, this creation cannot be viewed as employment, even if this creation takes place in an environment otherwise classified as commercial.

The application of the seventh component is how care or actually, assistance with the activities of daily living, (ADL), is to be provided.

It must be understood that the focus of the entire community is to create an enriched living environment for the still active senior—this is not a one building complex designed for care-requiring elderlies. It's not a retirement home within its present definition, and for sure not a nursing home (LTC). Instead, it will be a place which is a very attractive alternative to today's available living options—and the way of how seniors are housed today.

Since we know that older folks want to stay in their own homes, it is foreseeable that the general perception of the community is that assistance and care giving is what's being is offered. It should be noted here that this is not the main feature of the community. However, as said earlier, the threshold between independent living and assistance provided is a grey area, and may change at any time. It may even fluctuate from one week to the other, depending on how the resident feels at any given time. Today, he or she may feel like a million, the next day, however, they feel lousy, and perhaps cannot make it to the bathroom in time. It is hence necessary that at least a portion of the community is set up to assist, in order to be able to provide a seamless level of comfort, if it becomes necessary.

If serious care is required, then the proposed community has few choices but pass on the care-requiring resident, who is now considered requiring care beyond the capacity of the community, to places which are able to fulfill this need, as it is sometimes but not in general practised by retirement homes, but for certain provided by LTCs. Once this stage is reached, paid care giving staff, including specialists, therapists, nurses and doctors are all needed. But it is the lower level of assistance where the community is able to provide, and is able to provide at less cost to the resident than in retirement homes. It is only in this area where it is possible to save money and therefore, to bring down living costs, as opposed to retirement homes. This is possible with the assistance of younger people living onsite, and getting only indirectly paid as in fringe benefits, i.e. in form of lessened or free rent, and only small food expenses, since meals are commonly prepared and served. While this concept sounds great, I may cautiously raise the finger and point in the direction of rules and regulations, which may or may not, depending on the province, pronounce this kind of low level care giving including medication management as nothing short of illegal. As I said repeatedly in regards to regulations, and their dismantling, lots of work still ahead.

Further labour provided will be reimbursed directly by the resident. Barter style. There is no employment per se, and no employer-employee relationship, which cuts out a number of additional expenses. While the few seniors who are able to live in this model community will not require care as defined elsewhere, they surely will benefit from socializing by living together and thus, enable them to mingle as much or as little as they like, while at the same time know there is always a helping hand nearby. This helping hand lives right on site, and does not have to be called in, and paid for, as is the case for home care workers.

As we all have a purpose in our life, more often than not it is obscured, and only very few are able to see their purpose in life. In this model community to be created, it's the very same. It's a new purpose, and it is much more obvious and can be recognized by each individual. Even if that purpose is not the greater life purpose, but just the present need of peeling the potatoes. Each and everyone's input is needed and appreciated, as far as possible, of course. And so, with this given purpose within the functioning of this community, there is also a new purpose to life. The passion for living is being rediscovered. The very passion for life.

Once the state of health by senior residents is such that assistance with daily living is required, this also can be provided by younger people living on site—to a certain extent. It is this extent which is difficult to define, but it is exactly this grey area where the idea of community living shines.

Today's trend is the exact opposite. People are paid for every move they make for a senior. Even the most mundane tasks require people to be licensed and therefore, must be paid for. Making beds comes to mind, which has to be paid for, so does the idea of paid companionship. It is here that community living would be able to reinstall ideas which apparently have been forgotten by some of those law makers who are coming up with these ideas.

Assistance providing, then, will be spread out between younger folks living within the same communities, who receive benefits in terms of reduced or zero rent, and also, common dining. Call it room and board provided in exchange of service provided, but one has to be careful that this word is not used, otherwise once this classification is applied, there would be a ton of other regulations kicking in. This arrangement is for "light duty care", companionship, running errands, even "tucking in". It goes without saying that a certain amount of training is required to fulfill this assistance provided. However, the fact that the assistance providing person is not paid for does not mean that this person has no education and pertinent training.

There is more. The very concept of community also enhances bonds and friendships. One is looking out for the well-being of the other. Basic human instincts are fostered. By nourishing and helping each other, to a certain extent of course, real friendships develop. It is foreseeable that this fact alone improves the general living atmosphere, as opposed to retirement homes, where this aspect is not given. In fact, it is not allowed. We are not permitted to allow such simple things to happen, as one resident pushing another in her wheel chair. What a set-up! Community would encourage simple acts of caring for each other.

The next level of "care", which is still no care in the proper definition of the word, but which is very casually used, is really still under the umbrella of "assistance". This might be in the form of more pronounced application by live-in people on site, now becoming more a paid occupation, and takes on the role of employment and earnings. However, there is no employer, just older folks directly paying some younger folks for their work. The advantages are still the same. No travel to and fro is required, hence cost, fuel and labour time is saved, as opposed to how it is practised today by home care workers. Constantly changing home care workers due to changing staffing requirements and scheduling is avoided; change which would otherwise cause undue stress to the resident, who must now be looked after, washed and dressed by constantly rotating people, which is a sharp ingress on anyone's personal dignity.

The next level will be paid for professional care providers, holding a training certificate similar to Ontario's PSW's, Personal Care Workers. This home care is either privately paid for by the residents, or, if income levels do not exceed established limits, will be paid for and supplied by the government agencies.

That of course only applies if regional legislation allows for the application of home-care workers, as long as these are available through the current set-up of this industry. See above section of "Home-Care Industry".

It shall be noted here that it is possible to create the proposed senior housing community without the requirement of licensing as a retirement home, at least today. This community *could be operated as a **not to be licensed** retirement residence*, if certain criteria are given. However, in the event that more older folks already in need of assistance are interested in living in such a community, there is no reason that licensing cannot be obtained. The criteria is the degree of assistance provided, and its regularity, that is, whether it is provided once in a while or scheduled regularly, as in daily or an ongoing basis. The decision to be licensed could be made once the degree of care requirements by prospective tenants/residents is evaluated and assessed. If the decision is made to apply for a retirement home license, in any event this should only include a part of the entire community, mainly because, if such a decision is made, this would include a whole new scenario in terms of requirements to be met. This decision would take away many of the proposed benefits over an unlicensed home or community. However, the option exists. For instance, one additional requirement is that a licensed nurse would have to be employed, and since there is no employer, it must be on a contractual basis. Just to name one of many requirements.

And the next component of where to draw assistance giving folks from is at first difficult to grasp—from the ranks of active residents themselves. Enter volunteers.

If circumstances were created, which enables people to assist elderlies going through their day, these circumstances and the resulting relationship between these giving and receiving people cannot be classified as employment.

Eighth component: Volunteers

For the purpose of applying this eighth component, I am almost ashamed to categorize the work of giving people in this way—it's just another example of how society tends to categorize everything. But for reason of demonstration here it is.

The way I see it, in the future, we will finally realize that all our basic needs are met. We will further realize that the way society constructed itself, we are constantly bombarded by mass advertising and marketing too persuade us, that we have needs, or we are supposed to have needs, which have to be satisfied. In other words, this is consumption. Reality is, these are no needs at all, but wants. But only if we succumb to these messages, if we allow ourselves to watch or listen. At one point, we will also realize that all wants have been also met. Unless we are listening and acting upon those messages, which will bring and create *new* wants. And there is no end. Until we get tired of all this, and are also get tired *of paying* for all this.

Compound that growing awareness with the fact that our unbridled urge to consume will soon falter, those messages will cease, as well. Not only because they are now not having effect any more, but also, simply because there will be diminishing resources available to produce all these goods. It is then when we will finally stop buying constantly, and stop consuming constantly. As a side effect, our financial situation will finally become healthy. Healthier, that is. Think of it this way; in the States, 42% of all consumer items are paid for by credit cards, which is nothing else but a debt for the future, a commitment to keep working and to keep making money. It is also instant gratification, a concept we have all grown nicely into. This evil circle must be broken, and when it does, we will wake up and actually *work less*. We may no longer need to. Moreover, we may have to, since jobs are diminishing at the same time. And all of a sudden, from a former hectic life style of holding 2 jobs to make ends meet, we will have more free time than ever, because there are no longer jobs to be worked at, but also, it's not necessary. Basic needs are met, and superfluous items will not be bought any longer. They are not desired or wanted any longer.

It is then when the thought will come to give back. First, we will give back time. It is then when we decide to do something for no remuneration. Yeah, I think this is what they call "volunteering".

Reality is, however, it's much more.

The exploding older population will initially consist of a huge potential of still available productivity, a potential still useful. Better than that, it is screaming to be utilized, and in this way the elderly will still contribute to the society by a huge margin. Actually, some of the older folks past retirement age will continue to work, because they might have to or because they might want to. Either way, they are still employed, most likely part time, but not necessarily so. There is still a lot more free time available. The ones who work part time or stop working altogether will have even more time available. There are other factors conducive to volunteering, at the moment almost unthinkable. This "more time available" in today's way of thinking may mean more time travelling or spending time with all kinds of activities offered, including visiting other family members, who may live further away. However, the shrinking available money pool, compounded with the fact that most of these kinds of activities become sharply more expensive, simply means they are not being pursued any longer, at least not at today's extent.

They are simply becoming too expensive. The sharp rise of oil price and hence gas price will see to it that traveling, by whatever means, will cost drastically more. But while this development may be seen first as a step backwards, as a diminishing or lowering level of life style, it will be soon recognized that this is actually not true. Traveling or consuming will no longer be desired as it is today—instead, deeper, more fulfilling occupations will be sought and pursued.

And yes, one of them will be volunteering to help elders in need of assistance.

This volunteering may take place in private residential homes, perhaps even in nursing homes, provided some regulations are altered, and finally, also in retirement homes or alternate living options. Simply because we are genetically wired to assist and help. We are driven to assist and help anyone who is in need of our assistance, be it animals, nature, the nurturing of the earth, or older people. There is no doubt that this urge—while covered up for most of us and most of our lives—will finally sprout and blossom. It is only with the current error of thinking, the thinking that consuming is fulfilling, that this basic need to serve is obstructed. Once this error of thinking is corrected, suddenly a lot of older folks who are still active will seek opportunities to exercise and apply this usefulness. And this opportunity exists in organized community, where still capable folks will assist older folks who need their assistance.

Again, in order for this concept to work, there are a lot of regulations which would have to be changed, if not downright scrapped. And also, courts would have to alter their way of thinking of accepting nuisance law suits, and instead, dismiss them. Which ones? Within the context of this writing, here is an example: If an older person, untrained and unlicensed, helps another person and something goes sideways, there are grounds, at least at the present time, to press law suits by family members—rest assured. That of course, could not be accepted in the proposed model community. It must be realized and expected that there is a certain risk of living, and not all accidents can be avoided. The harder we try, the more obvious it should become that it is in vain. As it is today, in situations like this everyone in sight is being sued as being responsible and made to pay if something drastic happens.

Now, as the gentle reader will notice, this approach of one elderly helping another elderly may be only short lived. That is, because it works only initially with the coming baby boomers needing assistance. Because as time goes by, the once 'younger' and more agile volunteers will be in need of assistance themselves, while the person receiving assistance will be now in a stage of receiving real care. Professional care, that is. So this shift is expected and has to be allowed for. When does the time come that we run out of volunteers, because they are now in a situation unable to help, but needing assistance themselves?

Running a couple of scenarios, I have calculated that it will be around 30 years after the main portion of the baby boomers will reach that stage, that is about 25 years from now, for a total of 45 years or so from now for the totality to have its effect. There are many components to be allowed for in this calculation; but it is safe to say that indeed, the bulging older population could conceivably look after their own, at least in the initial stages of assistance required. But it is certainly a huge component of providing such assistance, as opposed to today, where even the slightest move to assist a senior must be paid for, and actually is being paid for, including such silly things as paid home care workers providing companionship.

To conclude, the basic assistance given in such a community consists of 4 levels: first the residents themselves assisting the ones who need it. Second, the volunteers coming in from outside, not living within the intentional community. The third level will be younger folks of all ages living in this community, to a certain degree volunteers as well, but mainly, for indirect remuneration, such as reduced expenses up to nil for housing i.e. rent, heat, utility cost, food, providing meals, use of vehicle and others. These fringe benefits may include everything needed for basic existence. Once the service of basic assistance provided is exceeding this level, remuneration is paid. However, within the framework of this intentional community, an employer-employee relationship shall not be established, since otherwise strict labour laws will apply, and this element is detrimental to the overall concept. It is detrimental to all parties involved except the employee. Earning money by providing basic service to elders shall simply not be regarded as an employable industry. It is one thing for the elder in need of service to pay someone for some service to be done, because otherwise this time commitment takes away the earning capacity of the younger person or care giver, but it is quite another step to declare this giving and taking relationship as an industry, requiring the application of all labour laws, including paying taxes on all ends, employee's deductions, paying dues for workers compensation boards, insurances and all other bodies we have invented and perceived to be useful, including and up to insurance for unemployment. And who shall be the employer? The receiving resident? Their family? Somehow, this does not look right. Somehow, this is a pretty sad picture to paint, allowing our own older generation to be degraded and reduced to become a target of providing a base of taxable employment—again, that view is for basic assistance only. Today, even "companionship" is regarded as a chargeable service, and constitutes a job opportunity. In this case the government is paying for this. For instance, for the seniors who live isolated, and is at risk of getting depressions, because they want to stay home at all cost, the government takes on the view that this decision is supportable. The senior who has decided to continue to live on his or her own must have the basic need to socialize be looked after—by means of sending paid companionship to their home. How far are we carrying this nonsense?

To have these three levels actually "perform work" will require again a major step away from the present way of thinking in terms of liability.

The proposed way of providing assistance is fraught with risks. And where there are risks, there are law suits not far away. It is with great probability that things will go sideways, and it is then when finger pointing and fault finding will take place. Since our court system has established itself to support these views and actually listen to these kind of suits, it is essential that all co-habitants refrain from any law suits. The idea of an older person (or more likely, his family) suing another old person for his or her kindness given, when something went wrong, is twisted thinking indeed. Yet, I can easily picture these events taking place, unless laws change. Until then, only a strict, legally tight waiver to be signed upon moving into the community may, just may, be sufficient from preventing law suits to happen. Then again, it is also foreseeable that the entire court system, in its present set-up will more or less falter, as I have pointed out in my book about spiritual awareness.

A simple example, which could happen any given day, may serve to demonstrate.

Dorothy is trying to get up from that comfy but low sofa, and struggles to do just that. Emma comes along, sees her struggle, and gives her a hand. The following picture might be taken on camera, because it is usually quite hilarious, until the inevitable happens, and both of them fall. If nothing is bruised but the ego, it's funny for all, especially for the onlookers. If a serious injury is the result, all of a sudden the picture is not quite as funny anymore. That's life—and the risk of living—until the courts are taking it apart, and declare that this incident was preventable. Law suits are flying.

The forth level is that of actual employment of trained professionals. Professional care givers providing assistance and service which can no longer be provided by untrained individuals, comprised of the three levels described above. Now we are at the stage of real professionals. And I am sorry to say, in my personal view, Personal Care Workers do hardly fall within this category. The education given within this type of training is nothing else but common sense, and basic knowledge, which can be and will be passed on during the actual working with elders, taught by elders and educated professionals, as well as trained staff in the retirement homes themselves. And these professionals are nurses or practical nurses. We witness every day the work of PSW's, and quite often are amused by their level of performance. While some show very good indications of professionalism, others are not even able to make a bed properly or fit on pampers. Part of the problem is that today everyone under the sun can get that certificate, regardless if the personality of the individual is suited for the job or not. Only after actually working in the environment for a while the true suitability of a care giver for this kind of job comes to light.

This level of paid professionals might be home care services themselves, if they are still around at that time in the future. As described earlier it is questionable whether the home care industry at that time will still exist, at least in the way it is set up today. But if it is, this is the first choice, because the government might pay for it. If not, the second choice is to provide this service by either private home care services, or living-on-site staff. The bill which has to be paid by the receiving resident would be the same way as today's retirement home services are paid for, except on an individual level, something like a user fee. If today's set-up still holds true for this future picture, then a combination of both elements is to be expected. For the lower income bracket of the residents, the service by home care will be provided free, the higher end income earners would have to pay themselves. Another option would be in-house employment, that is, the intentional community itself, i.e. the managing body, will take on the role as employer. After all, they are already fulfilling this role by employing folks needed for the operation, like maintenance, repairs, lawn care, and snow removal. It's just a matter of adding more professional employees.

The level of paid professionals and executing of this kind of care level will in my view remain unchanged from the present model. All the way to the next step, the step of nursing home care. It is in the steps before where payroll cost can be saved. And the proposed model shows its benefit. Not on this last level.

But these three levels combined will provide for a huge workforce, and in effect, will be much more effective, and much less expensive compared with the current model. It's in the *giving*.

Tom Bender, an architect and economist, says this in a most wonderful way.

The Economics of Giving

Giving may sound like a ridiculous basis for economics. *In reality, the majority of our expenditures are for wants, not needs—things that connect with our dreams and our self-esteem, not our physical survival. They are not dealt with by the same dimensions of relationships as our material needs. If we change our relationships with others from a basis of taking or getting to one of giving, we begin to work with those dimensions, and amazing new potentials open.*

A giving economy benefits the giver as well as the receiver. In conventional buying and selling we often end up uncertain whether the other person is taking advantage of us or whether what we are buying is worth what we are paying for it. We frequently end up with the unhealthy feeling that we got a "raw deal", or the equally unhealthy feeling that we got a "steal".

In contrast, giving ends up with everyone feeling they have received a gift. Such win-win situations represent a far different economics of benefit than our conventional exchanges. Plus, we don't have to pay taxes on it!

When we give our time or possessions to someone, we do it because we feel better in the process. When we are given some thing or some help that we need, we feel grateful because it was something we couldn't take care of by ourselves. Everyone gains, and feels good towards each other.

In giving, the gift has different value to each participant. There is no way to "price" it. When we give something to someone else, it often is something we don't need anymore and which the other person does. Occasionally a gift is something we value greatly, but something we value the other person enjoying even more.

When we offer to give our time to someone else, we often do it because we expect to have fun being with them. Our real skills are also so familiar that we rarely really understand their value to others. But to someone receiving them, they have a very different value—an often-vital expertise which they are lacking. When we give "insights" to someone else, we both end up with them.

What goes around, comes around. *In a culture of giving, need is perceived by the community, and gifts appear when need appears. The gift economy of a community based on love and honoring fulfills our emotional as well as material needs.* The economics of giving enriches those inner resources. The power of those inner resources is vital in overcoming the diseases of the spirit so endemic in our society, in creativity and progress in every field, and ultimately in our own sense of health and happiness.

If 'What can I give in this situation?' is always in our hearts when we talk with or do something with someone, we not only leave a legacy of gifts in addition to our intended interaction, but we generate an enduring climate of trust, mutual caring, thankfulness and happiness which moves outward like the waves in the sea. This also provides the glue of love and trust essential to any enduring relationship. *Giving is an integral part of loving, and loving is the root of holding things sacred essential to sustainability.*

Borrowed from my book titled "*Spiritual Awakening—Applied to Daily Life*", I have devoted the following observation about volunteers:

Conscious Awareness 18—Serving Others

"*You are what you do, not what you say you'll do*" —Carl Jung
As it can be observed, we are all genetically wired to serve others. That is, genetically made up that way.

But when we hear about someone serving others, we have in mind some missionary in faraway countries to teach third world inhabitants, or perhaps help them with various techniques, or perhaps give out medications and so forth.

But we do not have to go so far to observe that people serve others. In fact, just look around you and you will see it everywhere.

Why is this important, anyway? Well, because we are made this way. In a God like way. And God is very good at serving others. Boy, is he ever! So then it comes as no surprise that, since we are made in a God like way, we do strive to serve others as well. Trouble is, for one thing, we do not recognize this connection. But also, for most of our time as adults we put a price tag on this—'serving others'. So then it can be said safely that while most of us for most of our lives serve others, we want to get paid for that. The question then becomes—how much. The amount we expect to get paid is a direct mirror of the level of spiritual awareness one has reached. Because making a lot of money is a direct measure of the level of ego in a person, and since the level of ego is the direct opposite and is contrary of the level of spiritual awareness, there is a direct connection in the level of reimbursement expected for someone's service to others.

But let's start with our observation even earlier—in childhood.

Obviously, mothers or parents are serving their child. But it is not labeled that way. Children, however, serve just as well. There are serving by being, not by doing. This is an important fact, and hold onto that thought, because we will come back to that.

Just by being a child, it serves the mother or parents. But it is also not labeled that way. Just imagine the child being taken away from its parents, and see what happens. This loss is a sure indication that the child served its parents. To be loved, that's what it's called. Its love it gives, just by being for what it is. And it is love it receives, and is grateful, just by being what it is.

As the child grows into adulthood, there is a multitude of people the young adult must serve. Not just the parents, but also teachers, trainers, foremen and supervisors in early employment and so forth. Again, we put different labels on the different relationships, but it's all the same—the person serves others.

Once this stage of making a living is reached, one does well to notice that the only way to make money and pay our bills is by serving others. Within the fabrics of our society, we only get paid by serving others. You only earn what other people are willing to pay you. Simple as that. That may be direct compensation, or it may be through an employer. Same thing. You serve in whatever fashion, and the employer pays you. He can do that, because he sells the services you provided through him to others. That's how things work. You cannot make money by squeezing it out of a rock. Something has to be of service to others, and these others pay you for the services provided.

Now, you might argue that there are plenty of jobs where this is not the case. True, but from the viewpoint of a society, this is not a desirable type occupation, because it's not productive. And from the spiritual viewpoint, for sure it is not. These are the kind of occupations which are of no value to the society, or to any other human being, or to nature at large. These are like leaches of the society. Sucking money out, but giving nothing back. Think about those jobs, and see how many there really are.

The question then becomes what kind of services are required by society, what kind of service is useful, what kind of service is well or not so well paid for. Interestingly enough, what is most required in society does not automatically fetch the highest pay. In many instances, quite the opposite is the case. Just think this through.

Think of high earners, and see if society actually needs them, or how badly. You will see what is really taking place. Someone is getting paid big money for useless service, or for no service at all. Again, you will come up with your own conclusions on this.

What we should be concerned about, however, is the level of spiritual awareness, or better, the lack of it, once we are talking high earners. It is for this reason that it might be totally okay to for instance to dismiss all religious TV show preachers, because the truth is obvious. They expose publicly a well-developed ego which forces them to make lots of money and so are compelled to do what they do. And everyone knows this. But they preach the opposite. The bible has a nice way of putting this: They are preaching water and are drinking wine. Or think of highly paid sportsmen, or highly paid singers or actors. Many of them earn obscene salaries for ridiculous efforts. Again, you can add to this list.

As we grow older, however, something changes. One day, all this striving will be regarded as useless, as not important. It might even be regarded as a great waste of time. And it is then when the question of the purpose of life surfaces. It is then that the realization sinks in that serving others actually has a different meaning altogether. Now this price tag thing becomes painfully obvious. All of a sudden, the realization sinks in that the meaning of servings others is becoming more like God.

And what I am referring to here is to what we will be doing once we leave the stage of doing something, like serving others, for a lot of money. Now we are doing something else, for free, if we can afford it, or we are doing something for a lot less money than earlier on. We acquire more altruistic thinking. And also, we might be doing something else, because we recognize what we did all along in all those years is really not important at all. And hence, we are doing something more like what God would be doing. It is not just the view of things, or the underlying belief which is changing, it is also the behaviour which is changing. Once the belief changes, the behaviour, the actual action will change as well. And we will adjust to that, if we are able. For many people, this is unfortunately not possible, for many reasons and circumstances. For those people, many job occupations which have been practiced for years all of a sudden seem not worth doing any more. One gets tired of it. There may be the desire, even urge, to change course, but that's easier said than done. Frustration sets in. And so, many people experience this kind of frustration in their jobs in later years. And the reason is simply a growing spiritual awareness, and the awareness that what one does is not fulfilling any longer.

Once we grow even older, there comes a point when it becomes painfully clear that doing anything will be harder and harder on the body, simply because the body is getting tired. It becomes more and more worn out. That realization is very hard to absorb for many. You may see this everywhere you go. But it is rarely admitted. Just attend any of the many events constantly offered for seniors. They come far and wide to be part of all that, and to not miss anything. Some of them will appear at these events for no other reason than just to be admired, for sure. But in many cases it is overdone. It shows that the person exhibiting to everyone "Look at me, what I still can do—I'm eighty-five, and still able to go to all these events and show you I can still do it"...This, of course, is ego speaking. Once back home, they pay for it, because everything is aching. Time for Rub A535.

And it is here that spirit replaces the loss of physical ability. Mental ability blooms. It is here that it will be recognized that proving anything to anyone is not important any more. Even doing something for others at one point is not required any more. It has been all done. It is past. It is not necessary any longer. Once we are in this golden stage, or perhaps golden age, we still serve others. How? It is now that we serve others just by being. By being who we are, because we are unique. We are built that way, simply unique. There is no second me or you in the whole universe. You do not have to prove anything to anyone any more.

And that is reason enough to be. Just as it was when we were a helpless child. Remember what I said in the first paragraph? We are back to that stage now. And that is ok. We are serving others just by being who we are. And if we are lucky enough to be surrounded by spiritually minded folks, they will be grateful to have you or us around.

And are grateful just for who you are, or I am. Because they know— and understand.

All we have to do now is nothing. And all we have to be now is ourselves. This way, we can look back at our lives lived, even if we overcharged someone else for services which we thought we should provide, and what we thought we should charge for, but was useless in the larger picture. We don't feel guilty because we know that this was necessary in order to be where we are now. And we learned the lesson. But then, with a more altruistic attitude, we can look back at the part of our lives where we served others with little compensation, and we can feel good about it. And now we can look at this part of our lives where we do nothing anymore, we just are.

And this way, finally, find peace.
We had done all we had to do.

Ninth component: Affordability

Listed as the ninth component, affordability is also a very important element. However, there are insurmountable obstacles to this requirement.

Given the fact that retirement housing costs are running away, there must be ways to slow down these spiralling costs, or perhaps even reverse them, in order to see that the 'silver tsunami' heading our way is able to afford future housing units–any units. As said elsewhere, the combination of increasing cost in retirement homes due to the various factors while at the same time the money available by seniors for their housing needs shrinks, it is easy to see that this trend cannot continue indefinitely. A solution must be found.

Hence the affordability is of utmost importance.

But what is affordable? How affordable? What is the definition? Well, it is more or less up to society to come up with a price tag which is considered affordable. This price tag is a direct reflection of the number of regulations in place today. The following is a short list of regulating requirements, and it will be clear to the reader that the implementation, application and ongoing fulfillment of these regulation can only be done by paying associated costs. I do not put a value on these rules and regulations, or suggest anything contrary to what is in place. Or suggest, although tempted, that some of these rules are perhaps even superfluous. I do not say that. But this judgment perhaps will be made by masses in years to come. Perhaps in the nearer future. Why? Because once the effect of oil, our main motor of the economy, becomes too expensive, perhaps then it will be too expensive to have everything we need, and we think we need to consume, coming from countries like China. If this takes place, it is just too expensive to have the stuff shipped half way around the world. So, then, we come to our senses, finally, pull up our socks and get to work. We produce our own stuff again, as we did in the past, and besides, we will do with a lot less. China will produce stuff for its own folks. And once we rethink what we do here to get our own productions going, all these folks today who have nothing better to do than to create yet another rule and another regulation, will then become employed in manufacturing, which makes a lot more sense. It is then when these folks are the first victims of their own creation, because it is them now who have to pay for their own makings. It is then when rules and regulations will be dismantled. Can't wait to see this happen.

Okay, there are regulations which do make sense, as an example, the implementation of rules regarding water quality, which is in my view very important. We are exposed to (well) water every day, and drink it every day. Contamination is a serious threat and can happen anytime. Hence I put value on this. The same cannot be said for the required application of fitting masks to prevent catching contagious air borne illnesses in the course of dealing with sick and contagious residents. The idea is, if a resident has a contagious disease, for the staff member to enter the room with only a personal fitted mask, to prevent catching viruses and from becoming ill. This is a risk which may be formidable in hospitals, or perhaps in nursing homes; however in the setting of a retirement home such a risk is surely small, too small to introduce and implement expensive measures of its prevention-like each staff member having personal fitted masks, to be fitted by trained specialists—all this comes at a horrendous cost. I have never seen or witnessed its application.

If we are talking affordable and the implementation of all regulations in the same sentence, sorry to say but one is contradicting the other. So, if we want affordability, we have to seriously ask ourselves where and how regulations can be lightened up., or dismantled. Will this actually happen? Will rules and regulation be dismantled, just for the reason of saving costs? After all, the regulations are in place to ensure safety and prevent loss of life, harm suffered, accidents prevented, risks reduced of all sorts, including that of fire and so on. So then, society should be proud to be in a position to have all these rules and regulations in place, in order for everyone to live as safely as possible.

This may be one view.

Another one would be to realize the price tag of all these regulations society has chosen to embrace, and forces its members to embrace, the realization that somebody has to pay for all this. And when money is or becomes scarcer, something has to give. This realizations sets in, which otherwise was obscured.

For instance, the introduction of seat belts as a means of saving lives in the event of car accidents is acceptable, although as many studies have found, it is only marginally ahead with having more benefits than disadvantages. But it is regarded as a safety feature. But putting this aside, it does not cost much to have seat belts installed at the manufacturing plant. The introduction of air bags is another story, because vastly more expensive. Plus, there is a real danger involved once they are activated. So here, the question again comes up, how much cost is involved for how little benefit. The more we try to protect, the more expensive and technically challenging it becomes, which is totally fine with the manufacturers, because now they have something which they can charge money for—after all, everyone wants increased safety features, and is therefore willing to pay for it. The safety factor is well received, and well propagandized. And as a consequence, it sells well. Nobody asks questions of the probability of this safety feature to actually work, and more so, to work as intended, which are two different things.

Relating safety features to a retirement home situation may be illustrated as follows:

You are Dorothy. After your husband passes on, you feel the crunch of living alone in this big house. Alone. Loneliness sets in. Shortly after that, health issues arise. You are scared of falling, with nobody there to find you. Your diet deteriorates. You are afraid to continue living alone. The thought comes up to perhaps look at alternative living options, like moving into a retirement home. Finally, after long contemplation the time has come to seek out a suitable retirement home. Your son will look into the different options for you. You look forward to new social contacts, to other people, to good—and regular meals. And since you have a good pension from the husband's company in addition to the government pension, you can afford it.

The last time you had thoughts of moving into a retirement home was with your husband about 12 years ago. Rates were then $1,600/month. So you wait until sonny comes up with a few options, and you start to look around, too. But, to your surprise soon you realize the difference a mere 12 years has made. There is nothing on the horizon any more for $1,600/month.

Now it's twice as much. The good pension, all of a sudden, is way too small to afford such a home. No way for you to afford such a place. There is no choice for you but continue to live in that big old house, and to be lonely, and to be fearful of falling. The only other choice is to sell the house, but you had intentions to give this to sonny.

This is a very common scenario. Until, just for demonstration purposes and not possible in reality, one retirement home would be able to operate its home without all the superfluous regulations which are in place today, and had to be implemented in the last 12 years. What would happen?

If this home would not have sprinkler system? And a not commercial stair lift? And no fire doors? And no unionized staff members? Simply, now this imaginary home would be able to offer its services for half the cost.

We are back to the $1,600. Or only slightly more.

That's the difference.

Once more: Will rules and regulation be dismantled, just for the purpose of saving costs?

The answer is a clear no. There is no way that all development will be reversed. Or is there?

But this is only a 'clear no' within our present mind set. So it will be necessary for our mind set to change, in order to move forward. We are in our own way. We are a victim of all our regulations we have in place—and it will prove even more so in the future to be in our way, at the present rate. We think we are so far advanced in terms of rules and regulations, but at the same time, are our worst enemy, because we are stumbling over our own feet. Regulations must be dismantled, and this change may become necessary one day. Once we realize that there is not enough money around to pay for all this. Once we do not know where all these seniors are going to live. Not if, but when this point comes, it is then we will finally dismantle regulations. We shall do that in the reverse order they have been implemented, the latest ones first, because they are the most superfluous ones. And by doing so, we will do ourselves a big favour. Because we will create affordable housing options for everyone, even as we are *re-introducing risks which we had all along anyway*, and most of us survived those presumed risks for limb and life just fine. And here is an important observation:

The smaller the risk, the more expensive it is to implement a way of its avoidance—and the less it is necessary.

But there are too many people in power today who are constantly on the lookout for even the smallest risk, and coming up with new regulations to prevent harm, and at the same time, have no idea who should pay for all this. They do so because they don't realize that they, themselves, have to pay for that soon. If not themselves, then perhaps by their parents, leaving them less to inherit.

Rules are something we've imposed on situations to regulate them. Right today. Wrong tomorrow. Yesterday's pattern of containment or risks of living may not be appropriate for the demands of tomorrow.

We can apply the same principle and say this:

If Mom is financially unable to move into a retirement home, in effect she cannot afford a very safe and secure place—this is what she is paying for. Instead and by definition, she has to stay at home, cope with life at home, and exposing herself to the risk of living at home—but she did this all along.

And this is where we are today:

As long as we have heavily regulated *operational* rules and regulations, the implementation of which and actual day-to-day performance of which costs a lot of money, the associated cost must be met, as well.

As long as we have heavily regulated requirements such as *fire prevention equipment and training, including big-ticket items like sprinkler systems and retro fitted automatic fire doors, automatic and back up pumping systems for emergency use to be powered automatically from generator stand-by systems*, to pick just a few of many, as long as all of these requirements must be met, the associated cost must be met, as well.

As long as we have heavily regulated requirements such as those found in *health and safety*, to pick just one of many, as long as all of these requirements must be met, the associated cost must be met, as well.

As long as we have heavily regulated requirements such as *protection for staff members through the application of masks to prevent contagious air borne diseases*, to pick just one of many, as long as all of these requirements must be met, the associated cost must be met, as well.

As long as we have heavily regulated requirements *for commercial stair lifts*, as opposed to residential stair lifts, the application of which and its associated costs must be met, this cost for the resident must be met, as well.

As long as we have heavily regulated requirements such as *increased level of quality of building homes, increased requirements as spelled out in LEED*, to pick just one of many, as long as all of these requirements must be met, the associated cost must be met, as well.

Add to *that the cost of future oriented fuel saving building methods, such as excellent insulation, passive solar application, not to mention the application of even more expensive technology, as in in-ground—source heating systems*, the cost of which must be met.

Add to that *staff workers who need to get paid, want to get paid well, but over and above, expect vacation pay, training time to be paid, off time, sick time, holiday time, all of the non-productive time to be paid*, and of course, the Workers Compensation Board, the cost of which must be met.

Add to that *staff workers who feel and are told that they must be protected from 'greedy' employers by way of labour unions*, to pick just one of many, as long as all of these requirements must be met, the associated cost must be met, as well. In Ontario, the labour force of already more than half of all retirement homes are unionized.

And these are just a few examples.

It is no surprise, then, when I say that only if we wake up and actually attempt to *reduce or even eliminate* any of these cost elements, the cost of housing may become affordable again. Today, we have to cope with all of these costs. That means the end user, the resident, has to pay.

The foregoing spells out details that, within the frame work of our society, there are few elements left which can be cost saving when applied, in order to meet the mandate of affordability.

When we try to think the entire scenario through, we immediately run into obstacles which, because of regulations, put a dead stop to this thought. In my view it is absolutely necessary to dismantle regulations in order to proceed into solutions of the looming senior housing crisis. Of the few options left with the current set-up, with this I proposed some of my thoughts.

Tenth component: Location

The tenth consideration is the location; the scale is tipping heavily towards the choice of a country like location, as mentioned earlier. Here I believe the maximum distance of perhaps 20 minutes travel time by vehicle is accepted, not just for amenities, but also for health related services, in particular, hospitals. And in addition to what has been said elsewhere, one important element has not being mentioned: cost.

While the cost of land is considerable within city limits, it becomes drastically less just outside city limits, in our assumed country setting. Country, not rural. Country, not wilderness. For the introduced concept, an acreage of perhaps 10–25 acres is envisioned. Also, all our lives we wanted water frontage. We are drawn to water. Now, in the last phase of our lives, why not experience living on water frontage? This is not a must, but in my view, it should be the preferred location. The theme is to enjoy what we can, for as long as we can. Even if the proposed property does not feature water frontage, an artificial pond is the minimum. You might envision problems with flies and mosquitos, and this is a nuisance, to be sure. For enjoying the outside, a screened in gazebo next to the pond is a must. However, I envision more problems with authorities than with mosquitos to get the blessing of such an idea. Here, I am not talking a 4 x 8 prefab pond, but one which can be bulldozed out in 2 days, and from what I have seen, such a pond maybe 100 feet across. At this size, nature will take over soon, and next year there will be frogs and water lilies, fishes and dragonflies. So with this set-up we will enjoy tranquility and nature as closely as one can get. We can observe nature and it's unfolding just by looking outside the window. How beautiful can life be? Or, once such a community is the newly chosen home, how beautiful can life become?

Did I mention that the creation and construction of such a pond is, at least in some places including Ontario, is illegal?

In terms of closeness to cities, the question is, how large has the city to be? It has been established that it should be big enough to have medial facilities including at least one hospital. From this view, a population of perhaps minimum 2–3,000 should be sufficient. However, keeping in mind at least at the present time a mere 7 out of every 1000 people choose to live in a retirement home, and a mere 9% of the senior population over 65 years of age choose to live in a retirement home, then it is obvious that a larger city is necessary. In my estimation, a population base of 10–20,000 minimum is required to establish successfully the proposed senior community. But then again, the proposed alternative may attract many more older people to live in than presently in a retirement home.

It is in alignment with my spiritual thinking, that humans have to go through trials and tribulations all their lives, in order to experience all facets life offers, until all this is done, until all this is completed. It is now that life can be experienced in a way which was not possible earlier, because life demanded too much. Too much of everything, between holding a job and raising the family, one only wonders how all this has been accomplished. And yet is has, and yet at times one could hardly breathe getting through the busy day. But now, it's different. It is now that we can finally find the peace we are yearning for all these years. It is now that we discover yet another angle of life, one which has not been experienced before. Now it is time to see the glory of God. Not (necessarily) in the religious way, but we see it in pure life, the unfolding life and its intrinsic workings, all around us. And the intelligence to keep it all in place. And make it all happen. This is God at work. And that can be seen and observed much more pronounced once we are surrounded by nature. Here, we are one step up from the Eden Concept, which strives to bring nature into the home. Now, this concept, living in the country, takes the home right to the middle of nature.

There is another reason that I advocate this view. Our residence, Golden Pond Retirement Residence, is smack in the middle of nature, although only 12 km from town. And we have witnessed and observed, that all residents are totally in wonderment with our setting. It is as close to heaven as possible. And here is the most astonishing fact about this observance. Even city folks, even folks who initially were not drawn to live with us, or in nature, have totally changed their mind. Initially hesitant, always liked the hustle and bustle of the city, have realized that this not important any longer. The city has lost its charm. And it is no surprise that this is so, simply because, as mentioned above, we are nothing but part of nature, part of it all. Folks who are not particularly taken by our surroundings, living in cities all their lives, and are rather partial about coming to us, have completely changed their view. Many people coming though our door, but mainly the family members of our residents have coined this place as being "one in a million". And so it is.

Combined with our motto of "We are driven to provide care giving to the highest level", we have indeed established a one of a kind retirement home. What's left is to improve on the very set-up, but there are many elements to be improved on which are outside our competence—it must come from society.

Given this insight, it is my conclusion to situate this future oriented senior community in a similar setting, which is a country setting.

Other considerations

Common building

The common building is the heart of the community—the heart of activity. It includes the common dining room and the kitchen. It further includes not just washroom facilities but also shower facilities. It may further contain, depending on the size of the community, one, two or more guest suites. They will be used by family members who stay over, and will serve well for a number of other occasions. I remember one particular intense ice storm we had a few years ago, and power was widely out for many days. On that occasion, we opened our doors for everyone in need of meals, and mainly, warmth. This had been announced by a local radio station we had called—to advise. And indeed, there were quite a few people coming who made use of our offer. It feels good to be of assistance. On occasions like these, it is good to have a few, or even only one or two extra rooms available.

Meals shall be prepared in the kitchen in the common building. Following other models, some, but not all seven dinners per week are being served. However, often elderlies (and sometimes anyone!) do not feel like eating with others, and so the adobes will also be equipped with small kitchenettes, fully independent units.

The common building will not only serve as a place to cook and dine, but also to mingle, exchange ideas, sit and rest, perhaps play and baby-sit. But also, where important mutual decision-making by the residents is done—today it's called concensus decision making.

In this common room, other activities shall take place; its future use is manifold and self-explanatory.

Car traffic

The community shall be designed traffic free, as it has been successfully implemented in other intentional communities. I have conducted some studies on those, and while admittedly I have not found one in particularly catering to senior oriented communities, there are quite a few catering to community resident families with children. The overriding factors are the same. In communities, there is a certain risk for mixing car traffic with playing children. But by the same token, this can be said for senior population, as well. In addition, in our proposed housing community will be children, just the same. The main reason, however, is not just added safety.

The car free grounds surrounding the homes or adobes do not just bring in an element of security, but also, an element of tranquility and peace. People can walk and sit on benches, watching and feeding birds and squirrels. Perhaps there is a fountain in a small pond.

And this tranquility is the main reason to propose having the traffic end at the parking lot. Reaching back to the past, further transportation then will be in the form of golf carts, as I have seen practiced in several communities in the States. I remember seeing a community in Atlantic City during the time I lived in North Carolina. The necessary traffic from the parking lot onwards was conducted with a number of golf carts, stored in a roofed-over area at the parking lot, and each condo house had a designated roofed over parking spot for the golf carts only. In addition, this particular community had also a pick-up and delivery service which brought people and goods back and forth. Youngsters were driving golf carts. They had to be called in for ferrying, similar to a taxi service. This might be seen as a complicated idea, but it really worked well. These youngsters were even, in the case of the community in Atlantic City, employed. It worked very well. For the purpose of this proposed community model these youngsters will be living on-site. Even for that part of the generation, who will know be able to realize that the computers and smart phones and associated games etc. are not all there is.

Emphasis to include visiting family members as part of the living community

As I witness again and again, it is disturbing to see how family members of grandma conduct their visits. Again and again, I have the feeling that this visiting is viewed as coming to an institution, perhaps even a hospital. It bothers me to answer questions as to the visiting hours, or if it is allowed to use the common living room to play a card game with Mom, or to bring fruits or flowers or whatever to grandma. What bothers me most is the widely shared view that the visits must be conducted in grandma's own room only; her bedroom.

Where do family members get those ideas from?

Even in the Victorian style retirement residence I once operated, and where the bedrooms were really small, visiting family members would cramp in there to visit Mom.

What's wrong with using the common areas? Even now, at Golden Pond, where we have plenty of different common areas, including private rooms like the library or the sunroom, visiting family members come and go straight to Mom's bedroom. I wonder if they did the same at a time grandma was still living in this big old house of hers! Now, as to the frequency of visits, this is something to ponder. While most family members visit quite often, some of them do not. And a few, I don't even know, because they *never* visit. Worse, some of them don't even have the intention to visit. I have had people, more than one, who said straight to my face,—"Here is my mother, the rent payments will be arranged for, take care of her, and don't call me, except when I should come to the funeral…" This is no cruel joke, but reality. This attitude is actually known of, and has been already recognized in other countries. In China a new law has been introduced: Family members, that is, adult children, *must* visit their parents living in assisted living facilities at regular and prescribed intervals.

So then, for reasons not understood by me, I have no other proposal than to encourage family members to do away with the thinking that Mom lives in an institution, or even in a facility, and that there are different rules, as they are necessary in hospitals, but certainly not in retirement homes. And most certainly not in the proposed living community of elderlies. Come and enjoy your stay in the wide open spaces of the common areas. Come often, and do not view these visits as a chore, to be reduced to as little contact as possible. Come and bring your teenage children and make them interact with grandma or grandpa. Teach your children that this next visit may be the last time they see grandma, or perhaps the grandma they know. Make them aware that visiting an older grandparent is not something to be endured, or to be performed out of necessity in order to pick up the promised 20 bucks, but make them aware that visiting grandparents is an opportunity to see what happens to a life which is getting older, and different. And as such has to be viewed with awe, and with respect, and not put away as being boring. Make them aware that all problems, once again, all problems which the youngster is going through now, has already been gone through, and experienced—and mastered—by grandma at one point as well, even though in different times and in different circumstances.

Rent Charges beyond Traditional Thinking

While it is true for any business to strive to achieve a profit, it then follows that every step has to be undertaken to pursue this goal. However, in running a retirement home, I do not necessarily share this view. Potential residents should not be regarded as another means to collect rent money. Residents should not be reduced to a means for a desired end. These are persons. There are stories behind each and every face. Life stories with all their highlights and dramas. And so we listen. And so it happens that people come through our door who are unable to pay the regular rents we charge. These folks, who knock on our doors, and need our services, and need to be looked after. And if circumstances seem right, more based on intuition than any other means and tools available to verify the stories told, we take these folks in. At rental rates, if other residents would know, would create tensions to be sure. However, we are looking at the bigger picture. If these folks need help, we provide it. We serve. This is what we do. And in some cases this help and assistance cannot be paid for at the rate we are usually asking.

Of course, this thought can only be carried so far, and at any given time we cannot allow for more than a few residents to enjoy this special favor. However, we believe that even in those circumstances, the rewards in the long run more than offset the initial shortcoming in rental income. This is law by the Universe.

Taking this thought one step further, it is questionable if the way we charge rent today, and the way we do business today, will be continued as it does. It may change, as well. The necessary change I foresee will be a more pronounced change of all of society in the way of running businesses. A change in our spiritual awareness must be the forerunner of such a pronounced adjustment. As it is, this change is already underway, as anyone can observe. From this view, it can be said that in the future, whatever that definition is, we may reach a point where rent charges are not set in dollar numbers, but residents may choose to pay whatever they feel like, according to their ability—according to their gratitude. Perhaps for the service they receive. Perhaps for the quality of care they receive. Today's way of thinking, of course, would be contrary, and it is a concept difficult to embrace. The common thinking is—the concept of personal 'me-first' thinking, that everyone would pay the least possible rent while gaining the most of service. I predict that one day this thinking will reverse; it is not what we will practise any longer. This is when spiritual awareness sets in. But also, this is where true competition lies. The best service offered is not necessarily related to the most money expended by the provider. Elements of passion, of compassionate care giving, of being kind and understanding will be of much higher valuated than let's say fancy meals or offering expensive outings. The monetary aspect fades—what's left are feelings of love towards another human, a competition of caring and compassion. A competition of which place or home is loved most, and whose staff is most caring.

At Golden Pond, I am proud to tell you that yes, we have residents who are not paying full rent. Simply because we feel and felt that our assistance was needed. And the money is just not there to pay full rent.

But I am equally proud to tell you that we have also residents who are paying more than the rent we ask for. These residents are grateful for the service they receive, they love where they live, and they show their gratitude also monetarily.

If you believe such a concept is in future dreamland only, rest assured that I have ample reasons to believe otherwise. We shall leave it at that.

As usual, this monetary exchange outside of tangible services provided which takes place runs contrary to established rules. For instance, in a retirement home setting it is not allowed for residents to give monetary rewards to staff members.

HARMONY VILLAGE
Authors proposed model of a future oriented senior living community, called *Harmony Village*.

So, no tips. It is not even allowed for staff members to handle resident's money without documentation. For instance, if Dorothy asks a staff member to bring her a few bananas and her favorite cookies, this already must be denied. What follows is the usual, "Sorry, I'm not allowed to…"

And of course, large amounts of money to be willed to homes, staff, owners or operators cannot be accepted. As I understand, there are a number of reasons behind this rationale, so we have to accept it as is. But it must be recognized that this willing of money is exactly what the giver intended to do, and her will stated who the beneficiary will be. Perhaps one day we should look into ways of accommodating these wishes, instead of nipping all these expressions of gratitude in their bud.

This is the beginning of the trend which will no doubt follow once we grow, as a society, just a bit more.

At this point I'd like to thank you of being with me throughout this book, and allowing me to share my thoughts with you. I believe deeply that every journey starts with a first step—let's get started.

SOME ADDITIONAL NOTES

I have been asked many questions, and many are the same; in order to answer the most common of them, the list below points out what this proposed, intentionally planned community is *NOT*:

- A modern version of a bunch of hippies living together outside of town and outside any laws
- A place for the lazy to hang out and enjoy cheap rents, or worse, have parties.
- A place for religious groups, practicing whatever these groups are practising.
- A place for extreme nature or environment minded freaks
- A place for a group of *any specific* interest, other than the idea of taking care of our elderly.
- A place for a group of *any alternative* life style
- A community in the *negative* sense of the word
- A funky place
- A survival retreat
- A mobile home park
- A senior group home
- A senior housing development
- A senior co-housing project, although some of these elements are included.
- A pocket neighbourhood, although some of these elements are included.
- An Abbeyfield Home within their guidelines, although some of the elements are included.
- A place consisting of so-called micro homes, tiny homes, although some elements of it are planned for the future in selected areas.
- Finally, a retirement home, although some of these elements are included.

www.ingramcontent.com/pod-product-compliance
Lightning Source LLC
Chambersburg PA
CBHW080410300426
44113CB00015B/2463